"Set in 1994 when the Crime Bill included The Violence Against Women Act, Florez's evocative, heartrending debut plunges readers into a moving exploration of grief, trauma, and the painstaking journey toward healing."

"Florez's prose is laced with solemnity and empathy while remaining incisive . . . an intriguing supernatural twist drives the narrative with eerie mysticism."

—Booklife

"Stellar storytelling, beautiful prose, and conflict that is deftly handled . . . engagingly seductive."

". . . a character driven story with strong psychological themes."

". . . solidly written, vividly drawn, and nuanced. I loved the way the author explores the world of people suffering from PTSD and the relationship between Irene and her mother."

—Readers' Favorite

"The Daughter Bond is a compelling tale . . . a well-crafted blend of psychological intrigue and supernatural elements. You'll be helplessly invested in the characters and the engaging story."

—The Book Commentary

THE DAUGHTER BOND

THE DAUGHTER BOND

C.P. FLOREZ

THE DAUGHTER BOND

This book is a work of fiction. Names, characters, places, and incidents are the product of the author's imagination or are used fictitiously. Any resemblance to actual events, locales, or persons, living or dead is coincidental.

Originally titled Irene's Girls
ISBN: 978-0-578-263-298
Copyright © 2022 by C.P. Florez

Cover Graphic: MonkiMatt2022
All rights reserved artstation.com/monkimatt
Cover background photo courtesy of canva.com
Street scene photographed by author

Revised 2024

ISBN: 979-8-218-104-580
Library of Congress Control Number: 2023901811

IRIDIUM

To my mom,
and to Lorraine, Rosa, and Rabbit

"... there are only two or three human stories, and they go on repeating themselves as fiercely as if they had never happened before."

—Willa Cather

PART ONE

September 1994

Heartbeat rapid as a startled rabbit's, Irene sat up listening for the thing that had woken her again, and for the last three days since the funeral. It was still pitch-black out; the clock on the nightstand said a quarter after four. She punched the pillow hard, blaming it. For it was getting to her—the persistent internal alarm stirring her hours too early, and the absurd sensation that someone else was in the room. She rose, headed to the bathroom, swished some mouthwash, and ran the cold water tap for a full minute. Towel in hand, she stood staring into the mirror, expecting to see Alma staring back.

Cold water took a while to flow from the tarnished spout. The plumbing in the nineteenth-century brownstone had never been replaced, and the pipes knocked like crazy. Irene wasn't going to complain. She was grateful for the owner's generosity and thanked him for allowing her a virtually perpetual lease that promised reasonable, modest increases every two years. He was wealthy and Beth's father. During their undergraduate years, she and Beth had been roommates in the third-floor apartment Irene called home. Beth now occupied the entire first and second floors with her husband, Alan, her dog, Charly, and two parakeets Beth believed were, for sure, a mating pair. Irene perceived a snooty aloofness in Beth's demeanor since she married.

The change was jarring. In less than a year, free-spirited, fun-loving Beth, who had traipsed around France and Spain with her one summer, had assumed a married lady persona: young-married who socialized with other young marrieds. At thirty-six, Irene was still single.

Well, okay, Beth and Alan Martin; I get it.

Drawn by an excellent public school and brownstone buildings of surprising charm, more and more couples with young children had been moving into her Upper West Side neighborhood. Most of the women were about her age. Irene didn't think much about it, about still being single, didn't think it should matter much to anyone, didn't think it mattered to Beth; maybe it mattered to Alan. However, she did wonder about the new tenant. Much like a faded soul, the fiftyish-looking fellow slipped through the wrought iron gated entry of his street-level quarters without ever saying a word or even nodding hello. Beth said all she knew about Peter Grantis was that he was an old friend of her father's and an adjunct professor of Anthropology at nearby Columbia University. "Dad said the poor guy is paying out serious alimony to his ex, who also got the big house in Short Hills and both cars. Only thing Grantis can afford now is a basement apartment. My father likes to help out if he can."

Irene got the feeling Beth was also referring to her.

Beth had attended Alma's funeral, but Alan had not. His father had died recently, and he'd told Beth he was never going to do another funeral.

Irene tightened the faucet handle and glanced into the mirror above the washbasin once more. She wiped the foggy glass; rivulets of tears were sliding down her cheeks. Not the first time she'd cried in the last few days, not knowing she was weeping. Taking time off to grieve had not been a good idea. She needed to get back to work, just needed a few days to regroup—that's all.

She was about to sit down with a cup of coffee when a solid thump against the door startled her. She looked through the peephole and saw the back of the delivery person, right shoulder hunched with the weight of a large black satchel full of newspapers wrapped in blue plastic. She opened the door, bent down, and picked up the blue packet that had landed upright by the side of her threshold. Irene discarded the plastic wrap in the tall Rubbermaid receptacle she used as a recycle bin and laid out the paper flat on the breakfast table.

Wednesday, September 14, 1994. The lead story, which always appeared in the right-hand column, unless a state of war or the impeachment of a president warranted a massive headline, did not interest her. Issues of the past six days remained in their blue plastic wrappers, scattered under the table. She'd been kicking them away with her feet.

This morning, she'd at least made an effort to open up the paper. Last week, she hadn't even searched for her mother's obituary. Although she doubted anyone outside of family members cared to learn Alma Míral had passed on, she'd gone ahead and placed the death announcement in her favorite newspaper. Delivered to the door of her apartment each day before dawn, *The New York Times* had been a constant in Irene's life since Journalism 101, when the dream of becoming an investigative reporter perked enthusiastically in her eighteen-year-old mind. Two years later, she'd decided to become a psychologist and proceeded to pursue her goal with exceptional tunnel vision. In less than five years, she had earned her doctorate—Dr. Irene Míral.

Last week, her mother's funeral had stripped her of her professional cloak, rendering her malleable, floundering through mists of memories as she struggled to regain the structure of her daily life.

She sat with a second cup of coffee and the sprawl of newsprint. A large photo of the president signing a new bill seemed important. The story was on page sixteen. Irene scanned the article perfunctorily, paused at the last paragraph, and read it three times. The new and controversial Crime Bill included the Violence Against Women Act. "Well, hallelujah, about time." For the first time in days, a spark of enthusiasm renewed her focus. With the dexterity of an origami master, she refolded the humongous pages several times until the story of interest appeared on top. Back in Journalism 101, she'd learned how to fold the newspaper to a quarter of its size and access any section without allowing the outsize pages to unfurl and invade the space of another subway commuter. Mastering the skill was *de rigueur*, asserted Mrs. Hirsch, the eccentric journalism instructor who had inspired Irene's early career aspirations. The woman was something of a fanatic, a fervid anglophile with two loves: *The New York Times* and the tragic novels of Thomas Hardy. Irene finished her coffee and got ready for work. She was almost feeling like herself again.

The IND train approached her stop. A woman wrapped in mounds of heavy fabric stared. Irene had seen her many times and once tried to start a conversation as she jotted down details about two shelters on the back of a business card. Homeless persons often ranted incoherently or said not much. Silent and intent on Irene's face, the woman reached out with a skinny hand, took the card, and shoved it deep into a soiled cloth bag.

Well, there she was again, in the same corner, leaning into the metal wall shared with the conductor's compartment, huddling under multiple layers of crocheted scarves and a dingy army blanket. Probably never called or showed up at either of those places, choosing to hunker down in a cold subway car instead of relying on a safe shelter. Whatever had driven the woman to ride the rails could not be fixed anymore.

That was never going to happen to her girls. And she needed to stop thinking of her patients as girls. They were women. For now, though, they were her girls, her responsibility. The PTSD unit she headed at Lakeside Hospital was barely two months old. The women needed her, and now, more than ever, she felt compelled to help them. She would share the article about the new law with her patients. Would they yell out hallelujah, too? Or would they protest it was too late, that it wasn't going to take away their pain because what had happened to them was indelible.

Irene rose, tucked the newspaper tightly under her arm, and rushed out through the subway doors. At her back, the doors banged shut with a fulminant gust, urging her forward. She headed east toward Lakeside, walked with urgency and new purpose, wanting to leave the memory of the funeral behind, wanting to put it out of her mind.

All had taxed her more than she'd ever expected. In an insane instant, she'd wanted to nestle close beside her mom in that casket. But somehow, she'd managed to keep both feet on the ground, somehow, remained tethered to conversation and eye contact as she fought through an insubstantial feeling of weightlessness. Maríanis' presence had helped. Ironic, a role reversal of sorts. But then, the death of a loved one had a way of disheveling the order of things, like a harsh wind that buffets the shutters, whips up the curtains, and scatters the mind.

Irene felt quite alone at that funeral until Maríanis Román showed up. And she was grateful she did.

Madre Ausente

MARÍANIS HAD BEEN ATTENDING the funerals of relatives, neighbors, and acquaintances since three days before her fourteenth birthday when she accompanied her mother to the funeral of a neighbor's twenty-six-year-old son. He'd jumped off the roof with two hypodermic needles stuck in his arms. All the women talked about were the hallucinations he'd suffered since the age of ten when he began to report that at night a young woman dressed in white appeared at his bedroom door, urging him to find his baby sister. The little girl had disappeared and never found.

That's how it had always been in her East Harlem neighborhood. People just kept dying, OD'd, got shot, or jumped because they simply did not want to live anymore. Sometimes, folks remembered an incident here and there, but most, except those tormented by nightmares and so-called hallucinations, just forgot, accepted, or did not care.

Evil lurked in unexpected places, surreptitiously spawning heinous rapists, child molesters, abusive husbands, and ex-husbands, men who beat and kill their wives and girlfriends, never get caught, never pay for their crimes, never admit they have done harm. By the grace of God, she'd narrowly escaped death at her husband's hands. Yes, but only to exist as an emotionally deceased—until Dr. Irene Míral.

"All this week's appointments are canceled due to a death in Dr. Míral's family." A feeling of dread encroached: Bad things don't happen to good angels. Marianis replayed the message and decided to call the clinic. She found out it was Irene's mom who'd passed and immediately called to ask about services.

A recording played, "You've reached the office of Irene Míral, please leave a message . . ."

"I am sorry for your loss," began Marianis, "I . . ."

Then, "Hello. Marianis?"

And in that quiet voice that had reassured, soothed, and grounded Marianis countless times, Irene provided the address of the funeral home.

On a Thursday, early afternoon, it would take an hour and twenty minutes from Grand Central Station to the upper Westchester town where Hillside Funeral Home was located. Marianis stared out the train's window as The Hudson River sped by in the opposite direction. A year ago, she would not have been traveling anywhere. A spiraling kaleidoscope of maddening thoughts and recurring nightmares tormented her. Despondency nearly destroyed her. She was thankful; these days, her thoughts were much clearer, calmer. The women who remained at Lakeside continued to struggle.

In her best handwriting, she added the names of seven women to the sympathy card: Melissa, Olivia, Amanda, Felicia, Carolina, Marta, and Ana.

She had no money for expensive flowers, but Irene would understand a sympathy card, a mass card, and a long-stem white rose. On Mother's Day, people in her neighborhood purchased carnations from street vendors to pin on their shirts and blouses: red ones for a living mother, pink ones for an absent one, and white ones for a mother who had passed away. She adjusted the ribbon that held the cellophane wrapping together and gently laid the white rose on her lap.

About six cabs were lined up in front of the Amtrak station. "Five dollars to Hilltop," offered the third driver. "Lady, it's usually ten. You heard those other guys." In less than five minutes, she was at the door of the funeral home. The ride was worth no more than a couple of dollars, and Maríanis could have walked if she'd known where she was going.

She gathered herself and walked in. A man dressed like an usher in a fancy theater directed her to the appropriate viewing room. An ornate floor-to-ceiling mirror overwhelmed the small reception area. Deep burgundy wallpaper, flocked in velvety scrolls, lent an air of solemnity; cornucopias of dark artificial flowers crowded the corners of the tight space.

Condolences

The black wool dress Irene chose to wear for the service should have kept her warm enough, yet the notion she'd never again feel the warmth of another's skin widened. She sat alone in the front row by the entrance of the viewing room. Cold moved through her like a silent snake, chilling her blood until her hands and knees began to stiffen like an old woman's. Her sister Andrea huddled with her sons, their wives, and her grandchildren way on the other side of the room. Everyone else, including her brother Jaime and his son Robert, sat towards the back of the small salon. Four rows of empty seats separated them from the front row and the deceased.

Were they allowing empty seats for guests? She doubted the distance had to do with hospitality. She looked around. Hillside had honored all her requests. A white ceramic vase stood on a tall console behind the casket. Baby's breath and big yellow roses. Framed photographs of children and grandchildren also adorned the table. Wreaths and flower arrangements claimed positions on each side of the woman laid out in hues of beige and gray. Alma looked elegant in her stillness.

Sconces cast a soft light, creating an amber glow over the metallic sides of the casket. The air in the room felt moist. Irene knelt and lowered her head near her mother's face, taking it in, engraving its contours in her mind and soul. She imagined her mother's skimpy lashes fluttered ever so slightly, that a wisp of breath rose from her lips. "Yes, I will look after Jaime and Robert, just as you asked." But no, her mother was not speaking; she couldn't possibly be uttering a sound. Quietly, Irene repeated the words of a childhood prayer. Pressing her lips on the stone-cold of Alma's cheek, she asked her for a final blessing: *La bendición.*

Faltering as she walked back to where she'd been sitting, Irene looked down at her feet, feeling as if she didn't own them, as if they were someone else's. Wanting to ground herself, she turned to an elderly woman who was about to sign the guest book, Alma's next-door neighbor. "Thank you for coming. My mom mentioned you often." The words, hollow in her throat, felt as if uttered from a distance. She didn't know if she'd offered a reserved smile or not; she supposed she should have, but maybe she didn't. She tried to concentrate on the signatures in the book and noticed Beth had been one of the first to sign. Irene looked around again. No Beth. She'd signed the guest book and left. Knowing so stung. It would have been nice to at least get a quick hug from Beth. Likely, Alan had been parked right outside, waiting, because he didn't do funerals.

She remained by the open book, poised to receive more guests. When she glanced toward the hallway, there, standing before the huge mirror, was Maríanis. A dark green coat complimented the auburn lights in her hair. Just last week, she had been a blonde; just last year, she'd been out of her mind.

Irene signaled her brother. He came over, looking uncomfortable in his new suit. Two days before, they'd had to go out and get him a black suit. He'd always been a strictly sportswear guy. "Jaime, why don't you stand by the guestbook for a little, please. I see someone I need to talk to."

Toward the end of July, Irene concluded her patient was ready to face life anew. The flashbacks were fading, and her resolve and commitment to regain custody of her children helped tilt the scales in her favor. The supervising psychiatrist signed off on her case three weeks before the date indicated by the treatment plan—the first woman to complete the new PTSD unit's program, the woman whose case seemed remarkably similar to Alma's. Irene often compared her mother's experiences with cases that came before her. Alma's stories, reference points forever residing in the lanes of her memory.

Providence, perhaps plain old luck, had brought Maríanis to her clinic. Irene encouraged her to call her by her first name. It had taken a while.

"Dr. Míral . . . Irene, I am sorry about your mother." Irene managed half a smile and reached for Maríanis' hand. They walked toward Alma.

"Her skin is smooth and clear. All the flowers are beautiful. The blanket of flowers at her feet is especially beautiful." Over the years, Maríanis had internalized the tone, the phrases of mourning that served to smooth the intercourse of the sad moment.

"Oh, yes. That blanket of brilliant red roses . . . from my sister. It is special, isn't it? In a way, I'm surprised."

"Surprised? Why?"

Irene hesitated before the woman who had divulged so much of her own pain over many hours of therapy. Yet the intimacies of grief had a way of softening boundaries, blurring a person's role. Right now, the woman waiting for a response was a friend, not just one of her patients. And it was okay. Irene appreciated her presence. "It's somewhat of a complicated story, Maríanis. It's kind of cold in here, isn't it?"

The chill in her extremities caused Irene to stand straighter than usual. She pulled at the long sleeves of the black wool dress wanting to warm her hands, her fingers, wanting to bring the neck of the dress up over her head.

"I like your dress. It's nice." said Maríanis, "Are you going to *guardar luto*?"

"No." The question surprised her. To continue mourning in black after a funeral was unusual these days. Irene picked up an envelope from her chair, and they sat. "Some poems I wrote for my mom a while back, thought I might read one or two after the eulogy, but I've changed my mind." She'd concluded it would be maudlin, a useless gesture. And she shouldn't be useless; everyone always relied on her to hold it together. "Don't know, even thought I'd give them to her, so they'd keep her company in her next life." With a peculiar expression, she put the little sheaf of poems in her purse.

"You mean in heaven, don't you? The poems might help her in her journey to heaven."

"Yes . . . in heaven."

Maybe her mom would be rewarded for her life's lot of suffering in the place people called heaven. "My mom lived two lifetimes. Maybe she will live another, somewhere." Irene was not a religious person, but the idea of her mother's soul existing in a beyond was comforting.

"Your mom, what was she like? Had she been sick?"

Tears hovered over Irene's long lashes. Her lips tightened, then she sighed. "Yes, ill for a year, lost lots of weight. Funny thing is, I think she was secretly proud of her new size. As a young woman, she'd been slender. She would say to me, 'You see, there is something good in this. I'm thin again. I need new clothes, new brassieres.' Pride, a bit of vanity, and the inner strength that helped her survive life's hardships, kept my mom from giving in to dying." Irene's voice quivered.

"I wonder if I'll miss my mother at all when she passes." Maríanis bit her lip, regretting what she'd just said. She placed a hand over Irene's. The cold of her doctor's skin sent a little shiver through her arm. "It's okay. Your mom is at peace now."

Irene's hand warmed, and the tightness in her chest receded. "My mom would stand in the middle of the room, arms wide open, modeling new clothes in her new skinny body as if things were still the same, as if she were showing off a dress I'd bought for her to wear for our Mother's Day dinner date. Every year we took her out to City Island to eat lobster. She'd grin like a happy kid as my brother Jaime photographed her wearing one of those ridiculous restaurant bibs; the big lobster logo, blood red and tacky." Irene wasn't aware she was shaking her head no, negating the reality: There would be no more silly photos of her mom in a lobster bib. She tugged down harder at the sleeves of her black wool dress. Tears showed in her gray eyes again.

Maríanis retrieved a clump of tissues from her bag. "Here."

"Thanks." Irene dabbed under her eyes with a tissue. She wanted to stop; she'd already said too much. She was leaning on her patient and she shouldn't.

"You're welcome, Irene."

A flurry of lashes dispersed the watery blur; she did not want to cry like a baby, not in her patient's presence. She tried to modulate her voice. "And the transformation, I suppose that's how it happens. An alert air about her, as though she were anticipating something important that would require her attention at any moment. It was like that for weeks, until she learned she'd need hospice care by the end of the year. Then she shrank, gradually creasing into a diminutive version of her former self. My mom became a fragile old doll, a special child sitting on the edge of the bed, plaintively asking, 'Well, here I am, and what do we do now?'

One day around Christmas time, when she opened the door to let me in, we stood looking at each other without saying a word, the shocking recognition of the inevitable overwhelming us. We burst into tears, embracing each other in silent desperation. She told me she was dying and wouldn't last another year. She had accepted what I already knew.

By then, she could barely walk or stand on her own. I lugged in a beautiful fir tree and decorated it with red lights while she lay in the bedroom because she couldn't get up. I thought the tree might bring her life, that she'd get up and start to tell me stories again. Some I can't forget—sad stories, funny stories, stories about when she first arrived in New York City, and how she met my father."

Irene's pupils became stony. "Oh, also scary and terrible stories about her first husband. Sometimes she told me a bizarre story about a young woman in white light. I was just a kid when she first mentioned the mysterious girl. 'Who was she?' I asked. My mom just stared at me as if I should know. And why didn't I? By the time I was in my teens, she no longer spoke of her, and then a few weeks before she died, she started again. Except, this time, I think she was not telling the story but verily seeing a girl in white light."

"You mean she was like me?"

"Yours are flashbacks, flashbulb memories of past events due to your condition. What my mother described was different."

Maríanis said her own mom, aunts, and cousins saw visions and things. They were into it, the *brujería*. She blushed; she dared not ask if Irene's mother, Alma, was a believer. Anyway, Irene was a psychologist, and it was not likely people in her family would be into any brujería—not likely at all.

"My mother's parents died before she was four years old. Her older siblings raised her and made sure she received a Catholic education. Must be the reason . . . I have a feeling the strange stories my mother told me about a girl in white light were somehow linked to her experiences at the Catholic school. All the teachers were nuns."

"Then your mother must have been a religious woman. Might be the Virgin Mary she saw—the holy virgin in white light."

"Maybe. I don't know. I do know my mother was a good Christian woman, devoted to her family. But she wasn't at church every night with a rosary in her hand. Such things as statues of saints and virgins were not present in the house—just the usual picture of the *Sagrado Corazón de Jesús*. Ah, and a framed print of the Archangel Michael slaying Satan. It hung on my mother's bedroom wall for many years. As a kid, I remember I was fascinated with the long and dark reptilian features of the prone Satan cringing beneath the sword of the avenging angel."

"You were afraid of it, weren't you? You were scared of the black devil in the picture."

"No, just fascinated," Irene managed a smile. "Come, I want to introduce you to my sister Andrea. We look nothing alike."

Andrea was womanly-looking, dark-eyed, Irene, of large gray eyes and slender frame. However, the differences ran deeper than physical appearance. Even as a child, Irene sensed somber drama between her sister and her mother. She also perceived Andrea was Alma's favorite. With time, she came to understand that the attention Alma showered on Andrea was motivated by guilt, tormenting guilt.

Irene's thoughts drifted. She remembered an ugly scene in her family's living room: Andrea had been living with her father. Less than six months after she came to live in Alma's home, she asked her to sign permission to marry. Alma refused. She wanted to hang on to her daughter, wanted to make up for the lost time. She tried to negotiate. "Why don't you wait until you finish high school next year? Please! Why the big hurry? Andrea, what is wrong? I don't understand. Are you pregnant or something?"

Andrea's face gleamed red with rage, her words rising to a furious shriek, "Why all the concern? You've never cared about me. No! I am not pregnant! We are in love. We love each other, and I want to be with him, not just on weekends, but all the time, every day. But what would you know about love? You never loved my father or me." Alma relented. A young Irene cowered in her bedroom while her sister screamed accusations, and their mother wept.

Irene wondered if Andrea understood how effectively she had crushed her mother's heart back then. She never apologized, even after her marriage deteriorated and ended in a nasty divorce. Maybe Andrea was apologizing now. Her ample chest heaved, and the waves of sobs kept coming.

The woman's lids were red and swollen, long tips of dark lashes clumped together like small wet feathers. She whimpered, "I am going to miss Alma." Irene's eyebrows shot up. Even now, Andrea could not bring herself to say the word mother. "She's not my mother; she did not raise me," she'd repeated many times. The irony of it all was that Andrea never wavered in declaring love for her father, even after Child Protective Services removed her when she was sixteen. In a drunken stupor, he'd tried to molest her. Irene could never figure out how Andrea managed to forgive him. But this was not the moment to question her sister's demonstration of grief. She put an arm around Andrea and smoothed her hair.

"My condolences, *lo siento*." Maríanis offered her hand to the grieving woman. Lo siento sounded a lot more sincere than the usual "I am sorry for your loss."

People crowded the room now. Irene's nostrils labored under the fullness, the cloying fragrance of the funeral wreaths. She wondered why more funeral services were not held outdoors like garden weddings.

Three young men approached: Jaime's boy, Robert, and Andrea's two sons. Each one embraced Irene and kissed her on the cheek. Joseph, always with a quick sparkle of dark eyes, smiled widely, wanting to break through the heaviness of the hour. And ever the flirt, he eyed Maríanis like he was liking what he saw. John, his brother, was the more serious fellow. The men turned to Maríanis, and Irene introduced, "Maríanis, a good friend." She had to be careful to honor confidentiality, so she introduced her as a friend. And she was. Today, she was the friend she needed. It was nice to relate to her in a setting away from Lakeside.

She was thirty-two but looked younger. Little lightning rods of green in her hazel eyes glimmered as she greeted the nephews. Two spots of apricot appeared on the rise of her cheekbones.

"Robert is reading the eulogy," stated Joseph. John, Alma's eldest grandchild, gave a slight nod as if agreeing to cede the honor. If birth order accounted for anything, the honor should have gone to him. Irene, Maríanis, and the three nephews chatted politely. Between their words, moments of silence stood like sentinels.

Robert was most quiet, his mind likely on the eulogy. Only eighteen, Jaime's only child was intense, often emotional. He began the eulogy in a whisper, then his voice rose high to the ceiling—resonating through the sadness of the space. Some wept. Toward the end, he said Alma was just a mother and a grandmother and that he loved her very much. Tears streamed down his handsome face.

Bracing against a robust September wind, the kind that invariably precedes a rainstorm, the mourners gathered protectively around Robert. The ground was still soft from the previous night's downpour. Irene's black patent heels sank into the sodden soil. She bent over and wiped away the wet grass and soil in one easy swoosh. Rubbing her fingers clean, she thought of how inexorably the maudlin aspects of everyday existence dominated a person's life.

Smiling like a coquette, John's teen daughter held a bunch of big yellow blooms beneath her bosom as if she were a bride. That hurt. Irene wanted to snatch the flowers from the girl's hands. Even after she provided detailed instructions over the phone to the florist, she'd walked over to the shop and selected those roses herself, not fully trusting him to make sure that each stem was perfect, each bloom, newly opened, the yellow, fresh and bright. Irene turned away from the girl, and focused on Robert. The depth of her nephew's grief was concerning. But was there ever a monopoly on loss and suffering? No telling who could be truly hurting. No telling who would not be able to forget.

Irene gazed at the long rectangular opening and wondered how long it took and what the workers thought about as they chiseled out the earth for a new grave. The casket was lowered. A murmur of prayers and sobs. Some flung flowers and the loose petals dropped to the ground like ladened dew. Then it was over. Alma disappeared under clumps of wet soil.

Robert led them out of the cemetery. Jaime closed ranks behind the lagging procession; a bevy of newly fallen leaves whirled in the chilly air. Maríanis cast a sidelong glance at Irene, admiring how her profile silhouetted against the darkness of the lugubrious sky—long, rich lashes beneath a wide brow, and brown shoulder-length hair adorned with a dark silky scarf whose ends fluttered like the wings of a fragile bird.

The gravel on the path to the exit crunched beneath their feet. Maríanis turned to Irene several times, pausing, looking like she wanted to tell her something. After a while, she came out with it. "Your nephew Robert looks like he might have a bad fever. Did you notice the angel's kiss on his lip?"

Irene, nudged from silence, regarded Maríanis with a questioning frown. *What is she asking.* "An angel's kiss?"

"Yes, an angel's kiss leaves a trace, like when you have the flu, and your lips get chapped from the fever, and there's a burn on the lip."

"No, I did not notice, likely just a windburn." Irene wondered why Maríanis would remark upon such a thing, started to wish they could just say good-bye now, yearned for some distance. She felt a bit embarrassed. She'd revealed too much about Alma, exposed childish vulnerability that her patient shouldn't have been privy to. However, she did find this superstitious quirk of hers a bit intriguing. What an odd observation. What in the world was she getting at?

"Sometimes the dead leave a sign, that's all." Maríanis lowered her voice. "I sensed the wisp of a presence, diaphanous as a bride's veil."

"Oh!"

"Yes." She went on with considerable conviction. "Isn't that what funerals are for? We must help souls depart, otherwise, they might stay." Frowning, she told Irene about the first funeral she'd attended. "That little girl, the one who went missing years back, could not depart. Destined or dammed to remain in limbo, she sent an envoy, a messenger who drove her brother to madness and suicide. Some believe the angel's kiss is a warning, an omen, perhaps a curse. Others say it's evidence of a dead baby's visit to a beloved sibling, a protective blessing that will keep the bearer of the kiss from harm."

"Folk tales, Maríanis, folk tales and myths—a way to deal with what we fear or don't understand." Little *retratos* of a girl in white light and a dead baby brother surfaced in Irene's mind. She was tired now. This talk of dead babies had unexpectedly triggered a painful memory.

Maríanis changed the subject. "Forgive me, I had eyes on Robert because my ex-husband is similar in appearance, pale skin, dark hair, and the Japanese eyebrow—the ghost of ancient Amerindian blood. Except, my ex had a cruel mouth, I mean thin, hard lips. I'm sorry, but that's why I noticed. You know, I loved my husband once." She said I loved my husband once with the tone of a cold fact established on another planet. "Just that once, when I first saw him."

Apparently, Maríanis had a discerning eye for the boys—or a roving one. The nephews had intrigued her, inspired her to talk about love, to speak as a woman, not as a patient.

"Want to know how I met him?"

"Yes, tell me." It occurred to Irene that Maríanis was trying to distract her from the moment with girl talk.

"Six of us from the neighborhood did the Latin clubs. You know, we were like eighteen, but they let us in anyway. We were good with the makeup and slinky outfits, looked older, and the guys at the door rarely asked for ID. On Wednesday and Friday nights, we'd go to the Copa. All we ever met were married men looking to dance away the reality of being married by pretending to be single. It got so bad that we started dancing with each other." Maríanis studied Irene's face, wanting a reaction.

Irene was having a hard time focusing. Her thoughts kept drifting—Alma and a winged woman in white descending to bestow blessings and kisses that burned a mortal's lips. The tale of the angel's kiss had stirred her imagination. She smiled the empathetic smile and tried to listen.

"One week, we switched to Saturday nights, hoping to meet a better crowd. The place was packed with South Americans from Queens. One walked halfway over to me, crooked his finger, beckoned, and asked me to dance. And that was it."

Irene had never made such rounds; amazing how easy it all sounded. She wondered if her patient had any inkling then of how her journey with that man would turn out to be hell distant from easy.

"I was dying to get out of my house. Mother used to beat me with a broomstick. I mean big black and blue bruises on my arms and legs whenever I stayed out late or didn't do the dishes right, or whatever thing she wanted to pick on. Once she started, she wouldn't stop, her arms pumping over me with crazy fury. Only my pet dog's snarls and barks got her to back away. I had Samson since I was eight, and he was a puppy. If it wasn't for him looking out for me, she would have broken bones or cracked my skull open one day." Maríanis' hand went to her head as if she were trying to make sure her scalp was still intact. "My mother was a nasty freaking witch, a real bruja. After a beating, she'd drag me to her bedroom and make me kneel before an altar she had created from six shelves and decorated with bright orange and red satin fabric, an assortment of unlit candles, and a collection of ceramic saints she venerated with coins and sundry objects. She'd shove my head down hard, demanding I ask forgiveness of the saints and the spirits before they sent me to hell. Then, she'd take down a candle she said was meant to teach obedience. She made me kiss it, lit it, chanted something thick, and placed it right in front of her *santos*. Her face got a little weird when she got into stuff like that. I mean, it was scary. But you know what? Once done, she faced me with what I want to say was pride. I think she really, *really* believed in what she was doing, saying."

"You might too with all this talk of angels' kisses. Do you?"

"Hah. I suppose all of that rubbed off on me in some way, especially the part about the spirits. I do think they exist . . . You now, souls. But some . . . some are not saints. Anyway, the worst of it was when I started liking boys. If she saw me getting ready to go out, she'd pick a fight, just like a man. I mean she'd rip the clothes off me and pull my hair. She was awful, and I wanted out. Boom, I married him."

"You married him to get away from your mother. It happens a lot."

Maríanis looked down at the ground and laughed the self-conscious laugh of a girl who knew that back in that moment she had erred, made the biggest mistake of her life.

She had never spoken of such severe beatings and humiliation. She'd only mentioned her mother sometimes resorted to corporal punishment when she and her brother did not listen. During therapy, Maríanis delved on the emotional abuse she suffered during the marriage and the ensuing physical abuse when she fought to regain custody of her children.

The refrain "once a victim, always a victim" reverberated like an echo. Yet Irene did not believe such, not at all, didn't know where she first heard the cliché. What she did know was: It was a fight. A fight to strengthen the person to reclaim the capacity to heal and thrive and not become a victim ever again. Should she include the mother's violent abuse in the case notes? She would discuss it with Dr. Freile. He would shrug it off because, for him, Maríanis' case was done the moment the discharge to outpatient became effective. No matter, he was still the consulting psychiatrist. She would mention it anyway. Traumatic episodes of child abuse were not uncommon in persons devastated by PTSD as adults. However, it was the loss of her children and the events surrounding the separation which had precipitated her patient's breakdown and suicide attempt.

Maríanis looked as if she was intent on a thought. Irene had taught her a reflective technique, to count silently to increase self-control. Finally, she said, "Men make you do things, then wind up hating you for doing what they made you do. But I'm never going to let a man use me again. Never."

"The choices are yours to make." Irene had repeated such many times.

At Lakeside Maríanis had exposed every raw nerve, every tear of the fabric of her heart, and Irene had listened, lifted her, worked to help her recover the self-esteem the abuse had destroyed.

"I . . . I'll be seeing the children in a few days."

Irene sensed that Maríanis wasn't feeling confident about the visit. Subtle shadows were emerging under the light of her hazel eyes, and the rosiness of her skin was slackening to a grayish tone of beige.

"I bought Tina a dress, a pink dress with shiny gold moons and platinum stars on the skirt. It's like a little party dress, you know, one of those nylon party dresses with cupcake sleeves little girls wear, you know, like a little doll's dress. She's pretty, Tina, very dainty with a sweet face shaped like a heart. Oh, and I bought her a ring, a gold one with a small garnet stone. And Ricky likes . . . Well, he used to like hockey, so I bought him a pair of skates, and knee pads . . . and a helmet. I love them so much."

It was a huge step; Tina and Ricky had been kept from her for more than a year. Irene appreciated how her patient, even while struggling with heavy feelings of her own, had been able to extend comfort. "Thank you, Maríanis, thank you for coming. I need a little time to put my mother's things in order and won't be back at the clinic until mid-week, so come in for your regular appointment the Monday after. Don't hesitate to call if you need to speak to me sooner. You chose nice gifts for your children, but the important thing is you'll be getting to see them. It's been a long time."

Maríanis' eyes went moist.

"Stay strong for the visit. You can."

Yes, her patient was standing stronger now. However, Irene detected tones of fear in her voice. How Maríanis handled the supervised visitations was a test, and she damn-well knew it. Her resolve to continue to fight to get her children back could not waver.

Irene thought about sharing her mom's story, her struggle to reunite with her stolen children. But Alma did not succeed, so Maríanis need not hear it. Alma fought hard. Custody petitions came and went. Her allegations of horrific domestic violence and the affidavits she submitted to the court attesting the man was an unfit parent, and dangerous, were countered by the fiend's accusations that she'd abandoned her children to take up with a lover in New York. He denied ever laying a hand on Alma. There were no witnesses to testify on her behalf, no visible scars, no police reports. Alma's was a tragic story, a story that had molded Irene's thinking. She needed to rectify the world for women.

Small clusters of mourners hugged and patted backs before piling into their cars. One of the nephews offered Maríanis a ride to the

Amtrak station. A *velorio* would not take place. What was there to gather about now? What else was there to say about Alma? Even Jaime was unaware of what Irene held close to her heart, the sad bones of her mom's stories. It was only Jaime and Robert, and her. It had been that way since Antonio died. So why?

She knew going through polite empty motions would not help her grieve. She apologized to the neighbors, friends who cared more for her mother than family members who'd become strangers, whose presence at the funeral had been a mere formality. Her mom's friends were the only ones owed a wake's repast. They understood. "It's a lot, honey, and you need to rest. Just don't you worry."

She felt a momentary sense of closure. But closure was not something to order on a menu or check off on the list for a contrived buffet. She should know that. She knew. Still, she did not expect the churn of emotions as memories of her mother and her stories flooded her consciousness.

Stolen Children

INÉS HAD LIED. THERE was nothing special about being a married lady. Alma felt betrayed by her family. How could they give her to such a cruel man? He smiled deceiving smiles, uttered deceiving words, his lips hard put to bestow a kiss on anyone, not even a child. And Alma had been a child.

"¡Ese hombre es malo! ¡Muy malo!"

"¿Quién, niña? ¿Qué dices?" Inés put both hands on the girl's shoulders, trying to steady her. "¿Qué te pasa? What is wrong with you?"

Thirteen-year-old Alma shuddered, buried her head in the soft folds of her sister's skirt, and cried.

Enraged and indignant, Inés ran to Julio, "Cesar has tried to ruin our sister. I do not want him in the house. Tell him to leave! Tiene que largarse. ¡¡Ahora!!"

Julio walked over to the man he'd trusted as a business partner for ten years, a man he thought of as a brother. A Cain he was. The betrayal infuriated, and the adrenalin pulsed. Julio slammed the scoundrel against the wall and gripped his neck between his hands. When he finally let him go, he stated, "You must marry her. Allow us some honor." The family believed it was best. Young Alma had no voice, no choice in the matter.

At twenty-seven, Inés would barely escape spinsterhood when she married the following year. Upon her engagement, she'd appropriated the polished mahogany chest that had belonged to their grandmother, Agueda. The family was poor, and the chest was the most outstanding object in the faded wood house they rented on Valdespino, a narrow street south of the first plaza in old Mayagüez. Inés cast a wistful eye on the hope chest she'd ladened with stacks of embroidered linens, lacy camisoles, and scented soaps. She tried not to demonstrate resentment as she removed half her things and handed them to her younger sister. "Do not be scared. Being a married lady is very special."

With the improvised trousseau and the meager information Inés shared about being a wife, Alma moved in with her husband to a one-bedroom place a few streets down from her former home. She got pregnant every other year for twelve years, starting when she was barely fourteen. She ran away many times. Soon she learned there was no respite, no refuge.

To stop her from running back home every time he beat her, he moved Alma and the children to Aguadilla, the town where his mother lived, twenty-five miles away. And there, he abandoned her for months. Whenever he showed up, the beatings again, and the sexual abuse. She despised his erections and ejaculations, the forced entries, and ugly hardness that made her pitifully pregnant six lonely times.

His family was as cruel as he was. She and her babies were just more mouths to feed when he disappeared to who knows where. Alma walked around with her head bowed in humiliation. And always, a tightness in her chest, fearing he might return.

He claimed he was working. When, and if he returned with money, his family had first claim—nothing left for the young mother but another beating and a few miserable morsels for the children. Alma's breasts dried up for lack of proper diet. Her youngest babies died.

Desperate to provide sustenance for her children, she went out to work as a part-time domestic. As often as she could, she brought home the food left over by the children of the people she worked for. That too enraged him. And the rages were vile. In another of his cursing fits of fury, he snatched from her arms the bottles of milk she had brought home from the public dispensary and smashed them against the wall.

A child's death is the most heartbreaking of losses, confounding the order of things and creating desolate hollows in a mother's consciousness. Alma's fourth born, a boy who lived only to the age of three, died a strange death.

A sister-in-law, Hortensia, grudgingly agreed to look after the boy while the downtrodden young mother cleaned homes, washed other people's clothes, and swept other people's patios. Desperation and ignorance clouded Alma's judgment and kept her from detecting the woman's resentment and ill will. Hortensia would not share her children's food with the little boy, and while her children enjoyed full plates of green bananas, onions, and boiled cod, she fed Alma's boy only leftover briny broth. His innards calcified. The child hallucinated for many days. During death's delirium, he repeated, "There's a lady in the light, a lady in the light."

Alma wept for three days without stopping, without sleeping. On the fourth day, she began a conversation with a person she called Adriana. Her in-laws did not know what to do, so they locked her up in a room. Through the door they could hear Alma sobbing. *"Adriana, por favor, ayudame."* When they finally opened the door, they found Alma sitting quietly on the floor, her face calm, aglow with a strange pearly sheen.

Her husband was nowhere to be found. This time, the man had abandoned them. Her future looked bleak, yet in a small corner of her heart Alma harbored the hope he was gone for good. God and Adriana would help her manage.

But the *canalla* returned. And his cruelty began once more, plunging her into a pit of shame and despondency with every slap, shove, and blow. How many times would she be able to emerge from that pit alive and sane? Alma fled. She ran for her life. Terror, a primordial force overriding all other human instincts.

The separation would wrench to the root of her being.

One ticket to New York was all she received from her aunt Rita. Alma's heart raced when she opened the correspondence. "The family who is hiring you is expecting a single woman. I may not be able to help you again. Do not pass up on this opportunity to start a new life."

She entrusted her two boys, ages seven and six, to her sister. Inés was now eight years married but still childless. The couple was of modest means and generous heart. The husband, kind and hardworking, liked her boys, and her sister—her sister was anxious to mother any child. It was the best Alma could do for her boys.

Thoughts of the terrible things that could happen to a little girl without a mother's protection caused her anguish.

A godmother might be best.

Alma decided Fernanda, the child's *madrina de agua*, had the most to offer her little girl. The woman's home in Cerro Modesto, furnished simply with dark mahogany caned furniture, seemed perfect. In the mornings, a house servant scrubbed the small parlor's tile floor and polished the mahogany dining table until it reflected the cut glass vase of white *azucenas*.

In order to immediately safeguard the child's immortal soul, families traditionally assigned informal godparents to anoint the infant's head with holy water, lest the babe end up forever lost in limbo. A formal christening and celebration would happen later if the family had funds to pay the priest and feed hungry guests. Señora Fernanda was it; the only godmother Andrea would have. Alma wished with all her heart that she could bring Andrea with her, but she had few options and so would not delve on the nagging little concern: Fernanda was a distant cousin of the child's father.

"I will send for Andrea and my boys as soon as I can." Her young heart dared to trust, dared to hope, dared to look ahead to a future where she would reunite with her children.

⋯⋯◆⋯⋯

Alma arrived in New York penniless and underweight, with three dresses, photographs of her children, and a few samples of her needlework. Rita brought Alma directly to her new employer's home. Alma's insides coiled cold, and her palms perspired. She stood stiffly next to her aunt, who chattered away in broken English. "My niece intelligent, likes children, work good, hard." Awed by the sounds coming out of Rita's mouth, she stared at her aunt and paid close attention, yearning to pick up a smattering of words. Yet fear continued to scurry down her spine, making her want to grab Aunt Rita's skirt, hang on, and walk right out with her.

La Missy, a tall, blonde woman, showed a nervous young Alma around the huge house, the kitchen area, and the laundry room. She then walked her to a small room on the second floor, right off the children's bedrooms. The room, modestly furnished with a little night table, a pretty porcelain lamp beside a clock radio, a small dresser, and a twin-size bed, was to be Alma's. A single window looked out to the garden. Branches of a robust elm grazed the top panes.

The woman stared into Alma's eyes and saw something fragile, a girlhood unrealized. "I think you are just what our household needs." In the past year her daughters had rejected a string of rigid matrons. "Welcome to our home. I hope you will be happy here," and in her voice, a gentle plea that said she wanted the young woman to like her, like her children, and stay. Alma did not fully understand what the woman was saying but from her tone and demeanor, knew she was speaking kindness. Alma whispered a version of the first English words she'd learned, "*Tank you, gracias.*"

The situation was overwhelming. The reality of the extreme poverty she had lived in Puerto Rico shocked her. To her, the small bedroom was a luxury, the house a palace. She sat on the edge of the bed, numb and terrified. What was she going to do? How was she to communicate? They would likely dismiss her. And what would she do then?

She began work the following day. It was the home of a well-to-do physician in the Coney Island section of Brooklyn. La Missy y El Mr. (as Rita advised Alma to always address her employers) had two daughters, twelve and five. It was her job to care for them and assist in all aspects of housekeeping. The Bergman's was a liberal household, and the two girls were spoiled and capricious. But for the twelve-year-old who studied Spanish in school, and Mr. Bergman who bragged he was fluent, although he labored with her language just a bit less than Alma struggled with his, communicating would have been impossible for the timid housekeeper from Puerto Rico.

Lucy, the five-year-old, became especially fond of Alma. Maternal feelings emerged over the many hours she dedicated to looking after the two *Americanitas,* mediating their quarrels, listening to their chatter, complaints, and childish observations. The feelings fueled guilt. She was not mothering her own children.

Alma slept few hours between bouts of insomnia; phantom aches kept her awake, the emptiness in her heart unbearable. She'd rise, light the small lamp by her bedside, and, using her night table as a desk, imagined she was speaking to her children as she wrote yet another long letter. On Saturday mornings she was at the post office by seven-thirty, half an hour before it opened. The postal clerk regarded her with pity as she asked for more stamps than she needed for the letters she mailed to her children. Sometimes she sent gifts, presents which she lovingly shopped for on her day off. She also put aside money for the tickets that would someday bring her babies to New York. All she lived for. Her letters were never answered—not a thank you, not one note letting her know how the children were doing, not the photographs she requested—nothing. Not even from her sister Inés. The rapid racing of her heart told the truth, *"They are stealing your children."*

As she lay in the darkness listening to the elm brush its branches against the bedroom's window, she thought: It would have been better to kill him.

Hatred incubated in her heart, and every night she plotted her revenge. Who knows what Alma may have resorted to if she had not met Antonio. "I want to take care of you," he said. "Let me." It took time for Alma to trust him. About three years. He was a good man who loved her as unconditionally as he could, and he went the distance, standing by her side during the custody battles that began as soon as Alma found out the fiend was in Brooklyn with her three children.

The court appointed Guardians ad Litem. When the judge questioned the children in chambers, they denied abuse, deprivation, or neglect. Andrea said she did not know any person named Alma. The children seemed healthy, said they were happy, and insisted they wanted to remain with their biological father.

The law guardians requested psychological examinations. The judge refused, advised they should refrain from prolonging the legal process, awarded permanent custody to the fiend, and warned Alma to refrain from filing frivolous petitions.

Fortunately, by then, Alma was pregnant with Irene.

Still, it was not good. She cried throughout the pregnancy. When the baby girl arrived, she carried her around all day and stayed awake by the crib for a whole week, cooing like a sad mother pigeon. Then inexplicably, she stopped breastfeeding. She continued to take good physical care of the child and remained attentive. Antonio worried; it all seemed a sequence of empty motions.

"Do not worry. Postpartum depression is quite common. Be patient." The obstetrician assured the concerned husband his wife would be fine in a few months. Baby Jaime turned out to be the cure.

He was a beautiful, sunny baby, and Alma doted on him. She dressed both children like twins—Irene and Jaime, her pride and joy.

When Irene was four years old, Alma became pregnant once more. She had gained a measure of happiness; God was replacing her stolen children. He failed her, though. The baby boy was born with encephalitis and died eight days later. A piercing scream. Then silence. Alma did not speak for several days, not to anyone but the young woman in white light whom she called Adriana.

Retratos

BACK HOME, A DAY after the funeral, images of Alma's life rolled out in Irene's mind as though cranked from a crumpled movie reel—faint colors and lines struggling to take form, reflections emerging in an opaque mirror:

Alma sending Andrea presents from New York, lots of presents, pretty dresses, shoes, and all the things a little girl could want.

Alma showing her a photograph of a little girl standing stiffly on a narrow podium in a three-quarter pose, dressed in a fancy white dress, a white satin ribbon around her waist, and a big white bow holding soft brown curls away from her face.

Irene, at age seven, asking, "Mamá, is that me?"

"No, that isn't you. It is Andrea, your sister."

Alma had shown Irene the photograph many times, perhaps wanting to set things straight with truths she held close to her heart: "I lost her when she was three years old. Her father was horribly mean, and I had to run away because he beat me. I left her with a woman who did not turn out to be the godmother I thought she would be. I wanted Andrea safe while I was in New York and I planned to send for her as soon as I could. But when I tried, they would not surrender her. They told her lies about me. They told her I did not want her."

Andrea would not let go of the perceptions formed in childhood and honed by her father and his relatives. She refused Alma's account of how she had been stolen from her.

Three of her siblings had died of deprivation. But Andrea would not accept her father was responsible for their deaths. Irene urged Andrea to seek therapy. It could help her grieve, help her work through the inchoate anger of having an absent mother. But *that* would require forgiveness.

"I am not angry about anything. And I don't believe in therapy." Andrea stated she was happy with her life and stopped short of sending Irene to hell. The nasty sting of her sister's words hurt, but she concluded that Andrea was testimony to human resiliency and had inherited some of their mother's strength. She had to ignore how her words felt like a slap in the face.

Irene wished for a relationship, but Andrea kept her distance, smug in what she could not guess was a-soon-to-fail marriage. Alma desperately wanted Andrea to understand why she had left her behind. Irene wanted to cry out the truth. "Mamá loved you, loved you with all her heart. It was not her fault!" The plea never left Irene's lips. She knew. Andrea did not want to hear any of it and when her father died, she wrote her mother a nasty letter. As if his death had been Alma's fault. There would be no reconciliation.

Andrea had closed the door.

Irene did not doubt her mother's stories were true because she kept telling them, in the same way, each time, and the cant, "men are evil," became a litany, an echo in Irene's mind.

"But mamá, papá is not evil."

And softly, she'd say, "No, he is not."

Sometimes, Irene culd hear them making love.

Irene wasn't due back at Lakeside until Wednesday. Thankfully, she had a bit of time to sort out the business regarding Alma's estate, as Jaime, somewhat sardonically, referred to their modest inheritance.

There was a small parcel of land near the ocean, but its proximity to the shuttered Ramey AFB was not a selling point. The taste of military appropriation lingered metallic in the minds of the locals. Still, sand and ocean breezes might entice an American retiree who did not care two bits about island history and who might want to live near a new airport.

Alma was twice a widow and named only her three surviving children in the will. The whereabouts of the two oldest, Carlos and Eugenio, remained a mystery. They were either deceased or wished never to be found. Either way, they had excised themselves from the brutality of their childhood. Irene called Andrea to let her know about the will. Maybe this was finally the time for forgiveness. Irene was shocked by her reaction, although she shouldn't have been at all surprised that her sister was not moved by Alma's generosity.

"I do not need money. I relinquish all claim, I . . ." Bitterness barely reined in, Andrea's tone more than implied what she hadn't said. She did not need anything from Alma, not then or ever. Besides, the property had belonged to Irene's father. "Go ahead. Do what you need to do."

Yes, I will do that, and in a moment, I will ask you to relinquish in writing. For seconds, neither woman said another word; the phone wire absorbed the static, the tension. Because it was so true, once heard, words could not be unsaid, perhaps, never forgiven.

Irene understood her sister had issues. Alma had been constant in Irene's life, always present; the bonds of their mother-daughter relationship strengthened by Alma's sadness. Unfortunately, Alma had been an absent mother for Andrea—never once had Andrea referred to her as mother. Anger festered, a virulent infection seeping through layers of forced forgetting. Alma's absence, an empty chapter of Andrea's childhood story. Irene understood.

Still, she resented the distance between them, resented Andrea's stubbornness, resented the lack of a genuine sisterly connection, wished she was not a psychologist, did not understand emotions and motives, and could, like any red-blooded layperson, scream some sense into her sister. But of course, she could not. Well, she could, but she wouldn't. "Then it will go to Jaime. He needs the money." Irene sensed Andrea shrugging into the phone. And that was that.

As soon as he entered the apartment, Jaime checked the locks on the door and nodded approval. "Good. I'm glad you added the safety feature I suggested last time I was here. And who's the creep downstairs?"

"You mean Grantis? You know what, we've never spoken two words, but I suppose he's harmless. Beth said he's going through a rough time."

"Yeah? Aren't we all. You should have seen the look he gave me, like I was vermin or a criminal trying to break in. Funny, because he's definitely the type I would be suspicious of. Be careful with him. I mean it."

Irene laughed. "Must be your shiny Bronx Bomber jacket. You know how downtown people feel about anything Bronx." Jaime was a diehard Yankee fan, lived in a two-family house in the Bronx, with gates on most of the windows, and a big German Shepherd lookout. Although more vigilant than he needed to be, he did love the Bronx and constantly tried to convince her to move back, closer to folks who were more like them.

Irene had dealt with her share of bias since college. She'd broken out of the neighborhood only to have to deal with classmates and coworkers whose attitude shifted once they learned she was Puerto Rican. First, surprise, as if an intelligent Puerto Rican woman were an anomaly; then, remarks like, "You don't look like a Puerto Rican, and you're better off saying you're something else before doors start to close. And always, the steely determination expanding in her chest. "My foot is in the door already," she answered once. "And what is a Puerto Rican supposed to look like? Tell me." *That one* never spoke to Irene again. A point not well-taken by a bigot in disguise.

Alfredo Bryson, her mentor, had warned how everyone would not be accommodating or supportive. "But don't, don't you ever bow your head to anyone, Irene. Never."

"I won't." Yes, she would bow her head, but only before her parents. Their love and support had nurtured her confidence and strengthened her for life's fights. Although no one would describe her as having tough skin, for sure, there were some steely fibers in there, fibers resilient enough to shield her from the beast of bigotry. Yes, the armor was necessary. Especially because bias could rear up unexpectedly like a venomous Hydra, most hurtful when it came from people she'd trusted, people who should know better.

"Don't worry about me, Jaime Míral. I am tougher than you think."

Jaime hugged his sister hard and tried to hold back tears. She rested her head on the satiny fabric of his bomber jacket, and as he lay a hand on her head, he choked up. "Irene, you know you are our princess, the pride and joy of our family. Just be careful." She felt young again, wanting to go back to their days as little kids, when they went everywhere together, when they clowned for their mother, trying to make her laugh. The siblings held each other close for some moments, something which they had not done at the funeral. The finality of the moment had wedged between them, cold and black.

He pulled himself together. "I guess we ought to have the talk now." Jaime took off his Yankee baseball cap and headed straight to his favorite spot, the oversize leather chair Irene had tucked into the recess of the ample bay window of her apartment, the place he always claimed whenever he dropped in. She'd splurged on that chair and loved how its patina was enhanced by the soft light that came in through the three tall panes. The turret-like column of bay windows on the side of the brownstone faced north; and even though the light coming in was muted, she loved the window.

A colorful ethnic shawl she'd draped over the chair's fat arms welcomed. Jaime sighed as he sat back into the comfort of the soft leather. Irene sat opposite him on a forest green velvet couch, a find from a second-hand furniture place.

"I've spoken to Andrea about the land. She does not want in." There was a little catch in her voice. "Even now, she persists in alienating herself from the family we are."

Jaime shrugged. "Well then, we can go ahead and sell the thing."

"Or hold onto it."

"Don't know. Do you actually think it's going to appreciate any time soon? Or shall we build a family compound on it?"

Irene ignored the intimation of sarcasm. "Just a thought, Jaime."

Jaime was a practical man. She had always been the idealist. For her, it would be a way to hold onto Alma. "Just that it would be nice to build a family retreat, mom's legacy to the entire family." No reaction from Jaime. Irene was not going to insist. *The sooner I stop fantasizing, the better. An idyllic extended family scenario is just not going to happen.* "I suppose it's best to sell the property."

Irene knew Jaime trusted her like he would trust a parent, and that he felt confident she would handle everything well. She always did. He got up, walked over to the narrow foyer, and picked up the small valise he had brought with him. "Here it is, the rest of our inheritance. Do the best you can with the land thing." He dropped a little kiss on her cheek. "Now we are rich, right?"

She frowned. Jaime did possess a sarcastic streak.

"Don't look at me like that. Call me and let me know how things go." He adjusted his Yankee cap, smiling at Irene for approval. "Hey, how's our friend Beth? How does she like being married? *Beth Martin*—just doesn't sound right. Anyway, say hello for me."

"Okay."

Jaime was a bit of a flirt. He'd had the hots for Beth since he first laid eyes on her blonde head, barely controlling himself from coming on. Respect, Irene had said. "You're married." His dark pupils deepened as he nodded, "That's right, and I do love my wife."

He turned back at the door. "Listen, you must come up to the house for some rice and beans and those *maduros* you used to like. And hey, you could put on a little weight. We don't want you being a *flaca*. Call. Clarita and Robert would love to have you."

"Thanks, babe. Give them my love." She did miss her mom's cooking. Clarita's would do. Jaime and Clara had been teen sweethearts, and Jaime had become a dad at seventeen. Antonio and Alma were upset but lost no time getting the two married. And they did adore their Robertito.

⚊⚊⚊◆⚊⚊⚊

All the paperwork was in order: title to the land, death certificate, and other necessary documents. Their father was long gone—fifteen years. Alma had kept her inheritance in the same small suitcase. Irene placed it on the edge of her bed and opened it. A small, partially oxidized mirror hung loosely inside the lid; she peered at the reflection of her tired face. Irene supposed the valise, with its dented metal-capped corners, had accompanied her mother since Puerto Rico. She explored its contents tentatively and found something smooth and satiny, a small red pouch cinched with a thin lace ribbon. A bit of ribbon broke off as Irene untied it. She emptied its contents on the bed: a lady's Bulova watch with a gold-tone expandable wristband, pearl earrings with tiny diamond stones set on platinum wires, and a pair of sapphire teardrops set in gold. She held the earrings of stones the color of midnight in the palm of her hand. Her father's wedding gift to her mother.

Alma never spoke of how much she loved him, but Irene knew her parents had something special. His love made it possible for Alma to live a new existence. He'd been the ticket out of the hell that had once been her life.

Irene rubbed the small face of the watch on her wrist, a Swiss wristwatch her mother had given her on her eighteenth birthday, the one she preferred over the gold watch she'd received from her parents when she graduated from college. She loved the narrow leather strap, color of burnished saddle brown that flattered the beiges of her skin tone. "It's a good watch," her mother had said. "It has a diamond movement." She'd been right. It had only required two trips to the jeweler in all those years. It still told perfect time. Irene wore it every day and saved the gold one for dress-up occasions. The Swiss wristwatch marked a special hour, marked a rite of passage, the moment she'd become an adult and understood. She and Alma had gazed into each other's eyes. Understanding shared, unfolding in layers like the cloth folded and unfolded by generations of women.

She found more jewelry in the zippered compartment, custom, dangling silvery things with dullish rhinestones. No necklaces or bracelets; her mother liked earrings.

A creased manila envelope contained a small collection of photographs, her parents' fancy gilt-lettered marriage certificate, and a document that resembled a passport, faded green, and embossed with the seal of the United States. A photograph of her father was stapled inside.

According to Alma, Antonio had arrived on a ship, issued the document at Ellis Island, and was required to carry it on his person. Her mother must have been confused because her father hadn't been old enough to arrive before Puerto Rico became a U.S. territory and before its residents were granted citizenship. But if he arrived on a ship, maybe he *was* processed on Ellis Island. There had been some brouhaha about whether Puerto Ricans should be included as ethnics in the exhibit at Ellis. In the end, the powers that were determined Puerto Ricans belonged in the Latin American section with the rest of the *hispanoparlantes*. Irene examined the document closely; it was not a passport, but it looked like one. For sure, some kind of official identification. A faint musky fragrance like pressed flowers in an old book lingered over the document; she held it close before carefully returning it to the envelope. The black and white photographs, now yellowed, creased, and frayed around the edges were fragile. Maybe some could be restored.

She examined one of the larger ones: Alma was holding a three-year-old Irene in her arms; her father stood beside her, smiling, his right arm a protective circle around them. Her mom stared out from the photograph with the detachment of a lifeless mannequin. Irene shut her eyes, wishing to remember the moment, but if the memory was in her, it was too murky, too distant. She wanted to, she wanted to return to that place in time, kiss her mother on the cheek, and make her smile.

Hand to temple, she walked over to her small home office. The sunny second bedroom at the back of her apartment had a win-dow like many found in brownstones, original stain glass still in the transom. Picture frames of all kinds and sizes reposed beneath the window wall. Some lay on the floor, others leaned against each other, along with a few art prints and two newly framed posters.

She wanted the small frame she'd discovered in an antique store in San Francisco when she was last there for a conference. The frames were a hobby of hers, and she liked to think she had a knack for finding unique ones. She found the one she had in mind, a delicately carved cedar wood frame with a violet moiré fabric backing. The backing was a little torn, but the glass was intact. Irene inserted the photograph in the frame—nice, perfect. She turned to her desk and placed it next to the peculiar brass lamp that she'd also picked up in the antique store in San Francisco. The little monkey sitting under the palm tree seemed to wink.

Weariness settled on her shoulders. She continued to gaze at the photograph of her parents as if expecting them to speak. Alma's eyes were large, her best feature, even if heartache had stolen their warmth. Irene supposed she looked more like her father, but for eyes that were more like her mother's. Except, Irene's were startingly gray, not sad and dark. Antonio often said, "We should have named you Iris for the wonderful light in your eyes." Sometimes, he playfully called her his *bruja*, his *brujita* of the beautiful eyes. Antonio, a man with the smile of a matinee idol and a ready laugh, was a handsome, amiable fellow whom everyone liked. Jaime had inherited his sunny disposition. Irene was the quiet one.

Fate had dealt Alma too much of a heavy hand. The loss of yet another child had disabled her, robbed her of the capacity to demonstrate affection. With a young child's intuition, Irene sensed she should keep her distance from a mother once too many times visited by the unholy angel named Grief. Antonio compensated as well as he could for his wife's lack. Irene missed him too. His love for her had been full, untarnished by sadness.

And he loved Alma as fully, quietly—steadily.

How did she ever live through that first marriage? How did she bear ordeals no one should have to endure? What had sustained her back then? Therapy, if available, had not been an option for poor women like her mother. There were no shelters or laws to protect them. Friends and families blamed and spurned, turned their backs on victims. Adriana—her only refuge.

Years later, in need and ignorance, Alma had turned to Irene, unknowingly using her as a sounding board. Just last week, Irene had come across an article that ascertained abuse could be imprinted on a mother's genetic material and transmitted to her offspring, making a child susceptible to similar experiences. Irene hoped not; she had faith. She knew there existed in every human at least a kernel of resiliency.

The phone rang loud and shrill, jarring Irene from her cloudy stream of consciousness.

"Helloo, how are you? I'm sooo sorry. Did you see my flowers and the mass card? You know I can't take funerals. How was it? Are you okay?" There was sniffling and whining from the other end. It was Laura. They'd been best friends since elementary school. Both her parents died in the same year, and she'd crumpled.

"Don't worry about it. I'll live. I feel, well . . . I don't know, remembering . . . a lot. I suppose it's what always happens when a loved one moves on. You know that." Irene sat with Laura for many hours when her parents died. "I have to get back to work soon. I'm trying to tie up loose ends."

Irene glanced at her agenda. She scribbled: Send out thank you cards. Tonight, she had to, *had to* go through the guest book and the sprawl of mass and sympathy cards occupying the top of her desk. Some had drifted to the floor, and as she leaned over to retrieve them, she eyed the pile of unread newspapers she'd stacked against the file cabinet. Would she go back to last week and pick up the pieces of news she'd missed? Maybe that would be easier than picking up pieces of unsorted feelings. She did not regret much, but she worried about all sorts of things, like should she use blank cards and write personal thank yous, or just send out preprinted ones. Like what was happening with Robert? She imagined him still crying, had stupidly forgotten to ask Jaime how his son was doing. Underlining the words thrice, she jotted down: Call Robert today.

"Laura, honestly, I'm just empty inside now, hollow. It wasn't like it was a sudden thing, except I can't help feeling like an orphan, abandoned."

"How was your sister?"

"Fine, fine, even cried a lot. It's just Jaime now. She's not interested in anything that has to do with our mom, Jaime, or me. There's not a thing I can do about it. I've tried." *Maybe Andrea was better off not knowing the tragedy of Alma's life.*

"She's a bitch. I'm your sister."

Good thing Laura didn't show up at the funeral. Knowing her, she might have said something to hurt Andrea. "She's got her reasons, her sons, and a life. I have Jaime and Robert. Sometimes things work out for the best."

"Lucky you."

Irene could hear the click of the cigarette lighter and the deep inhaling and exhaling of the first puff. Laura was a real nicotine freak.

"Lucky?"

"You're spared a big nightmare. I mean . . . you know . . . my brother. He was useless when my parents were sick, then he had the nerve to contest the will. You know . . . my father left me everything." With every "I mean, and you know," Irene could hear Laura pausing to take a long pull from her cigarette.

Laura was about to probe, likely getting ready to ask if Alma left any money. Typical. Her friend rarely overcame her natural tendency toward the materialistic. It wasn't she was crass, but although concerned, Laura was not a real terrific listener. If Irene did not offer the tidbit she expected, Laura would just ramble on about herself.

"You know I'm all alone in the world. I could have been an only child for all the good it does me to have a brother. My parents did not leave him anything because he did *nothing*, nothing with his life, only disappointed them, refusing to assist in running the grocery stores my father worked so hard to establish, and they hated that woman he married. I'm sooo glad they don't have kids because I'd be just *too* embarrassed. I'd have to rescue them from those two, and what in the world would I do with the children of two addicts? I mean . . . those two, they're junkies, and . . ."

"Codependents, Laura, codependents." She bet her friend had tried all kinds of things. Determined to keep up with the fast lane in New York City, Laura Martínez had to be fashionable. She wore designer clothes, said she had to dress to impress for her job at the toney Madison Avenue advertising agency where she worked as an administrative assistant, and only shopped at Bloomingdale's and Saks. She kept telling Irene she needed to outgrow middling West Side boutiques and shop at more sophisticated places. "Laura, I like those shops, and I like my clothes. Thank you." Irene sometimes thought Laura only dressed to impress the mirror.

Laura tried hard to cultivate the style of artifice featured in magazines like Vogue. But Irene knew it was all superficial, the way she was choosing to face the world, her cover. Irene loved her quite a bit, anyway. Laura was a link to her girlhood *and* she was loyal. Different lifestyles, but always best friends. Irene wished Laura was more serious; Laura wished Irene was more fun. Irene worried about her friend's fun times. Laura had been fortunate not to wind up in her brother's shoes. Somehow, she'd navigated unscathed through the storm of drugs that flooded the rave clubs she frequented.

"I've invested most of the money my parents left me, two mutual funds, and I met a broker who's teaching me how to smoke cigars.

He's an expert on the new high-tech high yield things. Also, I've contracted for new bathrooms in the house in P.R. I want to put my parents' money to good use. They made the right decision not to leave my brother anything. What's going on with you?"

Laura had to know. Irene gave in.

"It's the land. We have to sell it. I must make reservations to fly out there."

"Is your sister going to be along? Do you want me to go with you? Stay with us. Our house in Isabela is *huge*."

It wasn't. Laura was prone to hyperbole. The house was quite comfortable, but it wasn't huge.

"No. I told you. Andrea could care less about the whole thing. She told me she did not need worries and wished me luck."

"Fuck her," laughed Laura.

"Yeah, well. Listen, thanks for offering to help out. I need some time to regroup. Then, back to the clinic. I don't want to take time off, not for a while. I won't be able to squeeze in vacation any time soon."

Irene could hear Laura mouthing a humph of disapproval.

"Are you still wasting your free time at that dumb lab doing weird research? You're slaving at the hospital all week, and now you've given up your Saturdays too. When are you going to start living a for real life?" Irene ignored the comment. To Laura, a for real life meant men, and Irene had no time for them. "Keep it up, okay. Keep on avoiding relationships and you're going to wind up alone, an old maid."

Laughing, Irene flipped through the pages of her leather-bound American Express agenda, hoping she could juggle and squeeze something in, thinking she needed to start using the calendar on her new Macintosh. Truth was, she resisted technology quite a bit. She found it all an unnecessary drain of mental energy. Computers were for work, case notes, research, and the office administrator who managed her clinic appointments. The leather-bound agenda made her feel like an executive.

"I can't make it till early next year, January sometime. That's it. I must let Jaime know and ask him if he wants to come along. He asked me to handle the whole thing. He should be more involved and not leave it all to me; don't you think?" Irene immediately wished she hadn't complained. On one of her last visits with her mom, Alma clasped her hand and implored, "Look out for Jaime and Robert. Look after them for me." Irene had hugged her and reassured, "Mamá, don't worry. It's all right. Don't worry about anything."

"So, as I said, you-are-lucky. That brother of yours is pretty cool, too bad he's married." Laura had nursed a teen girl's crush on Jaime for years, even after she too moved out of the Bronx and on to what she believed would be a better life. "If you need me, let me know. And Irene, you know why I wasn't there. Right? You know I will always be for you, always. Anyway, we should get together soon. How about next Friday? Wait. Oh hell, have to hang up. This new phone only holds a charge for about an hour. But I love it! You should get one. Cell phones are the latest thing. Hurry, the connection is fading. The usual place, or somewhere different?"

Irene sighed. "I don't think I can do Fridays right now. Never mind. Let's see, how about the twenty-eighth?" Laura was twice divorced, persuasive, very pretty, and kept a tight social calendar.

"Great. Irene, I love you. I'll see you then."

Irene understood why Laura had not been at the funeral, had not expected her to. The Beth thing, though, was confusing, how she left without saying anything. She called Robert's number and got voice mail. "Hi Robert, just wanted to know how you're feeling. I'm kind of still there, at the funeral. That's how it is—a lot. Call me back, Robert. Love you."

As far as social life was concerned, Laura was it. Irene hadn't been to her favorite cinema house on Second Avenue in months, and she had forgotten to purchase tickets for The Joffrey's fall ballet season. The Joffrey was her favorite ballet company; their repertoires were classical as well as innovative. Back in the 50s, Brunilda Ruíz, a Puerto Rican ballerina, was one of the six original founders. She'd moved on to dance for The Harkness. Knowing she'd been instrumental in founding a major American ballet company was inspiring.

She thought of one of the Joffrey's most famous pieces, *The Green Table*. She sighed. *Yes, death marches and triumphs, no one is spared.* She probably could still get single tickets for one performance or two. The only culture in her life these days were the soft sounds of 105.9 FM, the classical music station she woke to at six-thirty every weekday morning.

And she could not take on one more patient and did not have one free moment but for the time she dedicated to the ESP study she was working on at NYU. Alma's accounts of the girl in white light she called Adriana had engendered an obsessive interest in the paranormal. She wasn't a superstitious person; she didn't think her mother had been there either. It would be smarter, easier to hold on to a standard psychological explanation and accept that Alma's reality had been so unbearably cruel that she retreated to an imaginary sphere. Except, her mother dwelled there for only moments, moments when her Adriana had been human flesh and bone to her. Somewhere in the back of her mind, Irene sensed she could formulate a link between the flashbacks that impaired her patients and her mother's experiences with the girl in white light. Her mother must have suffered from PTSD, too. Although, the young woman her mom experienced was not a flashback. As soon as an opportunity arose to assist in a PSI project, Irene grabbed it, even if it meant giving up all her off time. Just as well, less time to cry.

She walked into her bedroom and opened the top drawer of the dresser. Silk and chiffon scarves of delicate floral prints rested softly on a layer of white tissue paper. Irene gently rubbed the hems between her fingers, removed one, and shut the drawer. She'd taken to using them as adornment for her hair. She folded the scarf into a narrow headband and tied it under her right ear, letting the ends rest on her shoulder.

Antonio had not wanted Alma to work, and although there was work in the garment district for women who sewed, he'd said no. So she began to take in piece work. She picked up sacks of unfinished scarves once a week and delivered them five days later, neatly folded and labeled. Antonio made enough to support the family, and Alma, obsessed with thriftiness for having been pitifully poor, saved all her earnings. Earnings that later helped with Irene's education.

Irene closed her eyes and saw her mother sitting, work on lap, hands rhythmically pulling a single strand of thread along the edges of nearly transparent lengths of fabric; the stitches running even and exact, meticulously tucked under the finger-rolled hems, Alma bending over, picking up tiny labels from a big brown bag, attaching and finishing the piece. The balls of her fingers, thin calluses, her neck curving.

PART
TWO

*At the intersections of reality and
imagination, strength and vulnerability,
one may find truth.*

Lakeside

Wednesday mornings at the hospital tended to be hectic: 8:15, staff meeting with the night crew assigned to the new PTSD unit, 9:30, case review with supervising psychiatrist Dr. Freile, 10:45, community meeting. Wednesday afternoons were devoted to annotating case files. Although each patient's metal-bound progress chart was located in the nurses' station, in her office, Irene kept copious notes for each case.

The patients suffered from chronic sleep disturbances and debilitating flashbacks. At times, they exhibited moments of unprovoked rage. Violent nightmares disturbed their sleep. The night crew provided support to the nursing staff in case of severe episodes. Irene had made a point of personally interviewing the six people that constituted her crew. Each had an associate degree in mental health; two pursued studies in the field. She trained them to use checklists, behavioral observation, and annotation.

Before the end of the shift, the crew met and recorded the evening's activities in a log. Irene debriefed them each Wednesday morning. This served two purposes: To encourage professionalism—no small task, as the patients could be insulting and abusive; and to develop a rich and detailed anecdotal record of what was going on with each patient during the evenings. The information was helpful in the maintenance and direction of each treatment plan. The unit was Irene's baby.

She hurried toward the first-floor conference room; the crew was giving up an extra hour once a week. She was glad she'd requested an ongoing reservation for the large, well-appointed conference room. Generally utilized for administrative conclaves and lectures by visiting doctors, the night crew appreciated meeting in the impressive space. Jackson was already seated at the head of the long table.

"Good morning, Gregory." He preferred to be called Jackson. Irene tested his tolerance level this morning, deliberately addressing him by his first name. The crew needed to remain objective, not allow slights to influence their performance, and although Jackson was professional and hard-working, one of the new patients had become problematic. Irene noted how both arms were crossed in front of his chest. "Any particular problem with the Amado patient last night? I understand there was a serious incident the night before."

Gregory Jackson rose from his seat, paced back and forth a few times and with an expression bordering on frustration, said, "She is extremely hostile. I think there's something about me that she truly, truly does not like."

His approach with patients was excellent. People generally liked him a lot, and Irene understood his ego might be feeling a little bruised. "Is it possible you remind her of someone?" She waited for a response. Jackson was familiar with the history of each patient, so he had to have a good idea as to why that patient might be having a problem with him in particular. Jackson uncrossed his arms and sat back down. A year away from earning a baccalaureate, he'd told Irene he'd been thinking of applying to medical school. She was sure he'd make an excellent physician.

"So, tell me. How many hours did Amado sleep without interruption? Did she see you last night? What did she do? Was she calm, agitated, robotic?"

He went to his notes. "About three in the morning, she came into the hallway, walked to the end of the hall in a trance-like fashion, then went back to her room. I don't think she saw me or anything else. She was like sleepwalking or too groggy. Then at about five fifteen, I heard her screaming, then blabbing. I don't think she was fully awake. I recorded it as a nightmare, although I did not step into the room to verify that she was indeed asleep. I was not going to provoke another incident."

Irene nodded approval. "Jackson, how do you feel about staying with this patient?"

Jackson rallied a wan smile.

"I think you can be instrumental in desensitizing . . ."

The smile broadened. "A challenge, but I've handled more difficult situations."

"Are you sure?"

"No problem." Jackson pulled back his shoulders, a gesture of restored confidence. "You know me, Dr. Míral. I don't shirk from any assignment."

"Do not go into her room unaccompanied until further notice. But do try to keep her in your sight in the corridors. She needs to see you're still present." Jackson nodded, indicating he understood. Amado needed to get over her hostility toward black men. He might turn out to be the key that opened the woman so she could begin to better process her feelings about the attack she suffered.

Irene shared a monograph with the group, as was her monthly routine, *Non-Adaptive Resolutions in PTSD Patients: Generalizations of the Anger Response*. She followed up with a medical update on Amado and then requested oral reports on the other patients. On the way out, Jackson asked, even as he knew what the deal was, "It's me. Right? I remind her of the rapist."

"Yes, I think so. Continue to keep detailed records of all her reactions when she sees you, verbal and non-verbal. But-be-careful. Although Amado is on a tranquilizer now, it's hard to determine how reactive she may get." Irene paid close attention to his facial expression. She wanted Jackson to stay with the case but also to be aware of what was being asked of him. "Feeling courageous? We want to help her process her anger and be cognizant of possible triggers. Hopefully, displacement will subside. You can help us test out her progress."

"I understand. Honestly, though, I thought this was going to be easier than the Crisis Unit at Bellevue. Thought I'd seen the last of such cases back there."

"You know our work is never easy. Keep in mind the sleep disturbances alone cause her to be hyper-irritable. PTSD makes Amado prone to display aggression in response to even mild stimuli."

"Good luck to us on this one," Jackson remarked dryly and walked down the hall, hoping not to bump into Ana Amado. He was going home to sleep. Pat Reid, his co-lead, patted him on the back. "You see, everything is back to normal."

"Yeah, well, I'm relieved. I don't need to be seen as inept by the rest of the crew. But I'll tell you what, although I know Dr. Míral isn't like that, the thought she might view the Amado incident as a lapse on my part had been rippling in the back of my mind."

Irene wished Dr. Freile would schedule the reviews a little later in the day; a bit more time with the night crew wouldn't hurt. Sometimes issues surfaced that required her to meet with individuals privately. She did not like to rush this. Irene was proud of how she handled those meetings, proud of how supportive the crew was proving to be of the unit's mission: to assist the patients to process their trauma safely, develop insight and self-efficacy, and without overreliance on medications, cope with environmental stressors. She read through the previous week's log again and then through the recent night's entries. She bit her lip—definitely a disturbing pattern emerging in Amado's case. Problem: Freile was no doubt going to dwell on Ana's ravings.

"Someone in my house cursed a blue streak, don't know if it was my mom or my bro, probably both. My family was nasty all around, like full-time *carajo*. For a while, I didn't know what words like that meant, didn't know Spanish curses, but I learned them. Sure did. So what does carajo really mean? It means hell, an infierno, a place where nobody wants to be, like the house I grew up in. Then it was like *coño* baby, fucking tastes good. Was it?? Who remembers if it ever was any good? Coño? Does it mean fuck? Or does it mean heck? I know what fuck means, it means to go up and down and then it means to kill, like to fuck someone. It means off him, like he's dead."

Ana Amado, recently referred from a detox unit at Cornell Medical Center, had suffered a psychiatric admission the previous year. The primary diagnosis should have been PTSD due to the severe physical abuse and violent rape sustained during a mugging in the laundry room of her building two years before. Dr. Freile believed she belonged back in detox. Irene needed to convince him that not only was Amado's case appropriate for the PTSD unit but that it would require extra time. There was much more to Amado's case than Freile would understand or care to.

From the start, Irene suspected the doctor viewed her Cognitive Behavioral Treatment modalities as inefficacious. Known to espouse the position that pharmacology was the therapeutic key to controlling and curing all mental illnesses, Walter Freile posed a professional challenge for Irene. He recommended sodium amytal injections for sedation, to facilitate desensitization, and to mitigate the extreme lability often present after nightmares and flashbacks. He wanted the new admissions to rest before starting them on anti-depressants, which he eventually prescribed for almost every patient. Irene knew sodium amytal was controversial, but it was the only aspect of his protocol that deviated from the norm.

Irene was not aware of how hard Freile had tried to push back on the idea of the unit. The moment he was assigned psychiatric supervision of the PTSD unit, he stated to certain people, primarily close colleagues, that he did not think the new unit was necessary. Professional cliques were generally protective of insiders. Yet inevitably, some remarks filtered out. She did know he was most alarmed about patients he considered psychotic gaining admission to the new PTSD unit.

She entered the doctor's softly lit office and sat in the blue leather chair opposite his desk. Walter Freile was a very blonde man with soft brown eyes and handsome features. She guessed he was in his early fifties, imagined his home was airy and spacious with ample windows and lots of sunlight. He was reading Ana Amado's chart, flipping through the pages with considerable distaste.

"Two nights ago, I received a call from the nurse on duty. Amado had to be tranquilized. You do know that. Don't you?"

"Yes, she became aggressive, directed her ire at Jackson."

"The reason she is on Thorazine now. I doubt the fluoxetine will help her," he said abruptly. Fluoxetine, an anti-depressant touted as highly effective in treating the whole spectrum of PTSD symptoms, was standard.

Irene blushed, a consequence of anger, not embarrassment. She sat a little more erect in the chair, ready to defend her patient. No doubt, Freile was aiming to write off the case. "Amado, awake at about three in the morning, came out into the corridor and bumped right into Jackson. In her state, she likely perceived him as an enemy, and his presence triggered extreme anxiety."

"That woman is psychotic, at best bi-polar. I am convinced it's due to her past substance abuse. I will continue her on Thorazine." He made an entry in Amado's chart, distaste still on his face.

"Amado needs to be taken off the tranquilizer. Jackson may resemble the black man who attacked and raped her in the laundry room. Already distressed after a nightmare, she bumped into Jackson and went off. We have to address the incident in session and in group, but she needs to be off the tranquilizer."

She knew sodium amytal should have sufficed to calm Amado down, but Thorazine was even worse for this patient; it wouldn't help her work through trauma and displacement.

Freile shook his head no. "She's too explosive. And you must know that symptoms of PTSD rape-related cases usually diminish without treatment within three months. This is now two years after the incident. So, what is her problem?"

The icy edge in his voice did not deter Irene from defending her position. "Her problem?? Really? The literature cites statistical evidence that after seventeen years—seventeen—*at least* sixteen percent of rape cases still have diagnosable PTSD. *And,* that percentage is only the tip of the iceberg because many women do not seek help, self-medicate, and endure dysfunction. Then there are the suicides. Doctor, I am positive the laundry room incident was only the most recent of a series of traumatic events suffered by the woman." Her voice had risen a notch too high, and she checked herself before offering a recommendation. "If not fluoxetine, perhaps lithium. It may inhibit her from reacting to stressful stimuli as if the original trauma were recurring." She went on. "Also, she needs something to modulate her somatic symptoms." Trauma wreaked havoc on a person's physiology, from elevated blood pressure to arrhythmia, ulcers, and aches and pains of all kinds. Irene pointed to the chart on Freile's desk. "Her blood pressure is very high."

"No. Amado's physiological response is typical. No lithium. Or do you now want to agree she is bipolar? I'll reduce the dosage to ten milligrams, and then," he cleared his throat, "perhaps consider anti-depressants. If her lability diminishes, her pressure should stabilize. By the way, how is Jackson? Shouldn't he be moved to the day shift?"

"He is excellent and completely on board. He's a very competent fellow." She wanted to say more and emphasize that Gregory Jackson was the most experienced member of her crew. But no, the crew was her call, not Walter Freile's.

The doctor smiled thinly, started to say something, changed his mind, and nodded what seemed to Irene to be half-assed approval. She now knew him well enough to recognize he was not approving at all, and she couldn't afford to alienate him—the whole thing was just too new and important. Yet she needed to emphasize the importance of permitting the patient to participate as fully as possible in a treatment plan which would help her process the trauma. Sedation was not going to allow it. Thorazine was not it, not at all. Not for Amado, or any of the women in the PTSD unit.

She feared he was heading toward a diagnosis of psychosis. He'd mentioned paranoid schizophrenia as the underlying pathology. Irene completely disagreed; the woman had suffered severe physical and psychological abuse. "I understand your concerns about the Amado patient. However, she demonstrates almost all the primary symptoms, particularly sleep disturbances. Her outbursts and inability to control hostile impulses are not necessarily indications of schizophrenia or any psychosis. Although, secondary mental illness is present, she is not psychotic. The projectives demonstrate disrupted interpersonal functioning, intense mistrust, and a sense of betrayal. Her symptoms are well within the parameters of DMS criteria for PTSD. A more accurate diagnosis would be CPTSD, Complex Post-Traumatic Stress Disorder. I suspect she was a victim of abuse during childhood, all making her especially vulnerable and unable to cope in the face of any significant trigger."

Pursing his lips like someone's prissy aunt, he said, "If you're convinced you can accommodate the Amado woman in your unit, fine. I will not change her medication at this time, but your suggestions will be considered. I have ordered additional blood work. I'm interested in looking at the cortisol and serotonin levels, among other things. Her adrenals are working overtime. A-blockers may be an option, although it's a long shot. I want to keep track of her endocrine mix. I assure you there will be more violent episodes. So, a blood test at least once a week and after each incident."

He took his time before he spoke again, pausing as he closed the file, looking at her long and hard. "Listen, Irene, I am concerned about your stamina. Do you realize what's happening? Hispanic women, mostly Puerto Rican women, now occupy all seven beds in your unit. Do you think that's fair to you?"

She was taken aback by his remarks. *Fair??* Was it fair the women had been misdiagnosed, their trauma overlooked, never addressed by an uncaring, dysfunctional system? *Concerned about my stamina. Is he?* Irene resented his condescending attitude. She kicked her left leg up abruptly before landing it on her right knee and leaned forward in the chair. "Doctor, I value my role as a member of the psychological community at large. But please understand. I very much cherish the opportunity to serve my own communities whenever the occasion arises." Anger was biting, and she needed to measure her words. She looked him in the eye. "If it's become known to the profession that a Puerto Rican psychologist heads a PTSD unit for females, and if it's become a factor in referrals, then there is reason and need."

"Fine, fine. No need to be defensive. It just seems like an overwhelming responsibility."

He was missing the whole point. Couldn't he see the unit was a therapeutic ideal? He may have stepped into Dr. Bryson's shoes, but he could hardly fill them. Alfredo Bryson believed people could learn to change behaviors within a supportive familial environment. He and Irene had worked hard to establish the groundwork for the unit—ethnicity and culture had been crucial factors in the paradigm. Irene had been trained by an exemplary behavioral clinician, and well, Dr. Freile was not Dr. Bryson. She missed him. The hospital did not hire a replacement for Alfredo and asked Walter Freile to assume responsibility for his workload. Maybe Freile resented the additional load, but it was not much of a burdensome assignment since she did most of the heavy lifting. The problem was they were not on the same clinical page.

The doctor repeatedly checked his watch, impudently signaling impatience, as if he could not bear to be with her one more minute. They still had six cases to review. He continued through the cases hastily, and Irene, who relished reviews even less than he obviously did, all but let out an internal yeah! Almost every case, but Ana's, had stabilized, and Maríanis Román was holding up as an outpatient. But then, there was Carolina Del Valle.

—She is startled by even cursory physical contact such as a handshake or a slight touch, demonstrating extreme discomfort around others. The girl does not speak, has not spoken a word for over a year. She came to Lakeside from the psychiatric ward of a large hospital in upstate New York. Initially, doctors diagnosed her as borderline schizophrenic. After two months at the institution, the diagnosis was changed to "Hysterical Reaction to Trauma." A patient advocate was instrumental in getting Carolina to Lakeside and Dr. Miral's unit.

When Freile first reviewed the case with Irene, he'd shaken his head no, stating the initial diagnosis had been benign. "My dear, the patient is schizophrenic, in and out of touch with reality, obviously beyond borderline."

The obvious is not always correct, thought Irene. The state hospital had approached the accurate diagnosis: PTSD.

"I see Carolina is still not speaking."

"No. She is writing a lot, though. I think she will share some of it soon." Irene wanted to move on. This was the other case with which the doctor dissented, the second case he wanted to dismiss. She sat back in the chair, expecting an ultimatum, wishing she could provide more significant feedback, but she could not—the girl was not speaking.

He raised an eyebrow and jotted down: Pathology persists; PTSD diagnosis to be reevaluated.

Irene needed to choose her battles carefully. She'd been on the brink of totally losing her composure. She said nothing else about this case, hoping her silence appeased Freile and bought her time to proceed with Carolina's case on her own terms.

Five more cases to review.

"Oh, by the way, Maríanis Román attended my mom's funeral and shared her mother had frequently subjected her to violent beatings. Should I include this new information in the case notes?"

"New? I see here corporal punishment by the parent is already on record." He seemed tired now. His tone softened, "Irene, I'm so sorry about your mother. Do you need another day or two? Losing a parent is hard."

"Thank you. I'm only doing rounds for the next two days and expect to be back on a regular schedule by Monday. Getting back to work will be good medicine. I'm fine."

The meeting ran ten minutes longer than usual. Irene smoothed down her skirt and rose from the leather chair. "Thank you for your patience with the Amado case." Ceding, she added, "She is a difficult one." He nodded agreement. This time the nod seemed authentic. Irene took a few short steps to the door, reached for the ornate brass handle, hesitated, and smiled politely before rushing out.

Walter Freile

Walter Freile had selected the ornate handle from his prized collection of antique knobs, door knockers, and handles. A collection he began back in his late teens when he thought he wanted to become an architect like his father. The hospital's head custodian had installed it for him the day Walter arrived at Lakeside. The brass handle defined the office as his, more than any plaque could. For a moment he'd experienced an intense desire to start a conversation with Irene about its uniqueness. But the tension between them, the differences in professional opinion, defined their interactions, precluded even mundane intimacies.

Irene was a highly focused young woman, obviously proud and determined. And *very* attractive. When she crossed her legs and leaned into him to make her point, he noticed the ample curve of a firm thigh. He ignored the hardening between his legs—it was only his autonomous nervous system at work. What he could not ignore was that the woman sitting in front of him had been Alfredo Bryson's protégé. Bryson was not a theoretical ally, and rumors wafted, as rumors will, that Irene and Bryson had been lovers.

Not surprising. Likely that Bryson's affection for the young woman prompted his desire to to set her up before he left. And the prize had fallen on his lap. But it wasn't a prize at all, it was a nuisance. Míral was too intense, a bit of an upstart, and he did not believe her cases were worth it.

He'd been careful to suppress his real opinion regarding the clinical model Irene and Bryson had developed. Instead, he produced detailed charts to prove to the hospital's board that outpatient treatment was a cost-effective alternative, thusly suggesting that the unit was superfluous. Two board members countered, citing the needs of the East Harlem community, pointing out how the hospital needed to move forward with new strategies. They were not going to be moved. He was not foolish. He stopped insisting. Times had changed.

His reputation was impeccable. He'd been with Lakeside since a year after its inception and had run the Adult Acute Care Unit quite successfully, the reason he'd been asked to take on additional responsibility. He certainly did not resent it and did not wish the board to consider his position on the matter as petulance. He would wait, confident the new program would peter out eventually. In the meantime, he intended not to waver from providing definite professional direction to Miss Irene Míral. He wanted to like her. She was exceptionally bright and, for sure, dedicated—too dedicated.

Community

THIS TIME OF DAY, some patients might be knocked out from the meds or just catching up with the sleep time they lost the previous night. Irene wondered if Amado would be lucid enough or at all cooperative during the community meeting. She walked along the perimeter of the common spaces and into the lounging area where patients watched television. She often thought there was something surreal about the lounge, a virtual living room with couches and club chairs spaced so far apart they seemed to be floating. A segment of *Friends* was playing, the cast's voices echoed in the empty space. Except for Carolina, sitting stiff as a cardboard doll by the grand piano, no one else was around. The instrument, a hospital trustee's gift, was seldom played by anyone. Carolina sat there for hours every day with a notebook on her lap. "She plays the piano well," mentioned her guardian. Irene had yet to hear the girl play one single note.

She put an arm around Carolina's shoulder and asked, "Where is everyone?"

Carolina pointed to the wide doors that opened to the garden areas by the lake. It was a little victory. She did not recoil as she usually might and did respond to Irene's request.

As usual, Olivia and Marta were engaged in a lively ping-pong game on one of two tables set up in the center of the immense atrium facing the lawns. Irene walked over. "I'm sorry to break up your game, but it's community meeting time. Would you remind the others to come in now? Thanks."

The women were sitting outdoors on metal lawn chairs, smoking their cigarettes, and enjoying bright morning sunlight by the lake's tranquil waters. Within minutes, all gathered at the east end of the spacious atrium. Some muttered as each grabbed a fold-up chair from the row of chairs leaning against the far wall. They took their time placing them in the customary circle. Marta and Ana fussed, repositioning the chairs several times until the circle was to their satisfaction.

"Good morning, ladies. Let's get started. Tomorrow at ten forty-five, you'll be meeting right here for a talk with the nutritionist. You can each make an appointment so she can work with you on an individualized diet program."

"I don't need a nutritionist. I need me some cigarettes." Ana Amado frowned feral, her voice loud, shrill. "When can I get me some more cigarettes?"

"When can you get you some manners?" retorted Marta. Ana whipped her head in Marta's direction and glared.

Irene intervened, "Ana, how are you feeling today?"

She appeared worn, her complexion dusty, skin tones opaque. "Bad. Real bad. I feel lousy every day. I want to go home."

"You wish." Marta did not like Ana. "After what you did, they're not gonna let your big ass go home for months. They'll lock you up forever. Watch."

"Bitch, I can sign myself out. I can sign myself out anytime I want!" Ana's features contorted; an angry rash rose from her neck to her cheeks, mottling her skin.

"Ana, the average stay here is two months. You are suffering from PTSD. It will take some time for your nightmares to subside, a while before you start feeling better."

Ana stared hard at Irene and with an arrogant grimace clenched her teeth. Marta laughed.

Irene looked around the circle. "Let's continue."

"I haven't had a nightmare in two weeks. I don't think I need meds anymore." Felicia's words sounded as hollow as a desiccated log. "And what about Neesi? Is she coming back?"

"Neesi?"

"You know, Maríanis. I call her Neesi."

Felicia had become friends with Román and cried when she was discharged. Clichés often ring true; maybe misery does love company. When a friend moves forward in life unexpected feelings can be confusing—human nature. But Felicia probably did miss her; Maríanis had been a bodyguard of sorts. Some of the women had lots of street smarts and could be aggressive. Although she didn't look it, "Neesi" was even tougher than Ana and Marta. She'd survived harrowing situations.

Irene took notice of the flat tone of Felicia's words; her meds might need adjustment. "Oh, Neesi—okay, got it. Maríanis is doing nicely. She's coming in for therapy only once a week now." She looked into the women's faces, trying to read their reactions. Were they happy for the one who was out there now? Skeptical? Envious? Or hopeful for themselves?

Melissa wanted to know if Maríanis had stopped having nightmares. One night, a screaming Neesi flayed madly at the air around her face as though insects were on the attack. Melissa called out to the night crew for help. Neesi broke into a run, then hid behind a door, crying, living a nightmare while fully awake.

"Yes, those terrors are mostly gone. And you, how are you sleeping now?"

"Not much. It's that stupid nightmare, the same one, night after night. I'm in my car, it's very dark ahead. I get off the highway onto a ramp, then I'm stuck there. The ramp becomes more and more vertical, the car is going airborne, and horror overwhelms me. I have no control over the vehicle, only know I'm about to die. I wake up drenched in cold sweat, waiting to die." Melissa had been in a terrible car accident, miraculously escaped any significant injury—except for the shock of her sister's bloodied head, impaled on the shattered windshield.

"My nightmares are stupid too, Melissa. They come at me from some gruesome hell just like yours." Amanda, usually stoic and contained, began to cry. "Damn." Angrily, she swiped away tears with the sleeve of her oversized sweatshirt.

"I want you to understand why you experience nightmares and flashbacks. The episodes are fragments of trauma. A catastrophic event can deeply disrupt the brain's processing, resulting in distorted and incomplete memories. They may come and go, horrific pictures and sounds you can't let go of because your heart, your entire physiology, is still struggling with the emotions you experienced during the event. You need to reprocess those feelings right here in the present and learn how to identify triggers that bring on episodes. It's difficult to work through the pain of the trauma, but it is necessary so your emotional brain can release the memories, and your thinking brain can integrate them. It may take time. The memories may remain, but they do not have to torment you. The trauma is part of your history, but it can be just that, an event in a history book." The women just stared at their therapist. Irene continued, "Amanda, Melissa, do you ever have episodes when you're awake."

"Don't know. Sometimes, it's like the verge of a flashback," said Melissa, "like something is trying to grab me into a place where I don't want to be. Then the terrifying moment evaporates somewhere—hope it stays there."

"It's the same with me, Melissa, said Felicia. "It can happen even when I'm fully awake, a helpless feeling, a sensation like I'm falling into a black space."

Amanda slid down into the chair and, like a guy, stretched out her legs far in front, creating as much space around her person as possible, distancing herself from the women's words. Irene waited for a response. But Amanda slouched down some more and remained silent.

Irene turned to Amado. "How about you, Ana?"

"Me? I want to know how to kill a black man."

Marta yelled out. "She attacked Mr. Jackson! Dr. Míral, you should throw her out. She's no good. Throw her out. What the hell do you think, Amado? That you're white or something, ha??"

"You know what, Marta, shut up. Shut the fuck up."

Irene took a chance. "Ana, you are safe here, safe to say what you need to say. So why do you hate black men? Talk to us."

"Because he raped me and tried to kill me. He trapped me in the laundry room, and when I tried to defend myself he put his big fat smelly hands around my neck. He was laughing the whole time, laughing. He said to open up and give it to him good, and I felt so dirty . . . his damn dirty penis against my skin! He raped me . . . He fucking raped me!" Ana was screaming.

The women looked down at the floor; several had been raped and beaten. Marta shook her head and whispered a sorry Ana did not hear. Felicia and Olivia wept. Melissa kept her face down and was quiet. Amanda said nothing.

Irene walked over to Ana Amado and held her hands. "Ana, look at me. I know how hard it is to remember and talk about such an experience, but he was *one* black man, not *all* black men. Jackson did not rape you. The color of his skin, his physical configuration, his voice, all could be triggers that cause you to overreact with fear and hate—your response to horrible trauma." Ana's hands were shaking in Irene's. The room was quiet. "Ana, think. He's not responsible for what happened to you, is he? It's fear, Ana, debilitating fear, which lives in our nightmares and disrupts our everyday lives. The fear surges when you see a black man, doesn't it, Ana?" Ana bowed her head and did not answer.

"Carolina, would you like to read something from your journal?" Irene had asked the women to keep journals, but as far as she knew, only Carolina was making regular entries in hers. The girl shook her head no.

"She can talk. She's faking," smirked Marta.

"And how do you know?" asked Olivia, "We haven't heard her talk. She's like zip all the time."

"Oh yes, I heard her. I heard her reading from her journal when she was in her room."

"What were you doing in her room? Trying to get in her pants? You're lying. You didn't hear her say nothing. You're just pissed-off because she won't let you."

"Whaat?? Olivia don't even think that. Don't ever."

Olivia and Marta were gay. Jackson had caught them in bed together twice; it seemed consensual. Irene wondered whether Marta was saying truth, that Carolina was speaking. She hesitated to question Marta because she did not want to encourage her to spy or imply she had power over the Del Valle girl.

"Ladies, keep in mind that you are not alone. You are all in this together. Each one of you has suffered a traumatic experience. Throughout your life, you may have experienced more than one event. PTSD is a serious condition, but together, we can work to process the trauma. You can gain the strength you need to get on with your lives. Yes?" Ana wanted to know if Irene had ever experienced trauma. "Ana, awful stuff can happen to anyone. Thank you. That's it for today. Don't forget the nutritionist tomorrow."

Irene wished she could have responded in a more personal way. But that was a no-no for a therapist. So immediately, she had curbed the impulse to share what had happened to her mother. She'd wanted to say, "No, Ana, I have not experienced trauma, but my mom was brutally raped."

> Alma extinguished the flame in the kerosene lamp and drew the mosquito netting close. Before she could lay her head on the pillow, her husband crawled out from under the bed, snatched away at the *mosquitero*, and pounced. The mosquito mesh tangled around her legs and frustrated his entry. He cursed. Alma struggled with all the strength of her thin body as her heart raced ahead of the impending hell. She pulled his hair, scratched his face, and screamed until the back of her throat was like a desert, until her jaws locked open with no sound. He punched her hard. In her left eye, she saw a purple light circled in red, and then all went black. She did not see or hear anything else. The netting was soaked sordid with the sweat of their struggle. Her face felt swollen like a million bee stings to the inside of her eyelids, her legs heavy, the sticky mess on her thighs foul. She lay as still as a corpse, the length of his body obliterating her soul. No one helped her. The babies cried, and no one helped her. He punched her once more and then he had her again.

Hard for a young Irene to fully comprehend those awful things, yet the pain in her mother's voice left an impression. "Mamá, he was mean to you. You should have run away."

"I did. I ran away, back home to my sister's. Even tried to hide in the hills where some cousins owned property, but there was no hiding from him. He always found me." And she looked at her daughter with a child-you-just-don't-know-what-it-was-like-back-then kind of look.

Irene couldn't remember how old she was when she began to promise herself that no man was ever going to hurt her, strike her, or rape her. No, it was never going to happen to her.

She closed her office door, grabbed a tissue, dabbed at the wet under her eyes, and sat at her desk to write a short memo to the day crew leader:

Please redistribute the rules regarding visits to other rooms. Thank you.

Respecting boundaries and personal space was paramount; a little reminder was in order.

Irene felt a headache coming on. Recalling stuff that had happened to her mom was painful. She wished Alfredo Bryson was still around, but he wasn't. He was in London. Just a month ago, he'd accepted a position as an adjunct at Kings College where he was currently supervising two clinical trials.

Alfredo Bryson

ALFREDO BRYSON MENTORED IRENE during her graduate studies and supervised her doctoral dissertation. Known as one of the best psychiatrists in New York City, he served as Clinical Director at Lakeside from 1986 to 1993. Irene adored him.

The afternoon they came dangerously close to carnal intimacy, he'd patiently stated, "I have two daughters who are about your age, a wife whom I do love, and you are falling in love with me." He recognized transference was at work; her father had died just a few years before. But Alfredo Bryson was not about to start taking advantage of psychological need. He knew transference could work both ways and came to regard Irene as a daughter who required direction. He also told her she was repressed then never mentioned it again.

"Irene, you are intense, intelligent, and slightly insane, but believe me, not any more bonkers than most of my colleagues and acquaintances." She laughed.

For a while she'd expressed a nearly morbid interest in supernatural phenomena. Although he admitted some individuals might possess psychic abilities and have telepathic experiences, when Irene insisted, he balked. "Most existing studies have little merit and are of no consequence. And especially, not in treating people who suffer psychological pain. You already know there's a dearth of dedicated clinical professionals and far too many people needing treatment.

Don't you think it would be an unaffordable luxury to waste time in laboratories conducting esoteric research? Instead, you can forge a bright and useful future for yourself and serve your community."

When it came to deceased individuals or spirits communicating with the living, he most definitely drew the line. He slid a hand across his desk, thereby emphasizing the boundary and his intention to dissuade her.

Yet he knew Irene remained convinced her mother did experience the presence of an other-world-being, a kind spirit who comforted her in moments of despair and guided her in moments of confusion. Alfredo reminded Irene that Adriana always became apparent when evoking a superior presence facilitated a critical juncture in Alma's life. But Irene persisted, searching parapsychology books and professional journals, intending to incorporate aspects of pertinent documented phenomena in her dissertation. She submitted several summaries for review. The answer was always: No.

"Why can't you accept? Your mother is not normal." Irene looked pained. "I'm sorry. I'm going to be kind and say she's been hysterical sometimes. Not surprising, considering she's experienced some horrendous life events. Perhaps she needed to separate herself from the unbearable grief of losing a child, for example. Don't be foolish. Admit she may have been hallucinating due to some break in reality. Don't jeopardize your credibility by persisting with this."

Irene accepted Alfredo Bryson's guidance. She specialized in Community Psychology, and her Ph.D. dissertation, "Clinical Depression in Females Ages 19-25 and New Behavioral Management Models," was published in three national journals.

"You have great potential as a clinical leader," he declared. He knew that given her mother's background, Irene would be highly dedicated to working with women who had experienced trauma. Together, they developed the concept for the PTSD unit.

Researching the Soul

On Thursday evenings and Saturday mornings, Irene rode the subway to West Fourth, walked to NYU, and signed in at Jamison Hall. Not too many people knew about the research lab way back in the recesses of the fifth floor. In the 70s, members of the Paranormal Psychology Club became squatters in there, and no one had given a hoot. The galère of clairvoyance was free to do its thing. Members even published a few papers, which, not surprisingly, were also ignored. The place, now dusted off and refurbished, had morphed. A graduate fellow was developing a paranormal psychology elective slated to appear in the following fall's catalog. Sophisticated equipment had been installed in U formation in the center of the largest room, the place where Irene would devote serious time to paranormal research—Alfredo Bryson's advice mostly forgotten.

As a scientist, Irene needed to know the how and why. She suspected her mother's experiences with the young woman in white light were more than hallucinations. Finding a way to reconcile her personal theories with those grounding her profession was vexing.

If she had known more about it back then, she would have pointed out that many celebrated individuals, including Nobel laureates, physicists, anthropologists, and psychologists, had engaged in some aspect of Paranormal Scientific Investigation. Telepathy, clairvoyance, and precognition, studied over centuries, continued to be of interest to scientists worldwide. William James, author of *Prin-*

ciples of Psychology, became president of the American Society of Psychical Research. Evidently, the renowned psychologist had not been concerned about anyone questioning his involvement in such an organization. He had no problem reconciling the tenets of his profession with the exploration of psychic phenomena.

Irene kept in touch with Dr. Bryson, but out of respect, she did not let him know of her work at NYU.

Research in the paranormal was well and alive, and there were several reputable programs around the country and abroad. Some of the most illustrious institutions in the country, including Harvard and Columbia, sponsored or housed PSI programs at one time or another. Then, there were the activities of the U.S. Government. Within DARPA, The U.S. Department of Defense sanctioned and funded hundreds of research projects, including a handful on paranormal research.

Some years back, several internal memos regarding the exploration of paranormal activity as a new technology for use by the military made their way to the pages of two notable newspapers. The whole business disappeared from the public eye until an exposé by a not-so-reliable source insisted a Russian national, an expert in artificial intelligence and self-proclaimed psychic, defected and remained in the protection of the military for five years. Except it wasn't protection, it was exploitation. The government kept the individual in isolation and "groomed" his psychic abilities to develop "mind control weaponry." Somehow, all his official records mysteriously disappeared in or about 1991.

For a time, Irene dated a fellow who had worked his way up through the ranks of the NYPD and achieved the rank of captain. He complained about how it was impossible to complete some investigations and admitted his detectives sometimes enlisted psychics when working cold cases. Paranormal Psychology was still a discipline to be reckoned with. Maybe she could contribute something to the science.

Irene delved into the literature and spent endless hours perusing obscure monograms. A case study she came upon in an East European journal stopped her in her tracks. The article documented suicide attempts by an adolescent female hysteric. The girl, jilted by a suitor, wanted to die. The unusual aspect of the case was the manner in which she tried: by lighting many matches in quick succession and inhaling the fumes. Ineffective, to say the least, but quite dramatic. Alma's account of the girl in white light came to mind immediately.

Her mom told a story of a suicidal girl in her hometown: In the old colonial section of the cemetery, there was a monument, a glistening marble statue of a beautiful young girl people claimed had killed herself over a suitor she could not have, did herself in by lighting many matches at once and inhaling the toxic fumes. According to Alma, several young women had attempted suicide in the same manner. But wait then, was there a connection? Had her mom somehow come to know the story of the unfortunate East European girl? And inspired by the stories and the white statue in the graveyard, she'd created a luminous image of a young woman in her mind. But why did her mom believe so strongly in Adriana? Was it all a defense mechanism that held her together so she could go on in life? And had her mom experienced suicidal ideation as well?

To Alma, Adriana's presence had been real, palpable as skin. Her mom's accounts raised one too many questions in Irene's mind. Questions that drove her to explore possibilities beyond the prosaically scientific. Could her young lady in the light be more than an eidetic memory evoked to emerge from a time unknown? A being whose light eased the darkness of Alma's despair and soothed her pain. *Adriana may have saved my mother's life.*

Interestingly, the Bern Conferences of the early 1900s prohibited the use of white phosphorus in the manufacture of matches. White phosphorous, poisonous in its most reactive form, was utilized to fill mortar shells, artillery shells, and grenades. Irene noted the dates covered in the study. By the time that sorrowful girl attempted to end her life, the substance had already been outlawed. Insufficient vapors of sulfuric acid produced by lighting the matches would not be lethal. The girl sank into dark despondency and refused nourishment and medication. Her parents interned the young woman in a sanatorium, where she died of sadness at age twenty-five.

Fascinated, Irene returned to the monogram several times. Surely a misdiagnosis. It had to be a case of endemic depression, a girl with a depressive personality since childhood. Unfortunately, incorrect diagnoses were still much too prevalent. Whether resulting from negligence, incompetence, or clinicians motivated by greed to dispatch patients with the quickest fix at their disposal, it was an aspect of her profession that Irene abhorred. Human error was one thing, but disrespect for a patient's sanity was another. At least three of the women in the unit had been misdiagnosed. The probability of such occurrences increased the longer a person remained entangled in the medical system. Walter Freile was particularly defensive about any claim of misdiagnosis. Professional loyalty to his colleagues, and his ego, would not allow him to retract an incorrect diagnosis. Invariably, he leaned toward pathology, the more profound, the better. He loved to medicate. After all, he was a psychiatrist and an opiniated purist who resented the taint of substance abuse. If a patient had experienced addiction, that was it—rehab.

Some of the women had experienced events so traumatic that no diagnosis satisfied Irene other than PTSD. Each woman clearly met DSM criteria for a PTSD Diagnosis—the reason she was at odds with Freile. He stated that even if they were dual-diagnosis patients, he did not want them in the unit. She did. She had to hold her ground.

The standard clinical protocol was to treat the substance abuse. Negative drug screens were the desired goal. Once the person achieved sobriety, that pretty much was the end of it. Another positive stat for the rehab program. Another individual walking away with a Band-aid that would soon fall off while issues that caused the person to use in the first place continued to fester. Few programs were genuinely invested in treating the root of the addiction. As Irene saw it, the standard treatment was ineffective triage, resulting in a high recidivism rate. Gaining sobriety and achieving long-term recovery were two different things.

The incidence of addiction and alcoholism among people living with PTSD was horrendous. Freile was blind to the correlation so very apparent to Irene. It was always a victory when he relented on a medication issue; those victories were rare. He held most of the high ground—anti-depressants, Xanax, benzodiazepines, and antipsychotic agents. Whenever she objected, he would offer his condescending yes Irene smile and, true to form, once again state: "Barring substance abuse, with appropriate medication, PTSD cases recover within a short time."

Bless his heart.

She intended to stand by her treatment plans at all costs. If she had to, she would push back against the time constraints that Freile kept shoving in her face. Yes, the unit was meant for short-term treatment, but imposing rigid parameters could be counter-productive, possibly unethical. Still, she had to tread carefully. He was in charge, well-known, and respected in the field. It was difficult enough to disagree with him on individual cases. If he even guessed what other theories were of interest to her, he might go for her license.

Just once in a while, Irene recalled Alfredo Bryson's warning: "Paranormal Scientific Investigation is considered the work of charlatans. You are now an expert on PTSD and cognitive-oriented treatments, do not jeopardize the standing you have already achieved."

Dr. Rosen, I Presume

David Rosen possessed an intense interest in telepathic communication. He and Irene first met at a symposium in Denver, *Symbolic Visions: An Analysis of Self-reporting Mechanisms*. They hit it off immediately and wondered how they had not bumped into each other in some psychology class when they were undergraduates at NYU. He'd been two years ahead of her and went on to do graduate work at Princeton. She remained rooted in the city and completed her Ph.D. at The New School. Both now lived on the West Side of Manhattan.

He was excited about what he deemed to be new findings in the field of telepathy and, courtesy of his very wealthy parents, had spearheaded the funding for the fifth-floor communications research lab. The rigorous designs of his research models persuaded the head of the Psychology Department to allow David to recruit graduate students as interns for several projects.

For five months, David engrossed himself in two experiments involving six volunteers who had reported auditory phenomena. He was doing exciting work tracking auditory cortex function with MRIs and recording actual voiceprints. This was possible thanks to a newly developed code interface and to the connections his family's wealth facilitated. Gaining access to equipment that could scan the brains of people who, medically, did not need MRIs was not an easy feat. David was deeply grateful.

He focused on the scans of two female subjects. Their MRIs revealed unusually distinct receptors in the areas of the temporal lobes responsible for advanced auditory processing. Since no two brains are ever entirely alike, it was more than curious how the receptors appeared identical in both women. David was excited about the findings. The subjects were unrelated, so the results were significant and worthy of further inquiry. He was convinced the two women possessed an exceptional perceptual gift—a gift capable of telepathy.

He would need additional rooms, ideally on different floors. Impressed by David's findings, the department head sequestered two extra rooms for David, one on the fourth floor and another on the second, where individuals would try to transmit mental messages through two floors of space. David felt confident he could at least partially prove auditory phenomena reported by the women were not hallucinations.

Considerable work had been done on telepathy, but not with subjects who reported hearing things. Once he'd set up his lab on the fifth floor, he called on Irene and invited her to drop in.

She and David had made love a couple of times in Denver; encounters which, if they had bumped into each other as undergraduates, would have happened anyway—the kind of coupling that often results in lifelong friendship. And they were good friends, friends with an avid interest in Paranormal Scientific Investigation. They kept in touch, frequently meeting at lectures and sharing notes on recent developments in the field.

She was the first to hear about his findings and his theory that the two women were perceptually gifted. "I want to expand a research design around what I've already discovered and I want you on board."

Irene could not contain her excitement and gave him an elephant's earful of her own theories, her work at the clinic, and her mother's stories of the girl in white light. "My mother may have been receiving communication from somewhere—"

"Whoa, girl, one PSI element at a time. Your patients' flashbacks seem internal, though I must admit the possibility their memories may continue to exist in some other moment, perhaps in another dimension, is fascinating. But way beyond the work we are focusing on right now. And your mom's visions, kind of a Victorian age construct. No?"

"Yes, it is fascinating. A moment from a previous time somehow transmitted to the present." Sadness crept into her voice, "David, I don't think my mom was a hysteric or that her Adriana was just a vision." Looking dispirited, she frowned, and lowering her eyelids, averted her glance.

"I'm sorry, babe." He went for an apologetic hug.

"Get away from me," she said, laughing self-consciously as she pushed him away. "Look, the important thing is we're willing to explore beyond the so-called normal. Any bit of significance can open new paths for research. Count me in."

David understood how on a personal level, it was about her mom and the girl in white light, but it was also about PTSD and her patients. He listened carefully to her theories.

"Some persons may be gifted with a predisposition to be telepathic. The gift could be corrupted by horrible trauma and, yes, exacerbated by drug abuse, medications, and personal histories of neglect and child abuse. Trauma disturbs brain chemistry, so an individual gifted in ways the medical community hasn't yet explored might experience more acute events than others, cataclysms of the brain, so to speak."

The intense conviction in Irene's voice signaled how much the opportunity to participate in PSI meant to her. It meant the world to David, too. "Yes, there is still much work to be done. So why not us? Who knows what we may discover? We're both willing to explore territory where the impossible may become possible. That's what all great scientists have always done. Men like Nikola Tesla. 'The day science begins to study non-physical phenomena it will make more progress in one decade than in all previous centuries of its existence.' Irene, we're going to live by his words."

Science had not begun to plumb the capacity of the human brain. There were huge premises yet to be researched in neuropsychology, frontiers to be explored. Perhaps boundaries perceived to be physical were not. Quantum physicists understood time and space could be transcended, magnetic fields neutralized or manipulated. If a space vehicle could hurl through the infinity of the universe, could not thoughts and images travel from one time to another—between two minds or many?

⸺⸻◆⸻⸺

David frequently placed ads in newspapers whenever he needed new subjects for his study. The last round of advertisements yielded a surprising number of people. The exciting thing was that, unlike the graduate students who signed up for the internship credit, the new subjects would receive no compensation. They were participating on an entirely voluntary basis.

"David, you well-know that sampling can be the bane of research, especially in such a soft field as we want to investigate. I'm concerned. We only have a handful of subjects so far."

"Yes, but validity will be on our side, thanks to you." Not only was Irene passionate about the study, but she was a certified psychologist—especially skillful in screening potential subjects. "You're smart as hell, Irene, and you do have the knack to keep me grounded."

He thought the world of Irene. For sure, there was an obsessive motive driving her, but that was not necessarily negative. Once in a while, he'd recall their lovemaking in Denver and regretted he'd so casually let the sparks of passion cool. But then, Irene seemed to want it that way. And it was okay.

Data Is Objective;
Feelings Are Not

As their research model evolved, Irene did not hesitate to point out potential weaknesses. Methodical she was, never losing sight of the possibility they could be labeled charlatans once their results were scrutinized by the profession.

She always asked the volunteers what motivated them to respond to the advertisement. Their responses had a common thread; they heard voices. As a matter of course, anyone who reported hearing voices would be clinically diagnosed as psychotic. Irene checked all available databases for psychiatric hospitalizations. But if any of the volunteers had significant histories, they had slipped through the cracks of the system, perhaps received treatment in private institutions whose records were not accessible. Not one reported ever being on medication for a "perceptual experience." Odd. Or they were exceptionally good liars, and why? After having them sign releases, she screened rigorously for other signs of pathology, took detailed histories, even thought of taking urine samples, then changed her mind.

Drugs posed another potential bugaboo. Research on acid and other hallucinogens was extensive. She and David were not about duplicating other studies and did not need the presence of psychoactive substances as a confounding variable. Of course, David came up with a brilliant idea: anyone identified as an experimenter of hallucinogens should be included in the database for a future comparison group.

"Complicated, difficult to match on other dimensions. David, now you're the one getting ahead of yourself, possibly losing sight of your original goals. Most of our acidheads will likely disappear into the dirty fabric of the city, but I might as well humor you." She went ahead and created a special future projects file. His iconoclastic approach to research was inspiring.

For two months of Saturdays, Irene worked assiduously at the research center interviewing off-the-street volunteers. Time warped for her in those rooms. Data was objective, feelings were not. She coded responses and created data tables. It all made beautiful linear sense in the somber reflection of computer screens. Crunching data and redesigning models of inquiry provided the escape she needed from the sadness—the relentless progression of her mother's illness.

Eighteen people signed up; fourteen kept the second appointment. Irene screened out three immediately. One had a history of psychiatric hospitalization; another was high as a runaway helium balloon. The third person was an Army veteran who had worked in communications and artificial intelligence before being deployed to the Middle East. A reticent fellow with a slight stutter and a persevering twitch in his right eye, he denied any incidence of combat fatigue and said he'd had the twitch since he was a little kid back in Iowa. Irene detected a faint foreign accent, not a midwestern one—maybe something he'd picked up overseas. She probed for additional symptoms of PTSD. Irene gave him her card and the phone number to the VA Clinic where she had a contact, Joe Martell. She urged the vet to give him a call. He made a sour face, put the card in his wallet, and walked out.

Minus the special-projects-file people, only eleven people made it through her initial protocol. All eleven would not make it through the following battery of tests. Irene focused on the young woman in dark glasses. Something about her seemed familiar, an aura that touched her like the faint vibrations of a forgotten song.

"Please remove your glasses."

"Prescribed sunglasses," she said with a smile. "My eyes seem to distract most individuals, so I choose to wear sunglasses indoors." Irene could see that she had a point, her gaze, well, quite intense and penetrating. She asked her to put the glasses back on.

Only four people made it through the second protocol. She asked David to place another ad. The response was immediate. Ten volunteered, Irene weaned out eight. By the end of the four weeks, they had six viable subjects. All matched David's first sample on age, gender, and educational level. None knew anyone in the original group of six. A sample of twelve was not much to go on, but it was a start. The compelling young woman in the dark glasses eventually proved to satisfy all the criteria.

Milk Chocolate Eyes

Even if it were only a few days after the funeral, Irene was anxious to return to the lab. David was not surprised to see her so soon. He asked about the flowers. "I would have attended the service, but you asked me not to. How are you holding up?"

"I'm all right, grateful for the distraction of daily routines. It helps. The flowers were beautiful. Thank you."

He was not one to dwell on sadness and simply said, "Good." He placed a hand on her shoulder. "Irene, glad you're back. I have news. It's time. We're finally ready to set up a classic experimental model."

"It's more like we'll be setting ourselves up to become the laughingstock of the psychology community. Seems a bit premature."

David frowned. "No. No one is going to laugh. We're about scientific research and we will report the outcomes accordingly, whether the results are congruent with our hypotheses or not."

"Critics can be cruel, but don't worry, I'm not deserting the ship." The study was happening, and she knew David would share the results with the community. Her enthusiasm was getting a bit soggy. Maybe it was the funeral, maybe Alfredo Bryson's words, which lately rang like a dull alarm, maybe Laura's insinuations that working at the lab was an excuse, a way to avoid meeting men—all of it was driving her to ponder the pitfalls of pursuing her esoteric avocation.

But she was as invested in the research as David, and they did shore each other up when either became discouraged, much like a wife and a husband in a good marriage might do.

"Are you having second thoughts, Irene? Worried?"

"We need to be skeptical, and I do have second thoughts sometimes, and especially since . . ."

"Yes, our research is unorthodox. But here, read this." He produced a current copy of *Modern Psychology* and turned to an article: "Recent Developments in the Field of Transpersonal Psychology."

"This," he said as he brushed the article with the back of his hand, "is the type of thing that keeps me motivated . . . And you." His eyes warmed.

"Me?"

"Yes. You." His pupils went soft, and he leaned into her as if readying for a kiss.

Disappointment scurried across his face as she turned away.

"Bottom line is you and I are scientists, Irene."

She smiled, then a quick peck on his cheek. "Thanks for the pep talk."

He bowed with his head. "Glad to oblige."

She admired his confidence, earnestness, and his vast fund of knowledge. He was an expert in the history of parapsychology, steeped in the work of William James, Margaret Mead, and the endeavors of scientists at institutions like Duke University and Stanford. The prospect of breaking new scientific ground was exciting, enticed Irene's inquisitive nature even more than David's intelligence and milk chocolate eyes.

Irene and David moved forward with their work. Since their sample was small, they tried to design an experiment that would turn out to be remarkably scrupulous, going back and forth, punching as many holes in the methodology as they thought others might see. Two weeks later, their research design was as tight as a perfect geometry proof.

It was almost seven-thirty on the fourth entire Saturday Irene had devoted to the lab. At first, it had been only a few hours on Saturday mornings and Thursday evenings. Although the process had been mentally exhausting, she felt a sense of pride, much like after the effort expended during a sprint in the park, and most especially, after a breakthrough by one of her patients. She started to pack up.

"Don't go. Let's have dinner or drinks or something. I know a new Korean place two blocks away. Are you free?"

She heard the subtle plea in his voice and thought, why not? She needed to snap out of the social stagnation that had settled over her since her mother became ill. She made a mental note to call Laura and confirm their girl date. David was standing close enough for her to feel him waiting for a response. "Okay, let's check out the kimchi bar."

The place was small, tucked between a confection shop and a bookstore, intimate in the way crowded small spaces could be. David said the owner was Korean and that the clientele of university students had made the place wildly popular. "We caught it at a good time. There's usually a long line at the door." He ordered two Korean beers. "This is what they come in for." He held up a bottle of Kloud. "Authentic stuff, only place in the city that sells it."

"Okay, here it goes!" Although she was not a beer drinker, she gulped down half a bottle. He laughed and put an arm around her shoulder. Then, in the simple intimacy of the moment, she looked into David's eyes, wanting him to hold her tight in his arms, hold her so tight that she would forget that her mom had died.

During that evening and all the next day, Irene and David engaged in their own little experiment in his apartment. It was good, and for many hours neither mentioned telepathy, experimental studies, or the transcendence of imagery, gratefully yielding to the release of their joining. Late into Sunday afternoon, over pizza and red wine, David began a spiel about the transmission of mental images.

"Whoa, David, we barely have it together for the auditory phenomena."

"Have you forgotten about the girl in white light? How we wonder if she might exist in a different dimension or in someone else's memory? It's quite possible the image your mother saw was a transmission from somewhere. Your mom may have been a gifted one also. Funny thing, because now you're somehow reiterating what I said about taking it slow when you mentioned your mother's perceptual experiences."

She screwed up her face like a kid. "Yes, David. In my gut, I believe what my mother saw was real, and the existential aspect of the whole thing gives me hair-bending chills. But I'm a scientist and know enough to also be skeptical. You know, the concept of a supernatural woman in white associated with tragedy is almost universal. They say there's one roaming around Durand Park up in Rochester."

"Irene, it's going to happen. There are waves of energy and electrical impulses all around us. We know sound can be transmitted through radio waves, through any medium, air, gas, or solids. In addition, there may be unknown venues through which thought, and yes, images can travel. And haven't we both been alluding to the possibility of an unidentified wave only the minds of gifted people are able to access? 'If you wish to understand the Universe, think of energy, frequency, and vibration.'"

Nikola Tesla was David's hero.

"Yes, David, I suspect it's something else also. But sweetheart, what you're dwelling on still sounds to me like plain old radio waves." Then deadpan serious, she said, "By the way, all the people in our samples have IQs of at least 150. So, tell me, what's your IQ?"

"Very funny, genius," he laughed and reached for her arm. "Come here, you. Stay tonight. I'm feeling frisky again."

She started to lean into him but changed her mind and got up from the couch. "I'm leaving. See you on Thursday."

Her index finger hesitated over the console in the fancy elevator. Wanting to turn around and head back to David's apartment, and not quite knowing why she shouldn't, she finally pressed the button that would take her to the lobby. She paused as she exited the Normandy. In the lights of evening, the mosaic tiles at the entrance of One-Forty-Five glittered like gold. It was a half mile walk of brownstones from West 86th Street to her place. The brisk nip in the air was helpful, and the lingering heat of desire receded.

❖

David knew what would happen next. Irene would disconnect sexually from him just as she'd done in Denver. He wondered if she might have other commitments, but she didn't strike him as someone who slept around. If Irene did have a serious relationship, she wouldn't have been in his arms today. He was glad it happened. He had not been in anyone's arms recently; maybe she hadn't either. Keeping it casual might be best. He respected the woman and was grateful to have her on board. Best not to complicate things, even if he did miss her on the evenings he worked alone in the lab, wondered if she ever missed him.

Sunday Night

SHE WAS RELIEVED TO be home and have some alone time. The weekend had been intense. She poured a glass of wine and dialed the answering service. David had just called, saying, "Thanks for a really nice time. Let's do it again, sometime soon." A smile like a timid Cheshire's hovered on her lips as she went on to the next message. Maríanis wanted to confirm Monday's appointment. She sounded a bit sad. Laura reported. "I'm going on a cruise with my new guy. I'll tell you all about it when I see you on the twenty-eighth." Then three messages from Jaime. Robert was in the hospital.

She called. "What happened? Is Robert all right?"

"Early Saturday morning, he was on the way home from his shift at the Port Authority, lost control of the car, and veered into a barrier on Riverside Drive, right north of the bridge. I had advised him not to take that job, told him to concentrate on college and his coursework. But he insisted, saying it was hard to get a part-time job there and that he was happy to have it. Anyway, no injuries apparent, but he was unconscious when the police pulled up. They brought him to Bellevue Hospital. He's under observation, and I have to get the car out of the pound."

Her hospital emergency pager was always on. Nothing came through while she was at David's. But darn, she hadn't accessed her answering service. Wonderful. She could have called from David's landline. *That's it! I'm going to get one of those new IBM cell phones and dump the answering service.* The first message from Jaime sat there for a whole day. How embarrassing. She'd allowed herself to be seduced into a time warp of indulgence, forgetting who she was.

She checked her watch; it was six o'clock. Sunday visiting hours usually went to eight. Besides, she could get in anyway. "I'm on my way there now, Jaime." She gulped down the rest of the wine, ran downstairs, and rushed past Beth walking Charly.

"Hey, Irene, Irene!"

She turned around, waved, hurried to Amsterdam Avenue, and hailed a cab.

Robert was sitting up in bed watching a basketball game. He smiled big when he saw his aunt rush in. His mom Clara was sitting by the window, leafing through a magazine.

"Baby, what happened? Why are you here?" Irene leaned over him, brushed a kiss on his cheek, and grabbed the chart hanging on the wall by the bed.

"I don't quite know, Tití. It was kind of foggy, and I thought I saw a woman up ahead walking into my lane from the side of the road. I swerved to avoid hitting her and lost control of the car. I don't remember anything else."

"Well, maybe you saved her life. What happened to her?"

"That's a good question . . ." Face serious, Robert looked down at his hands.

"Tití, what if nobody was trying to cross the road? Maybe I imagined I saw a woman. It could have been some shadowy branches falling onto the road. It was foggy."

"Do you think you may have fallen asleep at the wheel? Can you describe the woman you think you saw?"

"I've never fallen asleep at the wheel. Don't know . . . it looked like a woman in a white dress." Robert made a face. "Forget it, Tití."

Goosebumps rippled on her arms. She remembered the angel's kiss Maríanis had described and how it could be a warning of impending doom. With intent concentration, she examined her nephew's face and lips. If the burn of a kiss had been there, it was gone. Then angry at herself for even remembering Maríanis' ridiculous report of an observation she'd surely imagined, Irene flipped through the chart. "Everything seems to be okay. No concussion, no whiplash, no broken bones, bloodwork looks normal. How do you feel? I mean your head; is thinking about it bothering you?"

"I'm fine, Tití. I'm going home tomorrow."

"Okay, I think you're all right. Probably just a mirage emerging from weariness and bad weather on the ride home from a long shift. Robert, please drive safely. If you experience any dizziness or anything, get back here in a moment. I love you. Call me and let me know how you're doing. I love you, Robert." She hugged and kissed him goodbye. His mother, looking relieved, waved as Irene walked out the door.

She splurged on another cab and was home in no time. During the ride, she thought about what David had said earlier about the transcendence of images and the girl in white light. A horrible thought crossed her mind. Had some version of that presence tried to manifest itself to Robert? Trying to convince herself that her considerations were ludicrous, she blurted, "Jeez, I need to stop right this minute."

The cab driver pulled over to the curb, turned his head to her, and said, "Yep, we're here." She laughed, tipped two dollars, bowed her head to exit the cab, and when she looked up, Peter Grantis was standing like a specter at the top of the stairs in front of the heavy entry door of the brownstone. When he saw her step onto the curb, he rushed down the stoop and disappeared through the black wrought iron gate of the lower level like the invisible man.

"What the hell?"

The cabdriver was about to pull away, paused, stuck his head out the window, and yelled, "Ma'am? Is everything okay, Ma'am?"

"Yes, yes, thank you." *He must think I'm nuts, talking to myself. But what in the world is up with Grantis? Well, maybe he thinks he's guarding the place. Could have said hello or something instead of scooting away like a thief. What a weirdo!*

As soon as she got into her apartment, she dialed Jaime. His phone rang busy. She wanted to apologize. For what? What was she going to say? "I'm sorry, Jaime, but I needed to escape my life for a while and became so engrossed in a sexual encounter that I didn't even think of retrieving my messages." She finally got him on the line and reassured him Robert was okay, that he should not worry.

However, she'd been right to have been worried about Robert. A woman in a white dress crossing the road? *Grief can assume strange forms.* But had Maríanis really seen a mark on Robert's lip? A sign, a warning of some kind?

———◦———

Neither Robert nor anyone else ever knew. If he had not swerved to avoid the apparition, the car speeding from the opposite direction would have crashed into his—head-on.

———◦———

What a weekend! Well, for the rest of the evening, she'd try to unwind. She'd shower, have some green tea, and maybe a salad. She was not hungry at all. Just tired. She sipped tea, began to relax, and she thought of David. *That work-out with David had been . . .*

Work-out? Is that what it had been? They had made passionate love. He'd quieted her need. The waves of grief that had been washing over her for days receded to a distant sea, and she'd welcomed the eddies of pleasure, surrendering completely to the whorls of sensation that transported her to an exquisite orgasm.

The scent of him was still on her skin. The feel of his hair lingered on her fingers. *Umm, that David has a beautiful head of soft curls.* "Jeez, let me get into the shower and wash the nonsense off me." The spray of warm water only made her feel more sensual. She touched herself, closed her eyes, and tried to erase David's touch with her own.

Irene didn't have to be at Lakeside until Monday at ten, group at ten forty-five. Maríanis would be coming in for her weekly appointment at one in the afternoon, then sessions with Felicia and Marta. Although tight, Mondays had been easy because her usual early Sunday morning routine of a Pilates class at the gym, or a jog in Central Park, served to renew her, strengthening her for the coming week's challenges. After a shower, she'd usually sit with a cup of coffee and the Arts and Magazine Sections of the Sunday Times. Afternoons had been devoted to visits with her mother.

Alma was gone; her mom was gone. Sundays were going to be difficult now. She supposed she would have more time to jog.

The phone rang. She ran to it, thinking it was about Robert again.

It was Maríanis. "Hello, Irene." The line went quiet for a moment, then, "I'm upset. I think I'm starting to have panic attacks again. I couldn't sleep last night."

Irene checked her watch: 9:30.

She doubted one night's insomnia would result in panic attacks. "Talk to me, Maríanis." No response. "Are you there? Talk to me."

"I feel as if soon, I'll just suffocate."

Something had to have happened during the visit with her kids. Something that made her highly anxious.

"Maríanis, I want you to be mindful of your voice. Tell me again how you feel."

"I'm feeling as if I can't breathe so well . . ."

"Tell me where you are in the room."

"I'm on my bed. I ache all over."

"Get up. Put me on speaker."

"Okay."

Irene could hear her fussing for her slippers. "Let's do some deep breathing, ten deep breaths. Breathe in, hold, breathe out." The breaths came in, first asthmatic, then extended and steady. "Good. Now concentrate on the movement of your chest as you breathe in and out . . . in and out . . . Touch your hand to your chest, feel yourself exhaling, feel the regular beating of your heart." Maríanis was off meds for a month now. Irene could always phone in a new script, if necessary. "I hear you breathing easier now. Again." After several rounds of guided deep breathing, Irene asked, "How are you feeling now?"

"Better. Thank you, Irene. I'll be there tomorrow."

"Not so fast. What else is going on?"

"I'm good, honest. We'll talk tomorrow."

"Hey. Let me hear you breathe into the phone again."

Maríanis started laughing and huffed into the phone a couple of times.

"Excellent! You've calmed down. I'll see you tomorrow. I'm here if you need me. Call again if you need to."

In the Circle

MONDAY'S NEW LIGHT FILTERED through the blinds of her bedroom. She didn't have to be there till ten but was on the way to the clinic by seven-thirty. For about two hours, she sat in her office reading cases, mulling over the pros and cons of introducing video footage as an intervention. Many clinicians shied away from "Prolonged Exposure Therapy," criticizing it as too harsh a technique. Irene liked to think she could make bold choices, be brave enough to test the limits of possibility. However, she needed to be careful.

She'd considered a film about the suffering inflicted by the Pinochet dictatorship, authentic cinema which had won several awards. Carolina's trauma was uniquely related to the horrors of that despotic regime. The movie might serve to initiate some kind of catharsis, and maybe, just maybe, the girl would say something. Yes, there was risk. Flooding the women with visuals might retraumatize them, especially the patient who might benefit most. But something had to jolt Carolina from her silence.

Irene needed to provide evidence to Freile, and soon. While each woman was a victim of violence or a catastrophic event, Carolina was the one in most immediate danger of becoming the victim of an incorrect diagnosis again, labeled as schizophrenic, and discharged to yet another institution. Irene would not allow it. She would fight Walter Freile with all her teeth and all her nails if he moved to transfer her out of the unit.

Irene annotated Maríanis' file, summarizing the previous evening's phone call, then turned to the young woman's case.

—Carolina, nineteen, highly intelligent, and talented. Her aunt and legal guardian, Rosalía Mateo, sought medical help for her niece when the silence began. Rosalía narrowly escaped the Pinochet regime's horrors, emigrated to Argentina, and finally to the states. She married Ricardo Mateo, a successful Puerto Rican businessman, became a citizen, and offered asylum to her two nieces. Their parents had been tortured and assassinated, the mother, brutally raped. The extent of the violence the girl actually witnessed remained in question. However, the rupture, the sudden separation from her parents alone would have resulted in a profound sense of loss lodged in the child's emotional memory. Then, as if God had willingly ceded them to a destiny of grief, tragedy struck the family once more. During a home invasion, two men abducted six-year-old Miranda. Several days later, authorities found the little girl's body in a field six miles from her home. Carolina stopped speaking and, in a sense, stopped living. She'd been deeply attached to Miranda, rarely parting from her little sister's side. Even before Miranda's disappearance, Carolina awoke from nightmares crying, Mamá! Papá!

The girl had survived a war zone. Whether or not she'd been privy to her mother's rape—grief, fear, and loss resided in the foundations of her childhood. She had not been present during the home invasion, but the violent circumstances and the loss of her beloved Miranda caused her to shut down. Carolina's silence cloaked an avalanche of emotion, possibly fury.

Any experience of violence, direct or secondary, could result in trauma. As Irene saw it, Carolina's case was classic PTSD. Freile, who had a ton of experience with schizophrenic patients, continued to contradict her.

Already 10:15. Community meeting started in half an hour.

The women followed her into a large room. There were several rows of long tables and a big screen on the front wall. A tech aide was setting up video equipment.

"Oh, wow. Now we get to see movies. Cool."

"Shut up, Ana," said Marta. "You always have something stupid to say. Just shut up."

Ana started to give Marta the finger, then flexed out her arms in an uncaring shrug. "Yeah, so what?" Marta wanted to start something. Ana looked her up and down. The women saw a look on Ana's face that wasn't fear but a deliberate and hard pulling in of fury.

Irene walked up to the front of the room and spoke to the tech aide, "Sorry, I forgot to cancel the work order. We're not going to show the film after all." He said no problem, lifted up the screen and carted the video equipment away.

"Damn, this place is no fun," blurted Ana.

"Maybe some other time, Ana. Now, let's sit closer. And we want to listen to each other because we are all in this together. Carolina, sit here, next to me." The girl stared blankly at Irene and rose from her seat, getting up so slowly that she seemed frozen in the moment. Plaintively, she looked into the faces of the women in the circle as if asking if it were all right.

Ana reassured, "You can sit next to Dr. Míral, Carolina. We're not going to get mad." Several soft okay's came from the women. Carolina stood in front of Ana, lips parting ever so slightly. Expectancy was palpable in the room. Was the girl finally going to say something? Carolina's hand reached out for Ana's.

"Do you want me to sit next to you? I think she wants me to sit with her," said Ana.

All eyes turned to Irene. She smiled approval, and Carolina and Ana sat next to each other in the circle close to Irene. "You are safe here, with time to heal. Each of you has been hurt by an event, perhaps more than one incident, which has caused lots of pain. So much pain that you may keep reliving it or try to shut it out in ways that don't help to resolve or cope with the trauma."

Ana, focused on Carolina, asked, "Something real bad happened to you, right? That's why you don't talk."

Carolina's lips seemed to mouth the word, "Mamá."

"Something happened to your mother. You saw it, right? Did some fuckers rape her?" Now, Ana was quite agitated. "Somebody got raped, somebody!" Carolina's face lost all color, her eyes fixed on Ana Amado. She began to cry.

"Ana, I think you're scaring her. Maybe she's remembering. Carolina, what happened?" Melissa wanted to know. "Something very terrible happened to me, too. I lost my sister in a horrible car accident. Her head crashed through the windshield, and blood, blood all over her and me, and I can't stop thinking about it."

Carolina got up, let out an awful scream, and bolted to the door. The women rushed over; Melissa held her close. "Oh, my God, Carolina. I am sorry, so sorry. Oh, my God, what did I say?" She walked a stiff Carolina back to Dr. Míral's side.

Irene took a chance and repeated softly, "Miranda, Miranda." Carolina began to scream again for what seemed an eternity of seconds.

The women stared at Carolina and then accusingly at Irene.

"Carolina, we know you're in pain. Why don't you tell us what you've remembered? We're all here for you. Tell us." The girl would not speak and just cried. "Rape and violent events can result in trauma that may stay with us all our lives."

"Then we're crazy . . . forever," whispered Melissa.

"Speak for yourself, Melissa. I'm not crazy. Yo no soy loca. Not! Not fou. You know what's crazy, this fucking place. Lakeside is not a retreat. It-is-a-nuthouse. That lake is going to fill up with big black tears, tears from the dark places inside us. Dr. Míral, you want it all to be bright and sunny, but all you're doing is making us cry."

Ana was taking the lead and didn't even know it, didn't realize the dark place inside her saw light the very moment she expressed the anguish, the anger. But her bravado did not fool Irene. Ana was fragile also. Irene's gaze calmly took in her circle of women before facing Ana. "When something makes us sad, and if we cry, it's because we need to. But we also need to speak out about those feelings. It's normal to feel furious and sad about being raped, physically abused, losing a loved one to violence, or a horrible accident. Your emotions are valid, one hundred percent."

"I think you should give Carolina a pill to calm her down. I mean, I would need to do two lines of coke and half a bottle of vodka if I had to remember that my whole fucking family was killed." Ana leaned into the girl, looking like she wanted to hug her, instead, she pulled out a pack of cigarettes. "Do you want a cigarette, Carolina?" Carolina looked away.

"Ana, one of the problems often resulting from PTSD is a tendency to self-medicate. Alcohol and drugs, prescribed or not, become crutches, a way to bury feelings and avoid pain. Dealing with trauma is complex and ongoing. When we try to deal with it in real time, we can learn to cope so the trauma does not disable us or rule our existence. We can develop skills and learn techniques to help ourselves so we can have healthier relationships and better lives."

Ana was shaking her head no.

"You have a right to be angry, every right to grieve. But remember this: You have suffered losses but have not lost your selves. You are whole." Irene made a circle with her hand. She stood up, walked over to Melissa, and placed a hand on her shoulder.

"It's my fault. I made Carolina too upset."

"Melissa, what happened here today is not your fault. Moreover, you are not in any way responsible for what happened to your sister. Carolina, you are not responsible for what happened to Miranda or your parents. Ana, you are right. You are not crazy, you are hurt."

"Yeah, sure."

"Ana, you're a rude pig. No couth man, no couth at all."

Ana ignored Marta's remark. Instead, she turned to the girl. "Carolina, it happened to me, too. Twice."

Marta peered at Ana from across the circle. Something seemed to get to her. Maybe the way Ana said twice, or the way the woman's voice quaked as she spoke to Carolina. "Hey, Ana, are you hiding a daughter somewhere? A little sister maybe?"

Ana rolled her eyes. "You're too much. You know that? Too much."

Marta laughed, "Well, woman, maybe there's another side to hard-assed you."

Yes, thought Irene, there is a person there. The real Ana was emerging. Beneath the anger, sarcasm, and pain, there was a caring woman. "Ana, thank you for trusting, for sharing your feelings of rage and sadness. You've talked to us about the incident in the laundry room. Tell us about the other time, you said it happened twice."

"I can't right now." Ana bowed her head; thick dark curls fell like a curtain over her face. After a while, she looked up, "I'm sorry for being rude."

"Once you recognize your feelings, your fear, you can start to work on coping with triggers. You can own your lives again."

Even as she spoke to the women in the calmest manner she could muster, the dread of having pushed Carolina too far worked incisively at the back of her mind. Carolina's case was all tied up in her ego and the desire to prove Freile wrong. The thought that she wasn't any different from colleagues who misdiagnosed and overmedicated sickened her. *Am I being ambitious for Carolina's recuperation or for myself? For the satisfaction of proving a point? This thing is eating me up.*

Román

Monday afternoon, a pallid and tight-face Maríanis walked in close to fifteen minutes late to her therapy appointment. Irene said hello and asked, "Were you able to get a bit of sleep last night?"

She looked around the small office—the desk behind which she'd rarely seen Irene sit, the comfy chairs facing each other across a small table, and the row of ornate picture frames lined up on the top shelf of the wide bookcase on the far wall. The frames had no pictures in them but formed an attractive design all their own. She'd unburdened her soul many times in the now familiar room.

Irene asked again. "Were you able to get any sleep last night?"

She sat and placed her oversize purse on the floor. "Hardly. Irene, I hardly slept at all. Afraid that if I went to sleep, the jungle episode would come back to torment me. My heart began to gallop like in the old nightmares I thought were forever behind me, like I was still running." She'd dreaded the dryness that occupied her mind after those events. But as Irene spoke to her on Sunday night, as she exhaled each breath, an invisible weight came off her chest. The dread and fear subsided as the regular rhythm of her heart returned. And she'd gone to her journal. "I wrote some stuff in my journal, then finally fell into a dead sleep from being too tired to keep my eyes open. Talking to you last night helped. Thanks." She tried to smile, didn't want Irene to think that after all the hard work, all the effort to make her well, she might be sliding back to where she first found her. Loyalty, gratitude, and silly pride kept her from saying that what she'd wanted to do was sign out and just sleep. Instead, she'd picked up the phone and called. Then, she wrote. Irene had introduced journal writing as a therapeutic tool and encouraged her to use it. Now pretty thick, it was a record of her thoughts and feelings, and her trauma:

> *"Again, I felt the terrible fear, an ugly old horror that surged in my throat and raced my heart. I almost asked for meds but didn't. I can be strong. I know it. Irene helped me like she always does. I must talk to her about what happened at the visitation site. He plans to steal my children away again. I can sense it."*

"Sounds as if you fended off an anxiety attack. What do you think brought it on?" Irene waited for her to find words, but Maríanis, eyes closed, shook her head no. "Yes, on the phone last night, you were having trouble breathing, a sign of considerable anxiety. You were afraid the nightmare would happen again, but I don't think it's what caused you to be anxious. By the way, I'm glad you called me. Tell me, how did your visit with the children go?"

"Horrible."

"Horrible? Why didn't you enjoy the visit with your children?"

"No, I did. I loved being with my kids. They liked their gifts. Tina tried on the dress in the restroom. It fit just right." Maríanis picked up her bag from the floor and pulled out two polaroid photos. "Here. Here she is. She's pretty, right?"

"She's beautiful, and I see Joey, showing off his knee pads. They look happy."

"Yes, my heart felt happy too . . . But damn, it wasn't enough. You know, not enough."

"I know. You want more time. But what was it? What made you so upset?"

"I walked out of there alone, instead of with my kids. Then to make it worse, as I walked to the car, my ex pulled up right beside me, honked the horn hard, blasting it, then he laughed loud and mean. I felt like the smallest joke on the block. I hurried to get into my car. He parked right next to me. And then this crazy feeling, the urge to run. I reached for the passenger door wanting to bolt and run like hell." Maríanis' eyes were nervous, darting back and forth, and she was squeezing the knuckles of her left hand with her right.

"He frightened you. Tell me what happened next."

"I drove away, feeling terrified, confused, and humiliated. Should have done something, said something, but I panicked. It's . . . it's starting all over again. *All over again.* He's setting me up, provoking me to lose control so I'll lose my visiting rights. Worse, he's making me look like a fool in front of the children, like a freakin' helpless fool." She let out a little cry of defeat, folding over like a spent flower and cried hard. Irene waited. The frustration, fear, and fury had to come out somehow.

Maríanis finally raised her head, eyes fiery, face full and flushed from crying so hard. She leaned forward and tore at the tissue box on the small table in front of her. "He won. He won again, stole again, canceled out all my positive feelings about the visit. The supervised visitation thing is hard enough for me. And you know it. I don't want just visits. I want those kids with me. They belong with me!" She looked away, "I'm sorry, it's just that . . . he was like stalking me all over again. He was in control again. I felt sick and disgusted all the rest of the day and kept gagging like I would throw up."

"You felt fear, fear triggered by his actions, a normal response considering what he's done." Irene's gaze of gray eyes held her patient steady. "How can you stay safe?"

"I don't know."

"Fear and panic prevented you from thinking logically. It happens. Often, our first impulse is to run. Or fight. And Marianis, we are going to fight this. Let's look at this more clearly. Had the visiting site already closed? Could you have walked back in there and spoken to the social worker about what happened?"

"I hate him. I want him to die. I'm never going to get my children back as long as he's in the picture."

"Tell me again how you felt as you got into your car?"

"Irene, I backed into the seat like a cowardly dog because I thought he might get out of his car and hit me."

"That monster is not going to get away with it this time, not again. And you are not a coward. But you must stay safe. I want you to be safe. So, let's make a plan. Okay? Let's access the social worker at the site. You're aware that a report is generated after each visit and eventually submitted to the Family Court. Correct?"

Fists clenched hard now, Marianis punched her lap three times, leaned back into the chair, and raged at the ceiling. "Why am I so stupid, Irene? Why didn't I go back in there and report it? Uhh! I didn't think, just reacted—wanted to get out of his reach, and the hell away."

"You were afraid, and you wanted to run away. Don't call yourself stupid. You are not stupid. And don't be ashamed for wanting to survive. Never be ashamed. The best thing you could have done was to get out of there. But it sounds like you want to take some kind of action. It's not too late. The restraining order is still in place, isn't it? It sounds to me like he stalked. You can report it."

"No. He didn't get out of the car, he didn't say anything, all more like taunting, mocking, and he'll deny the whole thing. Believe me, he'll deny it. He has never owned up to anything, and never will. He'll just go on and once more try to make me look like a crazy woman."

"Listen to me. What about security cameras? Try to park as close to the entrance as possible, even if it means getting there a little early. The best route to take now may be an appointment with the social worker. Remember, stalking is aggravated harassment. You can march right to the P.D. and file a violation if it happens again."

"I should have shot a picture of his ugly face with the polaroid I had with me. He got close enough, and it would have been proof of his intent, the nasty threatening look . . . Know what he needs? He needs someone to kick his ass hard. I want to kick his fucking ass! I'd like to get a gun, fill it up with horseshit, squirt it in his face and force it in his mouth. How can I kill the fucker? How? How can I load the gun without getting my hands dirty?"

Irene sat back with a pleased expression on her face.

"How can I make the creep bleed without touching him."

"You want to hurt him, and he would deserve it, but guns are not the only way to kick ass or seek restitution. I'm glad you are angry, happy you want to kick ass. I want to kick his ass too! But the most important thing right now is to stay safe."

"Yes." Marianis managed a smile.

"Okay! Let me know how it goes with the social worker. Call me."

Irene rose from her chair, went over to Marianis, and put her arms around her. "I'll see you next week. Call me if you need to. Do you need anything else?" Marianis shook her head no. "Are you sure?"

"Yes, I'm sure."

"Next Monday, then."

Marianis was about to leave, turned around, and said, "Oh, before I forget." She looked in her oversize purse again and pulled out a package wrapped in brown paper. She handed it to Irene. "It's for protection against evil omens. You know, the spirits and all. The good ones appreciate the light, the bad ones avoid it."

Irene removed the brown paper and uncovered the gift, a tall votive of white pearly iridescence. "Thank you, Maríanis. I could use it."

"Then that makes two of us, Dr. Míral."

⸺◆⸺

Irene had learned about Santería in a course she'd enrolled in a few years back: New World Spiritual Constructs and Psychological Thought. Her mom was not a practitioner, but once a year, she conducted a cleansing of their modest apartment by burning fragrant dry leaves in a pot which she placed on the floor in the middle of the living room. No incantations or anything but she was solemn about it and forbid noise before, during, and after. She said she'd learned the sahumerío ritual in Puerto Rico from her sister, Inés. Maríanis had mocked her mom and her makeshift altar yet some of it had rubbed off on her forever. Her belief in the prophetic "angel's kiss" and the offering of that white votive proved it.

Burning candles and spiritual cleansing of spaces might serve as palliatives of sorts, something like comfort food. But spirits were not protecting women from abuse. Maríanis lived with her husband's emotional abuse, ugly words, and putdowns for several years, but his violence was unexpected, his perversity, shocking. He wanted to break her. And he did. When he took the children from her, she came face to face with helplessness, with the realization she might never see them again. It made her want to die.

He'd been brutal and gotten away with it. The man locked her up in the bedroom of their apartment for days, slapped and kicked her repeatedly; for hours forcing her to snort cocaine and perform fellatio, attacking her self-esteem in the worst way possible. Two days later, her mother found her. She'd soiled her pants and thrown up all over herself. The children were gone.

By the time she gathered herself enough to access the Family Court, it was already too late. The man had flown the children out of the country and beyond her reach. When she learned The Hague Convention of 1980 protected her parental rights, she realized her only recourse was to go to his country and petition their court.

Maríanis' efforts to get her children back were futile. Flashbacks disturbed her days, most of her nights. A recurring dream tormented her. She was running through a dense jungle, searching for her lost children, desperately trying to escape from the man who pursued her. The thicket of the tropical forest impeded her. Leaves heavy with moisture slapped against her face and arms, suffocating her, obliterating her screams for help. She woke up in a sweaty panic. She tried to get through her days with Xanax. An overdose almost killed her, and she ended up in rehab. Then by some angel's fortuitous grace, she was introduced to Lawrence Chase.

Lawrence Chase specialized in divorce law and represented wealthy clients. He rarely did pro bono work but well-recognized perfidy, and once in a while, he felt compelled to help out a poor client. Domestic abuse was a weapon, children, pawns in custody cases that rarely had to do with love for a child, only with a heinous desire to hurt and control the other parent. Money was usually an issue. A man often reneged on paying child support to a woman who was no longer putting out for him.

Maríanis' ex-husband returned to the states with the children, kept them hidden, and did battle in Family Court. The sight of him made Maríanis tremble like a newly planted sapling struggling against the gusts of a cold March wind. Her will crippled when the judge declared, "Parental rights terminated, permanent custody granted to the father." The sound that came out of her was the moan of a being mortally wounded. Chase held her up, kept her from collapsing, and tried to have her understand what had just transpired. Her ex-husband had accused her of abandonment. He'd provided documentation to the court that damned her, proof that she was a danger to herself and the children due to her addiction and suicidal behavior. Moreover, he stated he would have her committed. Chase wanted to help. "First thing is to get Maríanis appropriate treatment." His wife was a social worker, and her sister, Patricia, had begun work at a new unit for women who suffered from PTSD. It was headed by a psychologist named Irene Míral.

The demons that had driven her to near annihilation lurked like hungry predators, gaining nourishment from the scent of her fear. She had to overcome panic and cope with her situation. Irene believed the day's session had sufficiently restored her patient's confidence and motivation. Hopefully, she'd go ahead and talk to the social worker. Irene, tempted to call Angels' Haven on her behalf, knew it was best if her patient proceeded independently. It had been grueling to lift her out of despondency, doubt, and despair. Maríanis needed to hold on to the right of agency she'd gained through her time in therapy.

Not easy for Maríanis to hope; that well was nearly dry—depleted. Therapy had tapped into what remained of her strength, enabling her to summon the courage to petition the court for an Order of Protection and seek custody of her children for a second time.

Irene submitted a statement to the court substantiating Maríanis' status as a victim of domestic violence. His lawyer pressed, the whole thing went to trial, and Irene had to make an appearance. The Judge stated too much time had elapsed since the alleged attacks. Irene's testimony regarding PTSD made all the difference.

But the court only granted Maríanis supervised visitation. The onus was now on her to prove she was stable and could be a responsible parent. Irene understood how vulnerable her patient was at this juncture. Maríanis may have perceived a threat when there was only a stupid honk. Hypervigilance was typical for people who experienced PTSD.

No. That man could be dangerous and had begun jockeying to establish the upper hand.

Irene annotated the case notes: The patient demonstrates sufficient ego strength and is working on coping skills. No suicidal ideation. Protocol: Continue weekly outpatient visits; no meds.

Guilt Is A Useless Emotion

IRENE RARELY TOOK LUNCH. This Monday was no different. She sipped on green tea and meditated for a few moments before opening the next case.

—Felicia Monserrat lived on the Lower East Side and worked at the Sunrise movie house, cleaning in the mornings and selling tickets starting when the first show began at eleven in the morning to the start of the last show at midnight. She liked her job; she was off Mondays and relaxed by sleeping until one in the afternoon and smoking a doobie for lunch. Sleeping late was her favorite thing. In the summers, she frequently went up to the roof after work to smoke reefer. It was great when she was up there by herself, gazing out, enjoying the lights of her city's skyscape glittering against the cobalt sky.

But on hot summer nights, others had the same idea, and some nights, the roof was transformed into a community gathering space for the folks who lived in the building. Sometimes, there were guests. Like the night she tried to jump off the roof. She'd seen the four young guys once before, probably relatives of one of the tenants. They offered her some smoke, and she accepted. No one else was around. They were smoking and laughing and then the groping and forcing of tongues in her mouth and the forcing hard through other places. Although she struggled hard, they took turns with her in every way their perverse minds could think of. Felicia lay on the asphalt bleeding from the back, her lips and privates mangled. Four lubricious faces like those of satiated hyenas looked down at her, their laughter lurid as they pulled up their zippers. She got up and ran to the edge of the roof. One of them ran after her and grabbed her off the ledge. She tried to wrest away, back to the edge. He knocked her out, dragged her to the stairwell, and dumped her behind the door, her crumpled body, a discarded sack. The four raced down the stairs and out to the street. The lady who lived on the top floor heard the commotion, walked out to the stairwell, and called out, "Who's there?" The moans were heartbreaking.

Felicia, the newest case to the unit, was most clearly PTSD. She suffered from debilitating nightmares from which she awoke screaming, soaked in cold sweat. Repeatedly, daytime flashes of a suicidal jump from the ledge of a roof intruded upon her conscious-ness. She saw herself falling into a dark pit, welcoming oblivion.

There were two positives regarding treatment. Firstly, hers was an isolated incident in the recent past, so the case was conducive to EMDR and short-term hospitalization. Eye Movement Desensiti-zation and Reprocessing was a fairly innovative and effective treat-ment for PTSD. And Felicia was cooperative.

"Why do men rape us, Dr. Míral? Why?"

"All men don't. You were attacked by predators. At least one of them possessed a modicum of a primitive conscience because he did pull you from the edge of that roof, and you are alive. You are here."

"They deserve to die." She made a fist, her knuckles white. "I hate them."

"Of course, their acts were cruel, the crime unconscionable. The roof, tell me about the roof. Do you still go back there in your nightmares?"

Felicia's face darkened like a rain cloud. "No, the episodes happen in the daytime. Most nights I sleep okay but ... Dr. Míral, if I hadn't been on that roof with them, not smoking with them, it wouldn't have happened. It's not like what happened to Carolina's mother. It wasn't her fault."

"So, you think it was your fault."

Felicia turned her face away, "Yes."

"Felicia, look at me. Rape is never a woman's fault. It is a criminal act."

"The police wanted me to identify them, and I couldn't. I didn't want to. I couldn't remember their faces, still don't."

"It's not unusual to blank out aspects of a horrible experience like rape. Your entire physiology was in shock, and your mind doesn't want to revisit the pain. Felicia, I want you to forgive yourself, although there is nothing to forgive. Say it: 'Those men are crim-inals; I did nothing wrong.'" Felicia stated such three times. "Guilt is a useless emotion, useless and debilitating. When you let go of it, you'll be able to get on with your life." The euphoria induced by the marijuana was likely the cause of Felicia's guilt.

"By the time I said no, they would not stop." Felicia could barely get out the next words. "When those men began to grope, I felt pleasure and I pressed my body against theirs."

"It happens, Felicia. Your hormones were stimulated, and your response was a biological reflex. That's all it was. It's not your fault, let go of the guilt. You said no. It's on them."

Although the new anti-depressant protocol seemed to be working, Irene wanted to rule out suicidal tendencies. The falling-into-a-dark-pit daytime flashbacks were a concern. She wondered if hypnosis could extinguish the image of the looming dark pit and replace it with a girl running through a field of flowers on a sunny day. She had no practical experience in hypnosis techniques and would need to enlist a colleague who did. Walter Freile? He'd been well-known in the field, but that was years ago. Sure. He'd already indicated that Felicia should be discharged. So, he would not be hot on the idea at all. And how about poor Felicia? The image of her patient, helpless under Freile's hypnotic spell, made her cringe. Hypnosis could be a way to banish the falling-into-the-pit-flashbacks. Thing was, any changes had to be cleared with the mighty Dr. F. She entered a few notes in Felicia's file, twice underlined, med protocol to be reassessed with Dr. Freile; hypnosis a possible option to extinguish suicidal ideation.

The phone rang. David. "Hey, love. Did you recover from our passionate lovemaking? I didn't." If he were expecting a response, Irene would not give it. David ignored the snub. "Also, thought you might want to know some real upset guy came in asking for you. He complained he called the VA contact you gave him, and no one got back to him. He said he wanted to talk to you. Do you know him?"

She did remember the fellow and thought it strange Joe Martell, her contact at the VA, had not followed up. She knew him to be unusually dedicated. He was probably better off in private practice than in a federal agency, and she'd told him so. "David, I did recommend the VA clinic because he demonstrated symptoms of PTSD. He was not appropriate for our study. I'll give Joe a call about it. Have to go now, my next patient is due in five minutes. See you Thursday night." Hah! She had another ten minutes before her next patient, but after talking to David, she'd need to take at least five to cool her mind. Thursday night was a while away. Right now there were more important matters to attend to.

Each of her cases was different but also the same. Violence was traumatic, an assault not only of the physical self but of the psyche, an abuse of the skin that holds one's soul together.

—Marta, twenty-eight, tall and attractive, sports an elaborate tattoo of a rosary in the space between her clavicles. She grew up tough in The South Bronx, but although she tried, she had not been tough enough to fend off a vicious physical assault by her live-in boyfriend. Curious about the Mexicans who had recently moved into her neighborhood, she began to frequent the small storefront next to the building where she lived. The indigo blue and vivid orange on the walls seemed exotic, and the men who worked there always looked happy as they sang along with the mariachi songs coming from a small speaker tottering on a makeshift ledge close to the ceiling. Marta liked their nice black hair, wavy eyelashes, and ready laughter. So, she let one of the young guys with the long lashes and nice black hair move in with her. He worked in the kitchen of the small restaurant. She thought he could help her with the rent. Besides, she could get free Mexican food. Maybe, this was her lucky turn with a guy, maybe he would turn out to be different from the other men she'd known, maybe she could be happy. She hoped. And it was fun—until she got pregnant.

Marta was super-excited about the prospect of having a Mexican baby with pretty, dark hair and long eyelashes. She fantasized about a perfect family life with lots of children and wonderfully festive Mex–Rican parties with great music and fabulous food. It all got pretty sour, pretty fast. He started to come home late, sometimes drunk—sometimes disappeared for days at a time. Marta was pissed-off. One night, after being gone for two whole days, he barged in skunk drunk, turned on the TV to the local Univision station, volume full blast. Marta walked over to the TV and turned it off. He pushed her out of the way, turned it back on, called her stupid, and yelled he was paying the Con Edison bill and would watch TV anytime he wanted. He was not paying very much for anything anymore. "You ain't paying for nothing, liar. Get the hell out!"

The rage must have been there already, and she hadn't known it. He screamed obscenities in her face, smashed the television screen with a swift kick, and slapped Marta so hard she thought she went deaf. She put a hand to the ear, flung herself at him, and went for his face with her nails. That face was the last thing she saw for the next eighteen hours. The assault was vicious. He punched her, shoved her to the floor, and kicked her repeatedly in the abdomen. The neighbors did not hear her screams because his vile insults were so horrifically loud. They did find Marta in a pool of dark blood, unconscious. The door was open. The man gone. She lost the baby and her womb.

Marta hated men. Marta also hated herself and, like Felicia, was overwhelmed by feelings of guilt. She blamed herself for losing the baby. She suffered from a recurring flashback. Blood streamed down the man's face, down the walls of her room, and down her legs. Each time, she felt as if blood was choking her every breath.

Irene had planned to begin EMDR with her but decided against it. She wanted to hear more from Marta, suspected the crazy Mexican had not been the first to hurt her.

"I wanted that baby with every fiber of me, yearned to finally be a mom, could hear his heart and mine beating together." She hobbled over in the chair as if in severe physical pain.

"How sad you feel, Marta, so, so, sad."

"The first one . . . I was fifteen."

"The first one?"

"My mother made me have it, the abortion. Then for the next two years, she treated me like shit. So, I left. I left with a man who promised me all kinds of things, and all I got was slapped around.

Then, when I got pregnant, he made me get rid of it. He threatened I needed to do it soon, or he would kick the dirty piglet out of me. He did have perfect aim. It could kick in a face or a heart. He said pissing in me was like pissing in the East River. He didn't think much of my genetic material, my feelings . . . or my body."

"Two people you trusted hurt you when you were most vulnerable, drove you to make choices you were not ready to make."

"I could have run away and not listened. But I didn't. I did not do anything. Not a thing. Just gave in."

"It's done, Marta. You were still a child. Forgive yourself. Forgive the child who could not stand up to a punishing mother and an abusive partner. Forgive her."

Marta's arms embraced her abdomen, her plaint heartbreaking. "I can't have children anymore. Babies have padded little feet, little feet I cannot kiss because my tongue is dirty from sucking filthy men. I've slept with over one hundred men. Not one . . . not one, loved me. I hate them. The Mexican did not love me. I tried to fool myself that he did, that I could have a happy life. I realized too late he didn't want children. I should have never been with him. It's my fault, Dr. Míral, my fault."

"Your fault? How did you lose the baby? Was it not his fault?"

"I wish him dead."

"He might be, and if not, will probably self-destruct somewhere down the road." Marta was now rocking back and forth. "It's a lot. A lot of hurt. Yet . . . you are a strong woman."

Marta went still. "Sometimes."

"I know. Thank you for telling me about those two events. You buried all of it for too long. I want you to be mindful of the onset of a flashback. It would be helpful for you to write in your journal when you feel the event coming on."

"I don't know. It just happens. Don't know when and where it's going to start. So how can I write about it?"

"I see. You have no control over it. I understand." Marta gazed into Irene's gray eyes with an expression close to insolence.

Better than hopelessness. "By the way, when and where is important. Try writing about it after the episode, noting as many details as you can remember of the when and where. And I want to try something new with you soon. It might help those flashbacks disappear." Marta rose from her seat and said yes.

The intake screening had included the PTSD checklist and the Adverse Children's Experiences Questionnaire. Still, Irene suspected that Marta had more of a history of child abuse than she had already revealed. The ACE questionnaire had its faults; however, she decided to readminister the instrument before starting the EMDR protocol.

Tuesday's Child

In the blue of a perfect October day, the sun cast its magical sparkle over the landscape. A scintillating cornucopia of brilliant autumn colors framed the expanse of the lake. Tall buildings shimmered in the distance. Lakeside Hospital sat on prime Manhattan real estate.

Established by a wealthy philanthropist a few years after his only child, a daughter, committed suicide, Lakeside had an excellent reputation. Irene was grateful for the opportunity to work in a meaningful and challenging discipline and in an institution which provided sufficient resources to sustain her efforts. Nevertheless, she dreamed of someday establishing an independent clinic for women, not bound by timetables or preconceived notions about mental illness.

She headed to the greenhouse and admired how the glass palace glistened like a gem—a symbol of hope, a place sheltering new growth. The trustees hosted annual galas and fundraisers in the enormous space, ensured its pristine maintenance, and the careful cultivation of rare plants. Irene wondered how she might steal some moments to grow miniature orchids, but it was out of the question; her schedule was too tight.

She found Melissa busy tending an orange seedling in a small, repurposed milk container. She looked up at Irene and smiled. "I remember doing this same thing for a third-grade class project when

I was eight." Carolina sat next to her with a sketchbook, making broad strokes of leaves and blossoms with a thick charcoal pencil. She frowned and shut the sketchbook when she saw Irene. "She likes to sit in here with me," said Melissa apologetically. "Today, she drew my seedling and gave it a name." Irene was pleased. Carolina and Melisa had connected.

"What did she call it?"

"Little sister. She drew it in her sketch pad."

Some communication was better than none.

Irene had been contemplating utilizing EMDR with the patients whose trauma was in the recent past. However, Marta's case made her slow down. Melissa, admitted to the unit three weeks before, seemed a better candidate. She'd been describing nightmares quite coherently. Now, she needed to begin the work.

Melissa had no history of previous trauma. Nevertheless, she still experienced episodes of irrational fear, insisted she would never drive again, and once cried out she did not deserve to live anymore. EMDR could deliver Melissa from the raw memories of the accident. She deserved a chance to have a normal life again, the life she'd known before the tragedy. Melissa had a healthy support system and, before the accident, sustained a long-term relationship with a nice fellow she'd known since high school.

Melissa's guilt was more acute than the phobia about driving; both could be dealt with in outpatient therapy. PTSD symptoms continued to plague her because the horrible accident still resided up front, and the emotional baggage was unbearable. The technique could desensitize and help the young woman integrate the event as a rational memory. Irene was confident Melissa wouldn't require more than four sessions. The EMDR device tracked Melissa's eye movements as Irene prompted her to repeat the narrative of the accident's aftermath and, most importantly, to report the emotional and physical reactions she experienced as she spoke. As Melissa's eyes followed the light of the device, Irene asked, "Your heart, is it beating faster?"

Irene considered what she observed during Tuesday and Thursday morning rounds as valuable data crucial to developing treatment modalities. Once a month, she met with the social worker to develop activities that would help the women achieve competencies and confidence. She hoped her little community of women would thrive. She tried to connect with each woman every day—at least eye contact or a casual greeting of acknowledgement, even if were not the patient's day for individual therapy.

Olivia and Marta's table tennis monopoly was still in full swing. Irene went over.

"You girls compete well. Can I play winners?"

"Anytime, Dr. Míral, anytime," said Olivia. "Marta usually dukes me out."

"Maybe I will too! Let's go." Out of the corner of her eye, Irene saw Ana watching. Irene volleyed well and scored several times, but Marta's returns were focused and forceful. She won. The women laughed. Irene wanted to know if anyone could play winners. "Sure," said Marta, and she resumed play with Olivia.

Ana had drifted off to the garden. Irene followed and found her sitting on a lawn chair smoking a cigarette and gazing out at the lake. The morning sun enhanced the coppery tones of her complexion and the gleam of her thick curls. Irene saw how pretty a woman Ana was.

Irene dragged a nearby lawn chair and sat next to Ana. "Wow, those girls love to play ping-pong."

"They're gay."

Irene baited, "Is that why they play so well?"

"Nah, it's easy. I like paddleball. Bunches of us played in the projects, I was as good as the boys . . ." She clammed up and put out the half-smoked cigarette under the grind of her sneaker.

"How about if you and I play a game on Thursday?"

Ana shrugged, got up, and said, "Sure."

Irene had no illusions about her methods. She knew patients did not always reveal complete histories. Someone as mistrustful as Ana had to have a lot more to divulge. Any movement forward in her interaction with a patient was meaningful.

For people living with PTSD, social situations could pose tremendous challenges. Inexplicable outbursts of anger disrupted family life, strained relationships to a breaking point, and eventually resulted in abandonment by the people who'd cared most. Ana and Felicia, tormented by unresolved mistrust and paranoia, would have a hard time reconnecting to significant persons in their lives or establishing new relationships. The women needed to reclaim their human right to love and enjoy. Marta and Olivia had found each other, but there was a whole world out there they needed to face. Carolina, ensconced in silence, continued to avoid it.

It was a tall order. Irene could not hold her girls forever. In just several months, they had to make sufficient progress to be able to return to their communities, hold down jobs, begin to forge a future. Most would need to continue therapy as outpatients.

Marta and Ana's feuding was still a bit concerning. Irene concluded it was due to the similarity in their backgrounds. Both were tough, street-smart women. But that was part of it. Learning to live with the stresses of the streets, arguments, toxic home environments, and everyday conflicts was a challenge for many people. For these women, whose internal resources had been compromised by the insult of trauma, it was a question of emotional survival—possibly life and death.

Another Wednesday

THE NIGHT CREW LOOKED relieved when they saw Irene walk in. She figured they were anxious to get home. "Sorry guys, I'm running a bit late today." She was seldom late, especially not to the debriefing with her crew. Irene appreciated their professionalism and willingness to put in a little extra time. She made sure to encourage and support their efforts; theirs was not an easy job. Dedicated workers with potential to advance in the mental health field were hard to come by.

The reports they generated supported Irene's assessment that the unit was functioning well. Ana was sleeping through most of the night, although Jackson noted she was the only one still pacing the hallway after eleven. "She's been quiet. In fact, only thing she does is give me a long, cold stare when she walks by. Sometimes, she stops right in front of me as if ready to say or do something. But then, nothing. Don't want to provoke or push my luck with her, so, I haven't tried to engage her in any way."

Someone shouted out, "Coward!" Everyone laughed, including Irene. Ana was as tall as Jackson, robustly built; most people would avoid a confrontation.

"Okay. Let's see how brave you all are. I have special news. For the next two Thursdays, you are going to teach." Irene distributed folders and began her pitch. "As you know, CBT is the program's principal mode of treatment. Educating patients about their condition, symptoms, and medications is crucial, but they don't have to hear it just from me. What I have in mind is a presentation. I need four volunteers, two females and two males, and one of them will be Jackson." This time the laughter was a lot louder.

"You're kidding. Why me?"

"Volunteers will be compensated with two Wednesday nights off so you can be fresh for the next shift. I will need the rest of you to cover." Irene smiled slyly. "You may be familiar with multi-level marketing." The crew murmured questioningly. "Well, this is something similar, another layer of intervention. The women will see how people work together in teams—heterosexual teams, and they will learn more about PTSD and treatment. And . . . Ana Amado will see Jackson for who he is, an intelligent, helpful, and thoughtful human male."

The group applauded. Someone called out, "Stand up, Jackson, take a bow."

Jackson stayed in his seat, looking embarrassed. "You mean you want us to do this for Ana Amado's benefit."

"For everyone's benefit, and especially yours." Applause and more laughter from the crew. Jackson scratched his head and laughed. "What it is, is that I want you to do the first presentation along with a female volunteer. Jackson, you better shine! And let's have two more volunteers for the following week. You have ten minutes to take a look at the material. The content is all there for you with some sample visuals. If you like, we can do it once a month, on different topics, and give all who may be interested in doing a presentation a chance to do so. But that will be entirely up to you. We can discuss additional comp time if that turns out to be the case. You'll have use of a whiteboard and Xerox—whatever you need."

With a doubtful look on his face, Roberto asked, "Are you going to rate us on this?"

"I'm glad you asked. No. Again, your performance is voluntary. Think of it as a professional development piece you might include on a résumé. Whether you volunteer or not, or whether you shine or not," Irene smiled, looked over at Jackson, and continued after a quiet ripple of laughter from the crew, "is not in any way going to impact on how I view your job performance. Each of you is integral to this unit's functioning. I value your input and my opinion is not going to change due to this activity. Let me give you some space so you can discuss it." Irene walked out to the hallway. She guessed who was going to volunteer. For sure, Jackson would take the lead. She loved that guy.

When Irene reentered the conference room, only two persons were sitting at the table, Jackson and Patricia Reid. "Sorry, it's only us. Roberto and Sylvia felt the task was above their level of confidence. René and Joan stated they were too tired and pointed out they would need some extra time to prepare. Pat and I agree."

Jackson looked a little uncomfortable reporting the outcome.

"No problem. Let me know when you're ready. It's something new to try. You're gonna be Ph.D. candidates in no time." She tried to inject some humor, but the smile on her face felt stiff.

"We only need an extra Wednesday night so we can be ready the following Thursday."

"That's fine. Thank you." Irene was disappointed she could not get another two people. But just as well, Jackson and Patricia made a lovely biracial couple. She checked her watch: On time for Dr. Freile's inquisition.

<hr>

Walter Freile began with Felicia's case. "I think Felicia is ready to be discharged soon, don't you?"

"Well, yes, after a few successful EMDR sessions, we may be able to recommend outpatient. However, I worry about underlying suicidal ideation. Hypnosis could be a way to extinguish remaining suicidal thoughts. Anyone in-house you might recommend?"

Freile removed his glasses. "Aren't you aware that I authored several articles on the use of sodium-amytal and hypnosis twenty years ago? I can do it, but it is not necessary. She's likely to be one of your few successes, so why do you want to complicate the thing?"

Irene detected irritation in his voice. She guessed he hadn't anticipated pushback. The man was definitely annoyed. She'd known about his work with hypnosis and regretted having asked such a coy question. She wanted to apologize, but his arrogance grated. "I am aware of your expertise in the field. You are well-known for it. Anyway, what I had in mind was a recommendation, not necessarily that you take it on. I understand your schedule is full."

"Irene, stick to the plan so we can discharge her. How is Ana Amado doing? Her vitals appear to have stabilized. Any other outbursts?"

Oh well, no hypnosis recommendation from him.

"No. We must keep Ana's personality in mind and maintain an objective perspective. Volatility on her part is not necessarily a sign of pathology. For the most part, she's been able to modulate her reactions in group sessions. I think she's on the brink of working on her issues." Irene scrutinized Freile's face for a reaction—None. "And she's offered a hand of friendship to Carolina, an awkward attempt, but a good sign. The girl has touched her in some way. Amado is functioning in the here and now and has the capacity for compassion. According to Jackson, she's sleeping through most of the night without incident, only directs dirty looks, and refrains from any other interaction. We're playing a game of table tennis tomorrow."

"Congratulations."

"At this time, I think an anti-depressant would be sufficient medication."

He made a sour face. "Fine. Your recommendation is noted. Let's move on. So, is Carolina speaking now?"

"No, not exactly. She seems to look up to Ana quite a bit; I think she admires her feistiness. Also, she's established a quiet relationship with Melissa, a remarkable development. Both lost a beloved sibling to a violent ending. They are bonding over having suffered similar losses. I started Melissa on EMDR."

"Carolina is still not communicating, is she? You realize her treatment may require more time than your unit is meant to handle. PTSD cases should resolve in a short time, and if they can't, then it's something else."

Irene muttered an internal, "Oh, boy." Freile had a way of pushing her buttons. How many times was he going to rub the time factor in her face? Carolina wasn't speaking, but she was going to. She wasn't out of touch with reality at all. She was communicating in many ways, just not talking. "I will work with Del Valle as long as it takes, CBT, group, and individual desensitization."

"Well, since you are so successful with difficult patients, how about taking on one more. It's a charity case . . . My wife . . ."

"Your wife??"

He laughed, "No. My wife is not insane yet."

Wow, thought Irene, did he just say *yet*? She raised an eyebrow.

"Irene, she's fine. Mrs. Freile is active in a charity organization that assists Central American victims of human trafficking. She asked if there were anything I could do about a young woman who is in a shelter right now, withdrawn and terrified of everyone, branded like an animal."

"The unit has a limited number of beds, but we can certainly accommodate her once a bed becomes available. The intake will take at least a week, and we can begin by starting her in outpatient." She supposed Walter Freile was no longer concerned about her stamina. At this moment, he did not seem to have any qualms about the possibility that accepting such a patient would open the door to many more. The astounding number of just the known cases of human trafficking and the magnitude of harm suffered by victims was mind-boggling. The case sounded exceptionally horrible. The women's mental health clinic she often fantasized about was needed like yesterday, like right now.

"Thank you, Irene. My wife will be pleased to hear it."

The little comment about his wife's sanity had been a joke, albeit a bad one. Yet apparently, Walter Freile was a husband who cared to support his wife's endeavors, and the thought softened Irene's opinion of him.

He handed her a brochure. "Early next month, I would like you to accompany me to a conference in Santa Fe."

She was just too busy at the lab and the clinic. "I would, except I don't want to disrupt the women's treatment. I just recently took time out for my mother. It's too soon to be away. I just don't think it's prudent."

"Think about it. Let's discuss it over lunch. We need to talk about another matter but, preferably, not in the office."

During the course of their association, Freile had not demonstrated much simpatico at all. Now he was asking for favors, inviting her to a conference and lunch. Her antennae went up, sensing something nefarious. Yet an offer to attend a professional conference with a superior should be considered a compliment. Turning down both requests could be the death knell of their professional affiliation. *So why shouldn't she at least have lunch with Dr. Freile?*

"I . . . Ah, yes."

She headed to her office thinking Freile had seemed genuine for a few moments. Nonetheless, she regretted having perceived him as such, regretted acquiescing too readily to his requests. It would have been preferable to say she would get back to him on the human trafficking case. The victim was already in a sheltered environment, and the facility should be providing some mental health services. If she spoke no English, the women in the unit might exclude her, or worse, take advantage. On the other hand . . . Jeez, she forgot to ask how old? Human traffickers tended to target young girls; they were more manageable, more in demand. Someone real young might not be a good fit in a unit of grown women. Although—Carolina was just nineteen.

And what about the invite to the conference? Was he trying to sabotage her work by pulling her away for a whole week, even as he continued to pressure her regarding the time parameters? He wanted to talk to her about a certain matter over lunch. What kind of matter? Something was not right.

Yes, the unit was functioning well. Each case had moved forward; several discharges were on the horizon. Did he mean to derail the therapeutic process for the women by interrupting their treatment? She disliked the encroaching paranoia, disliked not liking or trusting the doctor. She must work on improving her relationship with Freile, if only for the sake of the unit. She wanted to discard the suspicion that he meant to cancel out her work, but the way he'd said "a certain matter" had thrown her into a bit of a spin.

Irene scheduled an outpatient screening for the human trafficking case. Then she proceeded to email Alfredo, detailing Felicia's case, asking if he thought hypnosis might help and, if so, to please forward the names of clinicians he might know in Manhattan who were experts in hypnosis. She'd have to delay Felicia's discharge for several weeks and it would entail more bouts of jousting with Walter Freile. She wasn't looking forward to it, but she'd made up her mind not to agree to outpatient until a referral was in place for hypnosis. Alfredo Bryson's network of connections was wide and deep. She was confident he'd find someone appropriate for her patient. No harm in checking in and asking his opinion about a troublesome case, no harm at all.

Tough Thursday

IRENE DONNED SNEAKERS FOR the big showdown with Ana Amado. She doubted she was going to win the match. Not the point, though. If Ana could be open enough to chance a game with Irene, unfriendly audience and all, it might turn things around for her with the others. All but one had looked askance at the woman's behaviors. Amado's manner had been abrasive; and as tough as she was, she was in danger of becoming a scapegoat of sorts. The women liked Jackson and resented Ana's attitude. She was improving, but another altercation, and she risked being bumped out to yet another psychiatric institution—or the street.

Ana seemed surprised when Irene strolled over with ping-pong racket in hand. "Bet you thought I'd forget and let you off the hook. No way!" Ana blushed. She followed Irene into the atrium, muttering to herself, "Guess I'll have to be polite and let her win. I know how to be polite, sometimes."

Irene turned around. "Did you say something, Ana?"

"No. Nah."

Olivia and Marta were at one of the tables volleying vigorously. They stopped and went over to where Ana and Irene were about to begin playing. The other women gathered in a noisy cheering section on Irene's side. Only Carolina stood by Ana, applauding limply each time Amado scored. Irene played damn hard, surprising the heck out of Amado and the women. Back in college, she'd been good at tennis. Tennis vs. Paddle Ball. Carolina let out a little squeal when the paddle ball master finally triumphed. Irene gave Ana a high five and put her arm around her shoulder.

Carolina gave Irene a big silly grin.

"I've got winners," shouted Marta.

Ana glanced over at Irene and Carolina and said, "Bet." The two women approached the match with a macho attitude. Irene laughed. Ana flexed her well-defined arms and held the paddle in front of her like a tennis player. Marta rubbed the small ball against her chest and then breathed on it with a grin.

"Hey, girl, stop with the showing off and play," yelled out Olivia.

Marta laughed, "It's for good luck!"

They played hard. Perspiration glistened on Ana's forehead. She repeatedly scored. Marta ceded. Ana had an arrogant I-won-this-girl-fight written all over her face. Irene hurried over and had them shake hands. She then put her arms around both women. "Ladies, congratulations. What you just witnessed here is called sportsmanship." Irene said this, even though the women had quick-time pulled away from the handshake. Then, with a big smile, she announced, "I think what we need around here is more activities, physical stuff that makes us sweat and builds our strength."

Ana piped up, "Yeah, Kickboxing and Karate."

"I'd go for some Karate. My brother got to brown belt, then quit, too much discipline, but hey, I'd go for that." Marta was face-to-face talking to Amado. "You and I would probably get to black belt." Ana Amado shrugged.

Irene continued with her agenda, "You know, I've been thinking along similar lines. How many of you would be interested in learning self-defense techniques?" Every hand went up. "Great. I'll get on it. Next Thursday, you will be attending a workshop in the conference room. Check the bulletin board for the time."

The women chit-chatted about how busy they were going to be. Irene loved the buzzing of their voices and silently thanked God the table tennis tournament had not deteriorated into a gang-girl-hair-pulling-incident. Yoga or tai-chi might help the women with spiritual healing, but they could also benefit from hard-nosed survival skills, skills that could save their lives. She would discuss objectives with the activities coordinator and ask her to come up with an instructor who could do both Yoga and teach self-defense techniques. Money was always a programmatic issue.

On Thursday afternoons, Olivia and Amanda came in for individual sessions. They were young, hard girls, victims of life and the streets, victims of the harsh, unforgiving environments that formed them and scarred their psyches. Irene pulled up their files.

—By age twelve, Olivia knew she was a lesbian, and it wasn't just a stage she was going through. That's just the way it was for her. She had no desire to be around boys. Ignorant of the real reason her daughter stayed away from boys, her mother liked to brag that her daughter was not turning out to be a skanky slut like the rest of the neighborhood girls. Between the ages of fourteen and sixteen, Olivia and her girlfriend Gladys were inseparable. Although not unusual for two adolescent girls to become super-close BFFs. Olivia and Gladys were much more; they were lovers. Even as the AIDS epidemic ravaged their sons and daughters, many Hispanic families continued to deny and reject their homosexual children, brothers, and sisters. Her father, Tomás, began to wonder about the endless hours the two girls spent behind the locked door of Olivia's bedroom. And why didn't his daughter have any boyfriends? Boys should be knocking down the front door for her by now. Questions and innuendos became an everyday occurrence, often escalating to nasty interrogations and filthy insults. Olivia could barely look her father in the face. Tomás was determined to straighten her out. Olivia spoke about what happened next in such detail it could make anyone's skin crawl. She wrote about it in her journal:

My father barged into my bedroom like a mad bull, like a freaking raging locomotive, steam coming out of his ears, contempt out of his mouth.

"Olivia, I want to show you something." He slammed the door behind him, locked it, took off his belt, and with the leather strap in hand, hissed, "I am a man, and you are a woman, different between our legs, with parts that fit together to make babies. God made us that way, and you're not going to go against God, and you're not going to go against the bible and this family. Olivia, do you understand? I will beat the nonsense out of you if you don't stop."

"I don't know what you're talking about. I don't know." I cried and hid my face in shame and disgust. He took his time reinserting the belt through the loops of his slacks, pulled it tight for emphasis, and walked out of the room, yelling, "I don't want your girlfriend here anymore!"

No way could I be in the same room with him, ever again. How could he stupidly resort to humiliating me in such a vulgar way? If he meant to change my mind about sex with men, he'd only made it worse. For a moment, I thought of calling the police and alleging that he had exposed himself. I was frantic. He knew.

Crying, I called Gladys. "My father is going to kill me. I have to get out of here. Please, let me stay at your house for a few nights." I was about to hang up when I saw him coming at me, his face, violent red. He lashed and lashed and lashed, pushing, screaming; the belt's leather, like a blade ripping at the skin of my arms and legs. "¡¡Mierda asquerosa!! Now get out! Get out, Olivia. Never come back."

Olivia spent two years in a shelter for homeless girls, where she became well-schooled in the art of homosexuality. Then after a year on the streets, she ended up in the Psych Ward of Bronx State Hospital. Difficult, impossible to tease out subsequent events from the trauma of the unspeakable violence inflicted by her father.

> A copy of the police report was attached to the case notes: Appears the subject was a sex worker for a pimp who controlled her with cocaine. A john called 911 and left in a hurry. Medics took her away in a straitjacket.

She'd been a sex worker that year on the street. A "fatherly" pimp promptly appropriated her and kept her under control with cocaine and promises of wealth. She convinced him to let her work with another girl, and they turned out to be his prize moneymakers. One night, her partner in crime ran away with a john. The creep who owned her didn't know it, but thanks to her partner, Olivia had been performing without letting the john penetrate. Now, she could not continue. The pimp slapped her around a couple of times, denied her the candy, and kept prostituting her without a buddy. Olivia went nuts.

Olivia was pretty and petite. If she had landed in prison, hardened homosexual women may have targeted her. When Irene pointed this out, she said, "Better than hard-dicked creeps. Those women would protect me."

Bronx State discharged her within days. The streets were waiting. Despite her aversion to sex with males, all she knew was the life. A nurse took an interest in her and convinced the halfway house where she worked part-time to admit Olivia. A lesbian herself, she worked with the site's social worker to direct the case to Lakeside.

Reoccurring flashbacks were sufficiently debilitating to keep her from gaining employment, pursuing training, and securing housing. Irene was sure she could free Olivia from the cell of her nightmares if only the girl could get past the seductive posturing that had become the script of her existence. Olivia told Marta she thought that Irene was as gay as they were.

"No, you're wrong, Olivia. She's not like that. She just cares about us a lot, that's all."

"Then why would she be working only with women? All that doctor needs is to give in to our sensual touch."

Each time she appeared for a session, Olivia held out her hand and delicately grazed her slender fingers along Irene's palm.

Today, Irene greeted her with the EMDR device. She held the metal apparatus in front of her. Before she could begin to explain its purpose, Olivia flinched and jumped away toward the door. She'd been hit so many times everything looked like a weapon to her. "What is that thing? It looks like a taser. I didn't do nothing."

Irene explained it was simply an instrument utilized to help patients process the trauma which impaired their functioning. She placed the device on her desk and plugged it in. A blue light began to blink.

"Is it going to take my picture? Turn it off." Olivia was eyeing the thing with more than ordinary suspicion, taking furtive little steps toward it, curious, but still in survival mode.

"No, the light just helps you to focus once you've selected a safe place where you want to begin."

"A safe place? What safe place is that?" Olivia was staring back at Irene with her thin shoulders hunched so high up they grazed the tip of her ears. Olivia had suffered so much trauma, beginning with the beating by her father years ago, that EMDR might not suffice.

"It's okay, Olivia. We can wait to start with this."

"Don't take it personal, but I don't like this place. The only reason I stay here is because of Marta. I think the reason I can't shake the fucking flashbacks is because this is a hospital, and that's why I keep seeing a fucking padded cell closing up around me . . . The medics, or whoever the fuck they were, put me in a straitjacket and forced me into an ambulance. At Bronx State they tied me down to a table, tied me down with belts, Dr. Míral, with belts! And all because I screamed at the attendant to take his fucking hands off me."

"I understand. I can help you. Let me. You were traumatized by stuff that happened to you recently, but you've been a victim since you were a teen."

Olivia laughed, a laugh old and worn. "My father wanted me to eat dick, so I did. And that is my nightmare—forever. Except when I'm in Marta's arms."

"It sounds like you need her. Do you love her?"

"Yes, I do. She's the best thing that's ever happened to me, and when we get out of here, we're going to hook up, get an apartment, and you know . . ."

"Before any of it can become a reality, you both need to be able to get through your days without flashbacks and get to understand how PTSD can affect all aspects of your life. A sound, a scent or a situation can be a trigger. Once you understand how it happens, you can learn coping mechanisms so you can have a life, hold down jobs." Irene hesitated to say anything about a concern. Olivia had always been a lesbian, but for Marta it was more like the end of the road. Maybe she would betray Olivia at some point with a man. That would be devastating.

"Can I see that?" Olivia pointed to the EMDR device.

"Sure, it doesn't bite. It's just a machine."

She touched the instrument gingerly as if it might burn her, then turned it on and off a couple of times. "I want to get out of here, Dr. Míral. I don't want to see a padded cell or a restraining table anymore. Help me."

As Olivia examined the EMDR device, the long sleeves of her smock slid down the skin of her arms, exposing ugly scars where there had once been bleeding welts. What kind of parent would do that to a child?

"It's all right, Olivia. Can you describe the table? The one with the restraining belts."

⊰◦⊱

At the last review, Freile's remarks regarding Amanda's case had rankled Irene to the core. Without much ado at all, he'd stated Amanda was fabricating flashbacks and nightmares. "Considering her antisocial leanings, the woman should own her nightmares. She deserves them. Believe me, she is looking to be declared mentally incapacitated so she can become eligible for disability benefits." The doctor made no effort to disguise his biases. If he, a psychiatrist, was prone to making such outrageous judgments, what could one expect from non-professionals? Freile had succeeded in revealing his bigotry at every turn. Amanda's PTSD was not fabricated. And neither was her story.

Amanda was as beautiful as the soft syllables of her name. She was graced with silky black hair and skin like the pale flesh of a new peach. No one would guess she was prone to episodes of vile rage. Her predisposition to resort to violence seemed endemic to her personality. No Love, Just Blood.

—A conviction for attempted manslaughter resulted in a ten-year prison sentence which, on appeal, was reduced to five years and probation. The Osborne Society advocated for her return to the community and arranged for a provisional safety net upon her release. She had two nervous breakdowns in prison, and although a condition of probation was that she participate in treatment, after two years of therapy, she continued to complain of flashbacks and night-mares. During a session with her therapist, she threw meds in his face, went behind his desk, demanded her chart, tore it to shreds, and raged out the door. The therapist lost no time notifying Amanda's Probation Officer that he was closing the case, stating the young woman was dangerous, likely to hurt herself or another, and needed psychiatric treatment. The P.O. gave Amanda a choice: admission to the hospital for observation or returning to court on a violation to face charges of disorderly conduct and attempted assault. At Bellevue, her nightmares and flashbacks worsened. The P.O. had a degree in social work. She could not return Amanda to court in such a fragile state and searched for an alternative. Bellevue agreed to arrange a transfer to Lakeside.

She seldom spoke about her past or her experiences while in prison. After a month and a half of group sessions, Amanda finally revealed she had been raped six times, beginning at age twelve, by relatives and various males who drifted in and out of her life. "There wasn't a seventh time. You know why? I stuck a sharp pencil in the creep's neck and nearly killed him." Marta stood up and applauded. Irene immediately stated, "The incident resulted in a criminal record, and Amanda suffered yet another humiliation, imprisonment." She thanked Amanda for her participation and asked the women to applaud Amanda's willingness to share and participate.

Life had trapped Amanda in a tough outer casing—armadillo armor protecting her from hurt—from feeling pain—her rages, a shield keeping people at a distance. She needed to work through the layers concealing her innermost feelings. Although there was a lot of bravado surrounding the retelling of the crime, the piercing of the man's neck haunted her. She relived it in real time almost every night. It had been the act of a desperate woman who could not tolerate one more violation of her body.

Alma was never far from Irene's thoughts. Despite the violence she'd endured, her mom had not become a violent person. Of course, fate had granted her Antonio. He made her feel safe and loved her, even when she was not loveable, even when she could not demonstrate love. But unconditional love from men, or anyone, was hard to come by, trust, hard to restore.

Irene made a few notes in Amanda's file. She needed to clarify how she was going to proceed with the case. She reviewed the psych eval: intelligent, paranoid ideation, depression. The results of the Rorschach test were surprising—no indication of disordered thinking, and the patient was not evasive about the bloodstain or copulative features of some of the inkblots. However, the last cards of the series made Amanda quite uncomfortable; fluid situations would likely be a challenge for her. The Thematic Apperception

Test indicated varying stages of depression, feelings of abandonment, and poor self-esteem.

Amanda needed to love herself as unconditionally as possible, before she could love anyone, before anyone could love her.

CBT would be the therapeutic modality for now. If rage could be processed out of her, then Amanda might have a chance at normality. Girls like her had trouble with even mundane relationships, so social skills were a big deal. Her arsenal of defenses worked against her, would not keep her safe in a hostile world, would only keep her from love and stability. The trick was getting her to see it. Amanda needed to live socially in her community, complete her probation, and never return to prison. Irene did not like the word conform. But the girl needed to learn to do it.

Irene looked up from the case notes. Amanda was standing in the doorway of her office, staring in.

"Hello, Amanda. Come in. Did you bring your journal?"

Amanda searched under the bulk of her Wu-Tang Clan sweatshirt. She pulled out the journal and a ballpoint pen from beneath the elastic of her baggy sweatpants. She pointed the pen in Irene's direction.

Was she being provocative? Irene did not fear her clients, but she was not naive. She held her pen under the chin pensively and then pointed it at the patient. "I was reviewing your case and treatment goals. It occurs to me that you should be the one formulating them."

The arch of a well-formed eyebrow peaked in response.

"We can start right now. What is goal number one for you? Take a few moments and record the goal in your journal, or just tell me."

Amanda riffled through the pages of her journal with disdain, snapped it shut, and offered it to Irene in a motion meant to be dismissive.

"Thanks for letting me see what you've been writing. Red ink was practically dripping from the pages. Um, it all looks pretty angry. Tell me, Amanda, do you think you're a violent person?"

"I'm a fat goose."

"You're not fat. Why do you say that?"

Amanda pushed her hair back, pulled down at the sweatshirt's collar, and exposed a creamy shoulder. The words Fat Goose #17-1990 were tattooed on the slope of her upper arm. "I joined a gang when I was seventeen. So, does it answer your question?"

"No, it does not. Many young people join groups in their teens. Some are just social clubs. What kind of group was it? Did you fight other groups, sell drugs, mug people? What was it?"

"You're funny, Miss. I like you. But you know, not everybody is your friend."

"True, Amanda. Not everyone can be our friend, but we all need friendship and love." Irene got the feeling she'd just been offered a subtle invite to join the Fat Gooses.

"Just a bunch of girls to walk with. We smoked weed, that's about it, hung out. You know what? The weed kept me calm, kept me calm better than the meds. I think meds make me have nightmares."

Finally, getting to the point. "It sounds like you want to get rid of those nightmares. Is it your main goal?"

"Yeah, well, it makes me real mad I still have them. Sometimes I think therapy is bullshit. I'm sorry, but that's how I feel. Some of the other women feel the same way. That's why I said, everybody is not your friend."

"Thanks for letting me know. Amanda, I understand how difficult therapy can be. For some people, it's almost impossible. But I do believe it can work for you. Let me help. Right now, you must focus on what's happening in your head, on how your body responds to the stress of the symptoms that upset you."

"Sometimes, I feel like I want to off someone, anyone. It always happens after I have the nightmare or even when thinking of how I stuck the pencil in that man's neck." Amanda struck at the air with her pen. "It just makes me more freakin' angry. I should have killed him, so he never tries to rape anyone again, and besides, it landed me in jail. I was the victim. It was self-defense. Do you know what happened to him? Nothing. NOTHING!"

The amazing thing about Amanda was how her facial expression did not change, even as she shouted out. Definitely a disconnect. She batted her eyes shut and turned her face away. "I'm sorry. I do get angry a lot."

"You have a right to be angry. Anger is not a sin. But what we do with our anger determines whether it becomes harm of some kind. Amanda, how do you feel right now? . . . Amanda?"

She shrugged. "Can I go now?"

"Do you want to write something in your journal while you're here?"

"No, not right now. You can hold it. I'll get it later."

"Okay, next week."

Amanda hesitated at the door, then left. Irene began to read the journal. The young woman wanted her to. "Jesus!" she exclaimed. She got up, looked down the hallway, and closed the door. She hoped Amanda had been out of earshot and not heard that.

Knives dripping with blood decorated every page. Some pages exploded with bubbles like those of comic books from the dark side, spewing obscenities and threats. Penises, sliced like sausages, catapulted into the air and regenerated as steel spokes on the wheels of black chariots. The entries were vivid with violent dialogue.

Irene read the page illustrated with a bleeding heart. *"No Love, Just Blood."* It occurred to her that Amanda may have been linked to the Latin Kings, possibly an initiate. She read on. Our girl had been in love at least once and loved deeply. Perhaps she was not as antisocial as her history suggested. Her journal provided more insight into her state of mind than any projective could.

Odd. The writing, scripted in perfect penmanship, prompted Irene to check Amanda's D.O.B. She was much too young to have been school-molded to form letters in such a formal and uniform manner. Irene remembered the disapproving little tuck of the tongue on the palate of the nun who taught fourth grade, and how she returned all her compositions marked with a heavy crayon-red comment: "Poor penmanship."

Irene did not want to label Amanda as rigid. Still, her hand-writing, and the precision of the stylized crew letters, pointed to a terrible need for order. Obscenities abounded, not only in the bubbles but also in the evenly perfect scribing.

"I used to be the pride of The Bronx Club, next in line to be queen, but not the reason why I stayed. I was happy to be his princesa until the bitch tore him from my arms like a vicious crow snatching a fledgling from its nest."

Amanda had drawn a crow, powerful claws dripping with blood over a broken heart. Then, sentiment became fury, expressed in the stylized graffiti of a crew member:

Bitch
Beware The Fat Goose

"My snatch is tighter than that old whore's; my tits beautiful, hers, under-inflated party balloons, who would want to suckle on them? A freight train could whistle past her hole, and she wouldn't know it. So how can he feel anything in there?"

Irene let out a slow "Wow." Amanda did not need knives. She could slice someone up with words. Yet, she was also capable of expressing love and loss:

"MISS ME. Please miss me. I need the strength of your arms, the warmth of your skin, your saliva in me."

The hierarchy of gang organization had ceded Amanda's place to the widow of a respected leader killed by the police in a raid. The woman had two children, and Esteban, the coveted king, vowed fealty. He offered Amanda a second rung as sister and servant. She refused. Esteban abandoned her. She lost his protection and got passed around from brother to brother to brother. Sometimes she was raped.

Soul Mates

IN THE SUMMER, IRENE often braved the wilderness of Central Park, across bridle paths, over footbridges, and east to Lakeside—kind of risky, although joggers and bicyclists were usually in evidence. She saved on tokens and the occasional cab fare. Alma had taught her to be thrifty. In no time, her legs assumed new contours of aesthetic definition.

On those walks, her mind's eye often revisited the image of two happy children: She and her brother Jaime smiling up at their father as he gently glided their rowboat over the north lake on warm Sunday afternoons. The small boats were inexpensive back then, and the Harlem Meer was a nearby place for local families to enjoy. Once she moved downtown, she enjoyed lingering at the Bow Bridge, looking out to The Lake, thinking she should rent a rowboat at the new Loeb Boathouse. Lately, a postcard image of David rowing and dreamily gazing into her eyes began to occupy her imagination.

Walking was good for the soul, liberating the eye with the leisure to observe and ruminate, unbound from the obsessive nature of jogging. She liked to speculate about the people she came upon along the way, wondering about the context of their lives, their wants and needs. Were they heading to work as she was, or were they unemployed, a walk in the park the only purpose of their day? She often came upon an older man bent over harvesting dandelions. "For wine," he'd say, "and there are wild scallions all over. I gather them for the Asian grocer in exchange for coffee and buttered rolls." The round of his back and the shabby jacket hanging loosely as he worked over the weeds and dandelions reminded her of a French Impressionist canvas. The ease of his words was comforting as an old friend's. Sometimes he'd make a bouquet of dandelions sprigs, offering them to Irene with a, "You have a good day, miss." The warmth of his words lightened her step.

The long subway ride to NYU twice a week served to disconnect her from the structure of her workdays—the regular roar of the rails, lulling, enabling her to daydream, to create vignettes about the people who occupied her range of vision. But once her mother got sick, everyone else around her receded to a gray blur. Life was not a daydream. The end could be a nightmare or a recurring one, like Amanda's.

Rush hour was well and over by the time she boarded the train to Washington Square. In an hour or so, she'd be back at the lab. On Thursday evenings, she and David shared takeout from the Thai place, a popular eatery a block from the subway station. Both were light eaters with a penchant for Asian-Fusion cuisine, deemed it to be healthier than pizza or a pastrami sandwich. She'd called in an order of W-4th chicken breast, four duck basil spring rolls, and a large papaya salad to be ready in an hour.

Years ago, she'd interned at the nearby American Express building as a Loss and Stolen Clerk. Often, she sat on the benches around the square with a brown-bag lunch and her friend Doris who worked in the same department. Although the corporate employee lunch-room was far more comfortable, she and Doris chose to avoid its big-screen TVs and the steady broadcast stream of sports events. The square, a lively vignette of funkiness and city life, provided more entertainment than any staid programming, so they opted for the spacious lunchroom only when it rained. Neither harbored any illusions about a career with the company. Doris was going to concentrate on finding a guy to marry her and give her babies. Irene was going to continue college.

The eye-opening internship experience served to steer her toward finally declaring a major. Irene had been thinking about journalism and a minor in business, then discovered her true calling before the end of her sophomore year. Always a keen observer, she'd become aware of the pecking order in corporate offices. To her, it reflected the nasty demands of society's hierarchal pyramid, a hierarchy which enslaved many. She sensed that some clung to their positions because at least they had a job. Of course, many people didn't; they floundered without skills, didn't know how to negotiate the obstacles society thrust before them. She understood futility resulted in mental illness and decided to choose psychology as her major. She seldom considered how her mother's history influenced her choices. The reason she was on the way to the lab this very moment. She'd never asked David why *he* had such tunnel vision about paranormal research.

Irene laid out the fare from the Thai place. The generous portion of chicken breast was a favorite of David's and enough for two people. He concentrated on the big portion of W-4th while she consumed most of the papaya salad. In between bites, she talked about her nephew and his near accident when he tried to avoid what he thought was a woman in the middle of the road.

"Was there a woman?"

She popped another chunk of papaya in her mouth and paused to savor it, "No, just someone he thought he saw. Eerie. And want to know something else? At my mom's funeral, a patient who came to pay her respects remarked she thought she saw something she called an angel's kiss on my nephew's lip. Then she went on about lost children and supernatural warnings from departed siblings, all voiced with utmost gravity. The other day, she brought me a tall votive, an iridescent white candle. 'For protection,' she said. Isn't that weird?"

"Um, what did you do with it?"

"I thanked her. I'm not past respecting cultural artifacts or the premonition of a patient. It's sitting on the ledge of my bedroom window, right below my dream catcher, the one I purchased in Tennessee two years ago, at their Sequoyah festival. I lit the votive once. The nimbus around the flame made me think of my mother and her Adriana and the dead baby brother I never knew."

Her words fell like a somber blanket over the room. David's face registered a little shock of surprise. "A dead baby brother?"

Irene stared at David, her gray eyes wide and naked. "Yes. Several of my mom's children from her first marriage died. One saw a lady in the light before he passed."

"Oh, Irene, how sad. How did your little brother die?" Melancholy echoed in his voice, perhaps a trace of a personal sorrow.

She wanted to change the subject. The whole thing was shameful. She'd told David most of Alma's story but never mentioned the horrific abuse, and she didn't think he needed to hear about starved dead children. "Know what else I brought home? A bouquet of dried sage and a handmade ceramic vessel. Once a year, my mom burned some leaves in a pot, said it was a protective cleansing. I thought I'd do the same with the sage. Of course, I forgot all about it. The sage, in its vessel, is sitting on the sill also, waiting. Funny how rituals can lose significance. Unfortunate. I think they do serve a therapeutic function."

"I agree. I'm surprised you ventured that far south, urbane soul that you are." He and Irene were big city people, although their interests and curiosity were not circumscribed by environment or dogma. Soul mates they were, in almost every sense. "And what demons are you trying to keep away from your window?"

"None. Just making sure my weird neighbor Grantis stays in the basement."

"Grantis? Who is he?"

"He moved into the street level apartment of my brownstone a couple of months ago. Grantis is strange, kind of skulks around and doesn't talk. So, it's creepy, that's all."

"Could be a peeper."

"No, he would need to be a vampire to peep in through my windows. But seriously, I'm fascinated by folklore, cultural artifacts, language, and imagery. Sequoyah is famous for a syllabary he created for the Cherokee people, enabling them to record spoken language and inspiring other groups to write down their oral histories. You may want to take a look—codes, symbols, sounds, phonemes, and the impact of language—right up your alley."

David put his fork down. He had never mentioned a thing about his own family tragedy. "Um, never told you my mother was a professor of English Literature at Smith, did I? Neither my sisters nor I followed in her footsteps. And it wasn't because she didn't try. She made sure we knew our English lit from Chaucer to Shakespeare to Dickens, all the romantic poets, Wordsworth, Keats, Shelly. . ." David's milk chocolate eyes darkened. "Anne . . . did I ever tell you about my sister Anne?"

"Uh-uh. I thought you were an only child."

"No, there were three of us, Anne, Courtney, and me. I'm the youngest. Anne was ten years older than I, a commissioned Army officer, a brilliant mathematician. My parents did not learn of her involvement in the Stargate Project until . . ."

"Stargate?"

"I didn't know anything about it either and couldn't figure how she came to end up in a psychiatric hospital for veterans. My parents were torn up about it. I suppose they still are. And my sister Courtney just shut down about it. Even now she gets angry anytime we mention her. I still remember the pain on Courtney's face when we visited our sister in that place. All Anne talked about was how the Russians could see what we were doing and how the KGB had killed two of our people who'd developed the uncanny ability to guess, with surprising precision, the various strategic locations of their missile sites. She kept saying she could predict when the Russians would relocate the missiles and insisted it was crucial she be allowed to contact her commanding officer. The hospital's report said she was schizophrenic. She died there, passed away five years ago."

"Oh, no. I am so sorry."

"Scary stuff, right? But not as crazy as it sounds. Previously classified information about the government's remote viewing espionage missions, and there were hundreds of them, became available to certain people. Stargate was almost exactly what my sister described. Our government's intelligence and military community, convinced clairvoyance could be developed to defeat the Soviets, invested heavily in the program. And it was not a willy-nilly operation. Consultants from The Stanford Research Center were involved since the inception of the project, instrumental in its direction. You know the Patty Hearst case? The FBI enlisted remote viewers to find her." David paused and swallowed. Rubbing the back of his neck with one hand, he said, "What I think is—my sister was involved in some aspect of Stargate the military wanted kept secret."

So that was it. Sadness and unanswered questions over the loss of his sister had moved David to pursue paranormal scientific investigations.

"I understand why we're both here . . . if my mother had not told me about seeing a girl in white light, I probably would not be doing this."

He looked at her with wet eyes.

"David, do you really think the U.S. government has totally abandoned such programs? Wasn't there also buzz about a secret

DARPA project? Maybe the Defense Department put the Army in charge of clandestine research and gave it a new name: Stargate. Do you truly believe they will release *all* the classified information?"

A trace of scorn marred his countenance. "No. Not any time soon. It's possible my sister possessed knowledge of something the government wanted to make sure remained covert. Perhaps she was deemed a possible risk, so they threw her overboard by having her committed."

"One of my patients came close to being committed, the same one who told me about the angel's kiss, the one who gave me the votive. Her ex-husband tried. It happens more often than we'd like to know, and predominantly to women. If he could have burned her on the stake, he would have. She just recently ripped off the scarlet letter he'd pinned on her personhood. So, suppose a nasty ex-spouse can get a wife committed. In that case, it's not at all far-fetched that the U.S. government could do the same to a worker they want to silence, someone deemed a risk to national security." David shook his head in agreement. The rest of their little Thai dinner wilted on soggy paper plates.

"Let's get to work, Irene. It's getting late."

Friday, Big Sister

At her dresser, Irene brushed her hair back, pulled it through a thin scrunchie, grabbed a floral silk chiffon scarf from a drawer, and tied it with a generous bow over the elastic band. She glanced at her reflection, a soft navy sweater, and a charcoal gray pencil skirt. Most of her wardrobe consisted of interchangeable dark neutrals, her mother's beautiful scarves, the only bright notes. She slid her hands over her hips. The skirt was kind of snug. She took it off. *I'll wear this one tomorrow.* Her mind raced forward to Saturday morning when she would be back at the lab with David. She was not fully conscious of the desire to be near him. It existed subsumed in layers of pretext, disguised as an urgency to complete the study, even though she damn-well knew David's money afforded them plenty of time to produce results.

The clinic was a different story. Irene was fighting time and Walter Freile. At any time, he could change a patient's diagnosis and recommend discharge to another facility. This Friday's sessions with Carolina and Ana would require all her focus and intellectual stamina. Their cases could turn out to be her nemeses or her most significant successes. She silently chastised herself for thinking in such terms. It was not about success porn. It was about helping two impaired young women heal so they could function with some level of normalcy and get on with living. It was about not ceding them back to a dysfunctional mental health system.

But all we do in life is in service of the ego. Irene admitted she would like to prove her assessments were correct, wanted to prove it to Dr. Walter Freile. "I should have scheduled them for the beginning of the week instead of Fridays," she said aloud. No. Mondays were for Maríanis.

Time tolled. Her unit was meant for short-term treatment. Ana and Carolina would have to be the exception *if* she could keep Freile from writing them off. Carolina's reaction in group had been heartbreaking. Irene had to be careful not to risk a setback by pushing her beyond where she wasn't ready to go. But bottom line was: The session produced more positive results than not. Ana had become a real person in the eyes of the women, and they'd rallied around Carolina as she cried out in grief and anger. Irene hoped it all proved to be cathartic, hoped it had not alienated the girl from the therapeutic process. Her reactions indicated involvement, not withdrawal. Too bad she didn't speak. *Success porn wishes again. I must connect with Carolina today or lose gains from the group session. Anything— anything to get Carolina to talk.*

Irene crouched to examine the bottom shelves of the bookcase that housed manuals, texts, monograms, and professional journals. Finally found it, buried beneath reams of bound case files, a medium-size sketch pad tucked inside a promotional folder from the New School. A gift from an art therapy workshop she'd attended there two years before.

She grabbed a No. 2 pencil and sat down to wait for her patient. Carolina walked in, clutching her journal like a shield. She rarely parted from it. Irene smiled and pointed her chin toward the chair across from hers. The girl always waited for permission of some kind. Irene worked in the sketch pad she held in her lap. She could draw reasonably well; shaded strokes soon gave form to a vase of flowers. Irene raised her gaze from the drawing. Carolina looked a little confused, a bit curious, a bit sheepish, as if sorry she'd allowed her curiosity to be aroused. She looked down at the journal, which remained closed on her lap.

Irene moved her chair over, next to hers. Carolina pulled back into the round of the seat. Irene smiled again and kept working on the sketch. Carolina demurred, as if making a decision, then opened her journal. Irene kept sketching, sensed the soft riffling of pages. She would give Carolina all the time she needed.

A mass of lustrous brown hair followed as the girl bent over the notebook, now fully open on her lap. Her slender fingers hovered over the pages as if she were reading braille. That journal was her heart. Irene was sure of it.

She showed Carolina the drawing, a large vase overflowing with vines and flowers. "What do you think? I want to give it a name. Big Sister." Irene handed over the sketch pad and the pencil. She asked Carolina to help her complete the drawing with a title.

A moist sheen glistened over the girl's dark pupils. She took the pencil and wrote the word sister in big scrawling letters on the bottom of Irene's sketch. Irene took her hand and repeated the word sister. *God, why can't she say something? She is present, she is here.* "Why don't you draw something for me in my sketch pad. I know you're talented, and I would love to have a sample of your work. Someday, you may be a famous artist." Carolina smiled. Yes, she was present. The smile faded, and the girl became serious as she began work in Irene's sketchbook. "Let me hold your journal while you're doing that. Is it okay if I read something?"

Carolina looked up from her drawing and offered three quick nods. After a few minutes, Irene realized she was drawing her face. The girl squinted as she examined her subject like a photographer concentrating, searching for the best angle.

"You write poetry . . . Oh. I see each poem is dedicated to Miranda." Irene read one out loud. "'Miranda is lost in the forest of dreams, the forest of abandoned children, quiet souls walking through dark backwoods of sorrow.'" Carolina *was* speaking. She was voicing her sadness and grief on those pages. *What right do I have to ask more of her?*

"Do you see Miranda in your dreams? Carolina, tell me."

She brought a small hand to her chest and started to cry without a sound. Irene understood. "Yes, it hurts. You loved your little sister very much, and you will always miss her." Carolina continued to cry softly, prone over the sketch pad. It slipped from her lap to the floor. Irene picked it up and saw the portrait. The girl had created a remarkable likeness of Irene, wise eyes dominated the drawing. "Carolina, your poems express your feelings, the pain in your heart. Read one for me." The girl frowned. "Would you like your journal then?" She nodded a yes. "Carolina, I think the reason you don't speak is that you've been too sad, much too sad to say anything. You've poured your sadness into that notebook. But now you need to say it. Tell me how angry you are about what has happened to your family, yes?"

The girl grimaced as though something had pinched her heart.

"Is that anger now? Cry out, scream, curse the bad men who hurt your parents, your sister." Irene took the girl's hand and held it to her chest. "Listen . . . listen, Carolina. My heart speaks, but so does my voice." Irene was going to take a leap of faith. "My mother died last month, and I miss her. I miss her because I love her, and it makes me sad she's not here." The girl's lips parted as if to say something, then closed. "Thank you for listening to my heart today. Carolina, I want to hear yours."

As the girl walked out of the office, Irene thought she heard her whisper the word sorry.

A therapist should not introduce personal material to a patient. It was about the patient, not the therapist, except this was about a child losing a mom, a dear sister—a family. Irene had never thought much about having children, but she had to admit she could be experiencing maternal concern for Carolina. Just as her mom had felt maternal toward the *Americanitas* she cared for when she first arrived in New York.

Irene recalled an amusing story, one of the rare few her mother told with any levity:

"Little Lucy was a bedwetter, and every morning I had to strip the mattress and lug the ruined bedclothes to the laundry room. Often, Lucy would show up right behind me looking miserable, her blonde head bowed, thumb lodged between her pouting lips. Veronica, her older sister, was not so nice. She insulted the poor child every single morning. 'You smell Lucy, and don't come near me. I don't want you at the breakfast table.' I could not understand all Veronica was saying but knew from the harshness in her voice and the tears welling up in Lucy's eyes that her words were mean. I began raising an eyebrow at each of Veronica's angry outbursts. 'She's doing it on purpose! She should sleep on the floor!' But despite my stern arched eyebrow, the girl invariably pulled away from the breakfast table in a huff, exasperated and muttering. One early morning, I felt a sudden gush of warmth against my left leg. 'Is it my period?' No, it wasn't that time of the month. Lucy had gotten into bed with me and urinated right on my leg. I glanced over at the clock radio: 5:00 a.m. From then on, I would be rising at four-thirty, an hour earlier than my usual wake-up time. I let Lucy

sleep with me often, and each morning, at
four-thirty sharp, I'd wake the child up and take her
to the bathroom."

Yes, quite a funny story, except, when she first heard it, Irene felt
intense envy. Why she wanted to be the one in that bed with her
mom! The one to piss on her leg and follow her to the bathroom.

Carolina had been cheated of the bits and pieces of the seemingly inconsequential family scenarios that lay down the first fabric of
a person's life—the context of relationships. Writing in a journal
alone would not suffice. Irene annotated the file: The patient is
attentive, responsive, appropriate, and oriented to time and place.

Ana Amado was standing in the hallway, smoking a cigarette,
waiting. Carolina's session had run an extra ten minutes. She
wanted to know, "How did it go, Carolina? Did you talk to her?
Did you talk to Dr. Míral?" Carolina shrugged her skinny shoulders. "You didn't do it, did you? You didn't speak. No good. If
you want, you can talk to me. I'm an okay person, for real. You
shouldn't be scared." Carolina's face broke out into a big grin. She
liked this new friend, this wild woman Ana who was not scared of
anyone.

Ana walked into Irene's office, shaking her head like she didn't
approve of something. "I just saw Carolina outside the office. Um,
she's . . ."

"Did she say anything?"

The look on Amado's face was saying, nope, nothing. "I want to
be her friend. She doesn't need to be scared of me. She shouldn't
be scared of anyone. It's too fucking horrible. Carolina is just too
sad and scared to talk."

Amazing. With not one psychology course, briefcase, or any certificates, Ana had come to the same conclusion as Irene. "Don't worry about it. I think she'll start talking soon. Glad you two are friends. Did you bring your journal?"

"You don't want to see what I've been writing in there, Dr. Míral. It's all . . ."

"Go get it. Hurry."

"Okay," Ana sighed. She offered a wan smile, then loped out of the office.

She returned, waving the journal in her right hand and sporting a tight face. Was she having mood swings? Women like Ana did not like to be told what to do, so maybe she was upset about agreeing too readily to Irene's request.

"Thank you for that. Ana, sit. Let's talk." Amado, looking like she was trying to decide whether to sit or stand, turned to the chair, made her decision, and sat. "Ana, I want to know if you're still writing about your nightmares in your journal."

She responded drily, "My whole life has been a nightmare. Hell, a suffocating *infierno* with no light, no exit just like that house I was growing up in when it became coño baby, fucking tastes good."

Ana flipped through a couple of pages of the journal, "You want to know some more? Why?"

"Yes. I want to know. Tell me."

"There's more, but don't ask me to read anymore." Ana stood up, all five feet nine of her vying for defiance.

"Sounds like it was horrible growing up in your house, and you are furious about all of it. Are you there in your nightmares?"

"I don't know. I told you; the whole thing is a nightmare." She sat back down. A tear trickled down her left cheek.

"Ana, bad stuff has been happening to you for a long time. What is the coño about? Did you want to have sex, or were you forced?"

She shook her head no, closed the journal, and again rose to leave. She hesitated by the door, fingers grasping the journal like a life preserver, face hard, knitted eyebrows forming a deep and questioning furrow as she studied her therapist's face, the face she'd just recently begun to trust.

"It was my brother. He said I needed to learn stuff so men would not take advantage of me. I complained to my mom, and she said I was a fucking liar and a dirty whore who needed to get fucked."

Irene's insides lurched like seasickness. Sometimes, maintaining an expression of neutrality was a challenge.

Ana continued. "Then he stopped. This sounds crazy, but he became like a coach and protected me on the street. We used to hang out in the project's paddleball courts. He was the neighborhood's best player, and I, second best. One day, he said I'd grown *cojones*, and he laughed, 'It's hard for girls to grow balls.' It's true. I managed one testicle, and the other one is stuck in my throat, like a scream, the scream I always wake up to, all soaked in sweat."

Now was the time to start Ana on EMDR—she was graphically describing an emotional state from the gut. But Irene hesitated. She needed to attend to the feelings, the content of Ana's words. She could lose her trust in an instant if she turned the equipment on too soon. Irene knew the child in Ana cried, forever confused about the treachery of a parent who failed to protect her, confused about her feelings for the brother who raped her. All along, Irene had suspected some kind of childhood molestation. In a sense, it was a miracle Ana was able to talk about it. So many victims of childhood sexual abuse have total amnesia about it.

"I can help you. You deserve to be healthy, to have a restful sleep without medication, to be free of rage." Ana cried now. Big drops spilled onto the journal. Irene recalled what Ana had said about how the lake would overflow with their black tears. She went over to Ana and put an arm around her. "Bad memories are locked within you. The rape in the laundry room unleashed feelings you could not handle. But you can, you can learn to."

There was an expression of disbelief on Ana's face, "I still don't like Mr. Jackson. But thanks. Dr. Míral, thanks."

Irene went behind her desk and sat with a sigh released from a silent place of knowing. She proceeded to annotate her patient's file, the whole time thinking she might want to kill too if all of that happened to her.

Laura

Unease gnawed like unsatisfied hunger. And it was not just the intensity of her work at the clinic, Walter Freile's demands, or the anticipation of meaningful developments at the lab. David and the persistence of her libido were throwing her for a loop. He was on her mind *every single* night, and she struggled with the sheets and pillows, turning and tossing herself to sleep.

Laura was the only connection she had to the levity of adolescence. Of course, her girlfriend always obliged with comically lurid details of her current and past relationships. No question, her BFF was a neurotic control freak. No matter, Irene could always count on Laura's devil-with-everything-and-just-have-a-good-time advice. Not that she followed it, but the vicarious possibilities were entertaining. Right now, she needed some laughs and a nightlong conversation about men, love, and lust. *Laura, you're on!*

The Cig, one of Manhattan's most popular cigar bars, was packed. It was Friday. While she waited for Laura, Irene placed a call to Joe Martell on her new, too expensive cell phone. It went to voice mail. "Joe, Irene Miral here. Want to know about a referral, a vet I thought needed follow-up for PTSD. Did he ever get there?"

Laura sauntered in dressed in an ultra-tight dark green Kamali number—fashionable as always, and a little thinner than the last time she'd seen her. The women kissed, hugged, and mushed over each other. Laura banged her designer handbag on the table like a diva. Irene loved stuff like that about her; she was ridiculous. Then with her usual dramatic flair, Laura pulled out a fancy cigarette case from her bright orange Furla, flicked a silver-plated lighter, lit up a smoke, and inhaled. Her nails gleamed vivid and red. All she needed to complete her act was one of those extra-long cigarette holders. Irene would get her one, except she objected to smoking in general. "Laura, you know I hate the odor of tobacco and especially don't like the smell of cigars."

Laura ordered two vodka martinis without even asking Irene what she wanted to drink.

"Shush, I don't smoke cigars anymore, but this is a great place to meet men, ten times better than that girly sisters' place where we usually meet. I mean, honestly, when was the last time you got laid?"

Irene picked up the martini and practically put her face in it.

"Hey girl, you're blushing. What's up?"

She didn't want to start right in about David. "So, you've given up cigars. Great." She patted down her hair and twirled the ends around her index finger as she sometimes did when she was being evasive.

"Yes, Ma'am, and gave up the man too." Laura downed the rest of her drink. Then, an evaluative stare. She had eyes like a hawk. "Classy earrings. For sure, you didn't get those at one of your little boutiques. They look expensive."

"My mother's, a wedding gift from my father."

"Nice, but that headband scarf thing takes away from their luxe. Makes you look like some relic from an old flick. Don't know why you insist on wearing those."

"Maria Felix to you." Haughtily trying to play the part, Irene repositioned the bow of the jewel blue silk, bringing it closer to her cheek. "Maybe Hedy Lamar, ha-ha." She rolled her eyes. "Heck, I thought the blue colors and the tiny gold flowers complimented my mom's earrings." *Creep.*

Her cell phone vibrated. Joe Martell. "Irene, glad you called. Here's the skinny: The guy showed up, gave reception my name, and asked for an appointment. Intake couldn't find any record of his military service. The receptionist buzzed up and said he was being obnoxious and paranoid, demanding to speak to anyone with ethics, anyone who was not a liar. I had like fifteen minutes, so I went down, calmed him down some, but he kept demanding to come in. I explained why we couldn't service him and referred him to Veterans in Crisis. They provide support without asking too many questions. He shoved your card in my hand and walked away, muttering. He is not right."

"Wow, sure hope he walked himself over there. Reception did take some info, right?"

"Yeah. He said he'd served in The Middle East and Eastern Europe, claimed he was a communications expert and fluent in several languages. He checked off Dishonorable Discharge on the intake application. Still, even after that kind of termination, there would be a record. He was indignant that we could not confirm it. He could be lying."

"Joe, are you sure? Government records are not always correct. I have to go now. Thanks much for looking into it."

Laura was steaming behind a cloud of cigarette smoke. "Damn, Irene, just because you finally spent some money and got yourself a cell phone, you don't have to go showing off. You're worse than a guy right in my face talking on the phone to a new whore while I disappear into a stinking sinkhole of humiliation." She made a pissy sound with her lips.

Whoa! Is she in a mood. "Jeez, grumpy girl, sorry. It was just a business call, and I wasn't talking all that long." Irene turned off the phone and put it in her purse. "What in the world is bothering you? I expected you to be all relaxed from the cruise, not all wired up and upset."

"Pervert, a freaking druggie just like my brother. Practically speed-balled right into the ocean after the third night."

Irene looked up from her martini, not wanting to register what she'd just heard. "Laura! What?"

"You know me, babe. I'll try anything at least once. Yeah, me too. But you know, I can't stay with it, can't live with it, won't." She ordered another drink and gulped it down as soon as the waiter set it down. "The thing is, I was falling in love with him. Maybe it was his money, not love, maybe my need to be loved. We'd done a few things, you know, but not anything I hadn't tried before. I spent the last two nights of the cruise on a deck chair, told him it was too much, hoping he would stop. I said we should try counseling. Irene, I begged. And guess what he did? He laughed like it was a stupid joke. 'Stop being such an old lady,' he said. 'You're a great lay, but you need a little help. You know, so you can move your hips a little faster.' Honestly, Dr. Jekyll and Mr. Hyde. God, how can I possibly be such a poor judge of character."

"Laura, he's bad news, an actor who needs to take his act elsewhere. Forget him." Laura's hands were shaking. She bit her lip and lit up a third smoke without finishing the second one. *What is happening?* Irene remembered Maríanis' tale of the angel's kiss. She peered into Laura's face. No trace of it. But why the hell was she looking for it? She needed to let go of the recurring notion of impending doom. It was unnatural. Her mind began to reprocess everything Laura had just said. An image of tell-tale tracks on Laura's skin flashed before her eyes. *I think I'll go out of my mind right this minute. This is like being back at the clinic with a patient.* "Listen, why don't you stay with me this weekend? We can have a what was his name marathon." Irene wanted to observe her friend for a while, desperately wanted to know Laura was going to be okay.

"Don't know. I want to catch up on my beauty sleep and plan my trip to P.R."

"Perfect. You can sleep over, and we can talk. I need to talk to you about . . ." Irene was stalling while she figured out what the hell was up with Laura.

"What? What is it?"

"I need a favor. Could you set me up with a real estate person while you're over there? My schedule is tight, my brother needs the money, and I shouldn't put it off. The problem is I won't be free to make the trip for months. So could we set up a transaction by proxy—namely you?" Laura's face lit up. There was nothing she loved better than being in charge.

After enjoying a spread of flatbreads, salads, and another martini for Laura, they headed to Irene's place.

Laura dedicated an entire hour to eliminating the pervert's existence from her cell phone, reciting with gleeful disdain each message she'd saved, mimicking his words, and interjecting insults. "You know what the creep can do? He can jerk off with a pair of tweezers. I'm done. Done!"

Then in the next moment, another call from the creep: "Miss you, honey, want to do tomorrow night?"

"Ugh!" Laura ended the call with a high-spirited go to hell and deleted his number. His request had pumped her up and restored her sense of superiority. With a glass of wine in hand, she danced triumphantly around the room singing some song called "Macarena," stopped to dial two former boyfriends, flirted like mad, and voila! The incredible Laura Martínez scored—a date with one of the former boyfriends in minutes. "Could have set you up with the other guy. He gives a great kiss. But Irene, know what? Since you always want to be a prig . . ." Whenever she had the chance, Laura bugged Irene about how she needed to actively pursue guys before younger chicks gobbled them all up. "You are aging rapidly, old maid."

Girlfriend never failed to bring out the worst in her. Irene stuck out her tongue and laughed, "Ha, ha, ha, shut up, or I'll show you my old maid."

"Come on then, Macarena, come on!" Laura held Irene by the hips and coaxed her into the belly dance thing. 'Dale a tu cuerpo alegría Macarena . . . alegría y cosa buena . . . Hey . . . Macarena!'"

Laura dipped low and moved with a natural rhythm that got Irene going and laughing. "Wow! Did you just make that up?"

"It's a song by Los Del Rio, new, last year, I think. First heard it in a club. Keep up with the times. Girl, keep up!"

"Okay." Irene turned on the radio and found a disco station blaring, "And now from the Digital Underground. Let's go!!"

Laura squealed, "Humpty Dance!" She grabbed Irene. "Come on!"

"Humpty Dance?? Okay, let's do it."

Three martinis, wine, and the triumph of ending the relationship had made Laura giddy as hell. Irene was not into disco, but no matter; she'd have stood on her head if it helped Laura disconnect from the jerk. Laura untied the bow of Irene's scarf, flung it away, and they danced to the beats, carried on with hips and booties for a whole hour, dancing like their bodies needed it.

Irene silently congratulated herself for having invited her over. Girlfriend was emerging unscathed from the jaws of that predator. She was going to be just fine. Flushed like she'd run a fast mile, Laura turned off the radio, got on the phone, and set up a conference call with a real estate agent in Aguadilla. Her executive function was up and running again. Irene picked up her scarf.

The agent was the brother of an attorney Laura had been engaged to for a big three months during a sojourn at her family's villa in Isabela. His office was at a reasonable distance from the property. He said it all could be handled by fax and proxy, and he would list the property *prontísimo*.

Irene called Jaime and put him on speaker. He liked the plan. "Sounds okay." Then he laughed, admonishing, "Just don't go spending my part of the money!"

Laura yelled out, "She's buying a mink coat and a Benz!"

There were no needle marks on Laura's arms or visible anywhere else on her naked body. Irene had asked her to strip, and she'd said yes, if you undress too.

Laura and Irene had been nude with each other before, starting about when they first showed pert little boobs. They measured up at least once a month, laughing and tweaking nipples, trying on new brassieres, and comparing cup sizes. So now, here they were, standing in the middle of Irene's living room, each surveying the other's body, as they had done when they were girls. Except this time, it was not a funny moment.

Irene proceeded to examine Laura, stopping short of armpits and the soles of feet.

"Satisfied?"

"Laura, I love you, just please be careful. No man is worth addiction."

She looked away and whispered, "Do not worry, Dr. Míral. I know that."

Irene produced pajamas and bunny slippers. She talked a little about David, and Laura actually listened. When Irene said she was afraid she might be falling in love, Laura jumped up from the couch and gave Irene a monstrous hug. "About time, girl, about time. Damn!"

By the time they called it a night, Laura and Irene had recovered what they'd always shared—the laughter of girlfriends.

· · ·

Perking fresh coffee was not doing it. Laura was still snoring. Irene hated to wake her, but it was Saturday—the lab was waiting. And so was David.

For sure, my cortical homunculus is grinning.

"Wake up, kid. Get up and brush your teeth."

"What is this? Boot camp?"

"Ha-ha. Good thing I forgot where I put the reveille bugle. Also, forgot to tell you, I have lab duty this morning."

"Don't worry about it. I need to get home and do some hygiene. Aaand, I'm gonna fast for two days. I need to get rid of all the poison I put into my body last week."

"Hey, you can hang out at the lab with me. How about if you volunteer for one of our control groups?"

"Are you kidding? Me? Irene, I have to tell you I don't get what you do there, not at all. It sounds like hocus-pocus bullshit to me, like you're looking for something which doesn't exist. It's a waste of time. Stop searching for ghosts. Grab that David and get married. You're free now, free of your mom, free of her ghost stories." Laura bit her lip.

The ghost comment hurt and made Irene reel like she'd been struck somewhere way inside where she lived. *Waste of time? You waste it with every man you meet! Where was Laura anyway? Nowhere but on the verge of addiction just so she could hang on to another man, one of many in a string of creeps.* Tears welled, and she gave Laura her back. She was right. Her mom's stories clung like vapor after rain.

Regret was immediate, and Laura croaked out an apology. "Forgive me, please. I'm sorry. Please don't cry, please."

"Don't worry about it, just don't."

"I am sorry. I carry my parents along with me too. I guess they're forever a part of us, for better or worse. You know I love you. *You know that.* Take care." Laura went to Irene and held out her arms for the best friend she'd ever had. "Thanks for having me over and putting up with my end-of-relationship-crazies. I'll call you as soon as I hear from the real estate agent."

Over the years, Irene often shared Alma's stories. Laura listened. Until now, she had never said a word about how she thought the thing about the girl in the light was nonsense.

El Péto

She was barely through the door when David came near and dropped a kiss on her cheek, his arm circling her waist a bit too tightly. For sure, ownership issues were surfacing, the kind of thing she had always been touchy about. Yet the nearness of him provoked an intense wave of pleasure. Probably residual horniness from her encounter with Laura; the woman had a way of stoking her hormones. Irene disengaged from David's hold and mockingly said, "No, please, not the angel's cursed kiss."

"Very, very funny, Irene."

"Sorry, just playing. Unfortunately, the dumb superstition keeps popping up in my day."

"The angel's kiss? As a matter of fact, it exists. I've seen it."

"You did what?"

"Came face to face with it a few years back, in BCN."

Irene had visited Barcelona once and explored the ancient quarter with its gothic structures, Puerta de Angel, and María del Mare. At the exit of the cathedral she almost tripped over a man hunched over on the stone steps, alms cup outstretched. A healthy blue-eyed white man could not be anything but an affluent actor auditioning for a role as a beggar. She remembered that an aspiring actor friend had divulged that the mendicant's role was standard in acting school. So, Irene gave him nothing. As she descended the stone steps, she sensed his cold blue eyes at her back.

"It's a not so well-known sculpture called *El Péto de la Morte.* A young man reclines in ecstasy, or possibly agony, as a satanic winged skeleton stands over his body and kisses him. A nineteenth-century Gothic style piece by a Catalán."

A cold chill crept up Irene's arms. "Are you kidding? The kiss of death?"

David assumed a macabre stance and mummy-walked toward her. "And now, I shall bestow the kiss."

She scooted over to the computer consoles. "Stop. I've been trying to brush it off, but it's not much of a joke. Remember the thing about my nephew Robert? Well, when I visited him at the hospital, I foolishly examined his lips for traces of the kiss my patient thought she'd seen back at the funeral. And that apparition of his, if that's what it was, now I'm thinking it could have been a warning." Irene didn't mention how, just yesterday, she'd searched for the damn sign of doom on her friend's lips.

"Sometimes myths and superstitions are based on human psychological need. The legend of an angel of darkness, or light, bestowing a kiss on a mortal appears throughout the Christian world. Different permutations show up in art and literature all the time. Some regard the kiss as evil, others as a blessing, a harbinger—an omen."

"An omen? That sounds a lot like what my patient said. An omen or a blessing."

"Stories of angels, good and bad, likely evolved from early Christian beliefs, the miracle of The Annunciation, and Milton's Paradise Lost. 'Blessed Michael, archangel . . . / be our safeguard against the wickedness and snares of the devil . . .'"

"You memorized Milton??"

"Yup. 'Millions of spiritual creatures walk the earth unseen both when we wake, and when we sleep. . .'"

"Are you kidding me? Do you truly believe in such beings? And why are all the Archangels men?"

"Actually, they're androgynous, but there are female manifestations, Archai like Lady Hope, clothed in light and energy, Gabriel's grand mirror."

The pupils of Irene's gray eyes deepened like darkness in a melancholy sea; her thoughts returning to her mother's description of the young woman in white light. "I ah . . . I should have asked my mom more questions. A lady of hope clothed in light and energy; it sounds so beautiful . . . David, could my mom have seen an angelus? Was my mom's Adriana . . . an angelus?" Irene was about to cry, and she shuddered as though the air around her were cold. He moved to put his arms around her.

David held her close until she stopped shaking. "Irene, you *are* asking the questions. You're asking the questions *here*, in this lab. And you're also trying to work out those questions with everything you do at the clinic, just as I'm here trying to work out questions about my sister's illness."

"I don't know what to think anymore. I've never been a spiritual person. Maybe it's time."

"Well, don't know if I am either. Anyway, I want you to know that the Milton was my mother's doing. Her lit thing and all. Lines like 'The mind is its own place' were bandied around the house like Ben Franklin's aphorisms. Seriously though, there's a good reason Milton's verses have perdured. The universe of human thought is profound, replete with paradoxical constructs, legends, rituals, and belief systems so powerful that anything is possible. At times, we may find ourselves straddling the worlds of reality and imagination, science and religion."

They stared at each other as if they'd just come upon something terribly meaningful.

Not one of the twelve subjects failed to show up. Unusual, really something of a phenomenon, as attrition in volunteer groups was not uncommon. But nothing was happening. Their experimental model was producing only continuous monotony. The excitement of the initial findings had faded. So perhaps there was nothing especially remarkable about the receptors identified in the two women, or perhaps the individuals trying to transmit the messages lacked sufficient psychic energy.

Irene and David worked through weeks of tedium, patiently monitoring the screens, scrutinizing the data for the slightest sign of significant activity, each looking over the other's shoulder, bodies close, breaths mingling, thoughts in tandem. And in the passing of the hours, days and weeks, the intensity of their focus fostered intimacy.

In the evenings of the days she was away from the lab, when the phone rang at about eight, Irene knew it was him, asking her for thoughts on one idea or another.

Besides David, Irene could count the men she had slept with on three fingers of one hand, and those encounters had not progressed past the physical because she just wouldn't let the men get too close. Right now, she was trying to work out her true feelings about David. Her yearning for him was more than physical, yet she was having a hard time accessing the pith of her emotions. It was eerie how much alike they were. She also knew her mother's passing had thrust her unto unknown territory. She was needy. Not a good place to embark on a serious relationship.

Advocacy

THE UNIT WAS FUNCTIONING well. The healing process was happening. Jackson and Patricia Reid's presentation succeeded in moving the women to more of a social milieu. It was like being in school. The women had an opportunity to ask questions and express opinions about the facts available to them. And they got to see an intelligent black man and an assertive, confident female working together. Jackson and Reid demonstrated how a man and woman could collaborate, work, and relate respectfully. They were obviously friends. Irene hoped it would make an impact on Ana. Maybe she could begin to consider Jackson in a different light.

Irene sat towards the back observing the dynamics, reverted to drawing a sociogram, and was taken aback when Ana politely asked Jackson. "Mr. Jackson, do men suffer from flashbacks, too?"

"Ana, anyone who has PTSD may experience flashbacks." Ana said thank you, Mr. Jackson, and wrote something down. Carolina looked like she was taking notes as well but was likely just sketching. Amanda and Melissa were involved in a lively discussion with Patricia Reid. Irene silently congratulated herself: *Yes, this went well.*

Jackson and Patricia agreed to do another workshop, and Irene got busy putting together new material for their next show.

There was a message from Maríanis, "I'm sorry, I cannot make this week's session." Irene worried but did not call to ask her about it. Perhaps the weaning had commenced.

Maríanis had been busy. She'd spoken to the social worker, called Lawrence Chase to inform him of recent developments, and she continued to write in her journal:

> *The fiend continued to taunt me. Taunt me? He wanted to intimidate me so I would back off the visits. Did he think I was so terrified that I would skulk away? No. Irene helped me replace the images of horror with images of strength. She had me visualize my Order of Protection as a lance and shield. Instead of the nightmare of a journey through the jungle, I saw myself winning a court case and reuniting with my children. Yes! And Lawrence Chase is still helping me. Without him, I would have never dared to investigate and rush to find my kids that time, a time I cannot forget. I flew to South America to retrieve my babies, but my ex-husband moved them to another location and hid them. So, in desperation, I called Chase. Within days I acquired the information I needed; the children were at my sister-in-law's home. I hired a driver and showed up armed with self-righteousness and the court order. The children ran to me as soon as they saw me. Our car was waiting. I sat in the back crying and hugging my kids hard. Within minutes, a black van was in pursuit. My driver swerved into a minor road, dense with tropical growth, but the van overtook us, two men and my ex-husband. He dragged me out of the car and pushed me to the ground. A vicious kick in the meat*

of my thigh crumpled me. All I saw as I tried to get up was his back. He was walking toward the vehicle that had followed us, tight grip on the children's arms. They whimpered and stumbled. Tina looked back and tried to pull away before he urged them into the waiting black van. Rage gave me strength, and I ran after the car, ran and ran like a madwoman going nowhere. My nightmare. But no more. Lawrence Chase advised that I should access the court once more and file another petition asking for full custody. This time I am going to win!

In a second call, Maríanis reported she'd completed two meetings with Alva Turner and that she was ready to again petition the court for custody of her children.

Her ex had tried to pull a fast one. He phoned the social worker to say the children would not be available for the following two weeks, maybe a month, as they would be out of town visiting their cousins. Mrs. Turner promptly instructed him to produce the children as scheduled or lose custody. He showed up furious and side-swept Maríanis' car, yelling bitch out his car window. A security camera recorded the whole thing. His unforgiving rage had provided her with the ammunition she needed.

Maríanis appeared for her therapy session the following week. She was gleaming with hope, sitting erect instead of bent over in pain. Irene warned it could be a long, drawn-out process that would test her strength. She should not hesitate to utilize the restraining order if necessary. Alva Turner had advised the same. "Irene, I marched to the police precinct to make a complaint and filed a Violation of the Order of Protection with the court."

"Awesome, Maríanis. Now, you are advocating for yourself. The strong woman in you is back."

Breaking Bread

WHEN IRENE WALKED INTO the fancy French restaurant on East 71st Street, she did so with a sense of satisfaction; her professional life was going well. The Maître d' escorted her to the second-floor salon and to one of four tables dressed in fine linen and set for two. It was an intimate space, upscale Country French, and a dense velvety carpet the color of absinthe. Walter Freile, intent over the wine list, stood at once when he saw her approach. She fully expected a professional, cordial exchange over a nice lunch.

She had already turned down the invite to the conference in New Mexico, so she guessed he might press her about the Central American case and Felicia. Sessions with Felicia continued to be worrisome. She'd already shared her concerns and would do so again today if he brought up the case. Maybe if she were charming enough, he would reconsider using hypnosis as an alternative treatment before going ahead and discharging Felicia, and she could always banter about the progress of the other patients and the success of the workshops. Irene dared to think he was rewarding her, acknowledging she was doing good work. Still, she had the feeling she should remain cautious.

He did seem different; a laxness of demeanor was evident. Maybe the man just needed to shed his rigid shell for a while. He ordered a bottle of Pinot Blanc. "It's a fine wine from Alsace. Have you ever been to France?"

"Yes, but never visited Alsace, just Paris and Provence, followed the guidebooks." Irene relaxed; work-related stuff looked to be off the table.

"My mother's family hails from Alsace. It's known worldwide for industrial production and pitifully underrated as a wine-growing region."

The waiter poured two glasses of wine and stepped aside as they considered the menu. Under the small table, their knees practically touched. Irene positioned her body a bit to the side of the chair to avoid contact. She examined the menu and found a salad similar to one she'd enjoyed in Cannes. "Laitue Frisée Aux Lardons, please. Let's see . . . for the entrée, Truite Amandine." Irene smiled and sipped the wine.

"I'll have Les Endives aux Vinaigrette and Scallops in Lemon and Ginger Sauce. Make that a subtle ginger sauce. Thank you." His voice had resumed its usual perfunctory tone.

"This is a lovely place." She glanced around; only one other table was occupied. As she returned to conversation, she was taken aback by how blatantly Walter Freile was staring. Maybe he was going to demonstrate one of his hypnosis techniques. She was about to make an amusing remark about it when his next question deterred her.

"You're an attractive woman, Irene. How is it you are not married?"

"I, ah . . . I suppose I've been concentrating on my career."

"No boyfriend? I find that hard to believe." His voice, throaty and thick, made Irene quite nervous.

Irene reached for the small basket of bread and selected a still warm, puffy little pain. She added an orange-poppy muffin to the bread plate, concentrated on cutting the little muffin in half, and began to nibble. The flecks of orange peel refreshed her palate. She wanted to change the subject or at least gain a moment to regroup. What was this all about? Too personal—unexpected. His bread plate remained empty. This was not about breaking bread. Yet she supposed he deserved a response. "No boyfriend. Just my work. It's intense but rewarding. Just last week . . ." She would talk about the workshop, redirect the conversation, but his hand was on her knee, his fingers stroking the left side of her calf. "Please." Her face was crimson. The table shook as he abruptly withdrew his hand.

The waiter set down their lunch. They ate in silence. Freile downed several large gulps of wine.

"Irene, I do have a serious matter to discuss with you. Human Resources received several complaints about you, alleging negligence and misconduct. I have ignored the matter, in deference to well . . ." He drank the rest of his wine.

Is he kidding? "Who, when, what about?" She felt the food might come up on her. "Who??"

"I am afraid I cannot say. It all landed on my lap, but it's been left to my discretion regarding how to proceed." He again stared very intently. "I've chosen to speak to you about it privately."

Well, he should come out with the whole thing. Why the hell was he holding back? Was she supposed to feel grateful? Was she supposed to thank him with sex? Foreboding crept up. "Dr. Freile, this is highly upsetting. I need to know, deserve to know more about the allegations so I can respond accordingly. Who made the complaints? About what? I have a right to know." She did not want to plead and hoped her tone had not betrayed her.

"Irene . . . Dr. Míral, do not be alarmed. You do not need to know. I will handle it. Go ahead and finish the trout before it is ruined."

Although artistically deboned, delicately flavored, and delectable, the trout remained half-eaten, languishing in its almond sauce, forlorn and forgotten.

The humiliation was subtle but real enough. Irene turned down dessert, folded the linen napkin neatly into a square, and placed it beside the dinner plate. Countering an instinctive inclination to assert her bruised integrity, she thanked him for a lovely lunch.

"Take care, Irene. It was nice having you." Walter Freile picked up the napkin from his lap and haphazardly tossed it on the table as he stood up to bid his unhappy guest goodbye.

Hubris

Harboring fantasies was not his style. So then and there, he let go of an image of him and Irene cuddling in front of the grand fireplace in his family's country home in Alsace. Instead, he concentrated on recalling a honeymoon, twenty-five years before, when he'd made love to his wife by the same fireplace. But the only images he could conjure up were those of the tiresome charity events which now consumed his wife's devotion.

The call from the director of Human Resources had surprised the socks off him. Two anonymous letters alleging Dr. Irene Míral was not fit to practice had landed on his desk. Not unusual for medical staff to be harassed by disgruntled individuals who had little ground for a malpractice suit but still insisted on pursuing a grudge in any petty manner that occurred to their warped sense of justice. He was sure the complaints were of no consequence. Besides, there was no way to follow up, no return address. He could not identify their origin, except by the postmarks, which were much too faint. Only one was somewhat legible. He could have shared that with her. But he didn't. He'd chosen to concentrate on the alarm in her voice, simply because it placated his masculine pride.

He guessed the letters were the work of a prankster. Teletype text, pasted on stock paper, probably one of her crazies or one of their relatives. A professional rival who possessed solid evidence would have been specific, more formal. There was one detail that did bother him:

- conducting - unorthodox - subversive- studies -

A preposterous allegation! While he sometimes viewed her as too resistant to direction, subversive was a harsh term. He recalled that her file contained a monogram she submitted in 1992 to *Paranormal Psychology, Yesterday and Today*. Irene could do a lot worse than allow herself the shelter of his protection. Yes, because he could easily send her to hell.

Impulsively, he poked his fork into Irene's plate, stabbed a chunk of trout, and swallowed it.

Why?

If her mother were alive, she would go to her and cry. Just when her sense of accomplishment had increased tenfold, THIS! Was he lying about the complaints, trying to get into her pants? Worse, could the complaints be real? Walter Freile's advances vilely opportunistic? Why did he refuse to discuss it any further? Was he going to hold it over her head to discourage her from challenging his recommendations? Beautiful, just beautiful. He planned to exploit the situation to get his way. If he could not, he might move to disband the unit; something she felt he'd always wanted to do. He could ruin her career. She never should have agreed to have lunch with him.

She recalled her mom's warning: Men are evil.

A call from Laura stopped her from succumbing to increasingly hysterical conjectures. "Irene, why don't you come over? I have news from the realtor—two offers. He faxed over some contracts . . . Irene, eh, I could use some company."

The address on Columbus Avenue was to be envied, a block away from the Museum of Natural History and the Hayden Planetarium, places Irene loved. She briefly wondered if David might enjoy a Sunday afternoon with her at The Hayden. The sweet thought promptly vanished, replaced by thoughts of Freile, his harassment and allegations.

Laura had contracted an interior designer, and although tastefully done, Irene did not like the minimalist décor of her high-rise apartment. Laura, ever-fashionable, had to be ahead of the cusp of things. Irene was a traditionalist with a quirky, bohemian streak.

She pressed the lobby buzzer—nothing. Again. Nothing. She called up to the eleventh floor. "Laura, I'm downstairs. Let me in."

The woman who opened the door looked like a dehydrated version of herself. "Jeez, girl, you look like you lost ten pounds. Are you all right?"

With a shrug, Laura turned away from her friend. "I'm fine, working out a lot."

Was she? She looked like hell and as pale as a waning moon. "Well, you sure aren't doing it outdoors. You look sickly."

"Thanks a lot." Laura plopped down on a white leather couch and let out a sigh of exhaustion before lighting a cigarette. "Irene, I ah . . ."

"What is the matter with you?"

"Nothing. I'm just tired."

"Well, I'm tired, too. You have no idea what I just went through. My boss is harassing me. Do you believe it? Me, harassing me!" Irene paced; Laura listened. Irene, always wise, sensible, and steady, was having a fit.

"He is a bastard, a real bastard." Irene asked for wine, gulped it down like water, and ranting about the scene at the restaurant, paced the length of the living room like an angry lioness. She was furious.

"At least he likes you. Sounds like he's trying to protect you, and that French restaurant sounds terrific. I may check it out."

"Laura! You don't get it, do you? The threat was there. I have information that could damage your career so let me put my hand up your skirt."

"Why didn't you? Why didn't you let him? Do you think you're any different from everyone else? It happens all the time. Men are men. If your career is important, do what you need to do. Forget your damn pride. There is no pride, no fucking honor." She got up, walked over to an elegant white lacquer desk, picked up a folder, and handed it to Irene. "The contracts." Laura lit another cigarette. "It's business, it's *all* business. You could follow up with Human Resources, but my guess is it will all blow up in your face. Play along with the doctor . . . that's what I would do, that's what I always do." The bitterness in Laura's voice grated more than the callousness of her remarks.

"No. No, I cannot."

"You can't? Really? You and your precious ideals," she sneered. "Why do you always have to be so good, Irene, huh? No one is perfect . . . No one." Her voice quaked, and her whole frame shook like she was out in the cold without a coat, the cigarette trembling in her hand. She started to cry.

Irene grabbed her by the shoulders and shook her hard. "You started with him again, didn't you? You've been using that crap again."

The sobs came hard. "I can't say no."

"Oh, yes you can! I'm taking you to rehab right now. Get dressed."

Laura, shocked, let out a yell, "Who are you?! You are not my fucking mother, Irene. And right now, I don't think you're even my friend." She ran to the door. "Get the hell . . ."

"Stop! Just stop!" The walls of the spacious room seemed to move in on Irene. Soon, there would be no space to breathe. In a matter of hours, her world had begun to crumble.

Laura sat back on the couch, crying, looking old and worn. Irene went into the guest bath, stared at her face in the mirror, and silently chastised herself. *Monster, you're a selfish monster. Laura needs you.*

You detected an undercurrent of fear in her voice when she called but all you can think of are your petty career problems. Irene leaned into her reflection to examine her lips more closely, fully expecting to find the angel's kiss—the curse.

Laura was still on the couch where she left her, slumped into her bony self.

"Look, it's okay. I'm sorry. I overreacted. I just can't stand the thought of you getting hurt. You know I love you." Irene sat next to Laura and held both her hands. "Listen to me. I know a therapist you can talk to, talented, very discreet. And you'll need a physical. He will recommend that first. Please. Do it. You can call for an appointment right now."

Looking away, and with a limp hand, she gave Irene the phone.

Irene made the call immediately; if it went to voice mail, she'd scream. It didn't. "He can see you Monday evening. If you want, I can go with you." She said this, knowing Laura had to mobilize sufficient motivation to get there without a crutch to lean on. Laura, always with an independent, spunky attitude Irene had admired since they were kids, sat on the white leather couch looking too weak to get anywhere on her own. It frightened Irene beyond the point of anxiety. Fear raised the skin on her arms and descended to her stomach. She would stay with Laura all weekend if necessary.

Laura was now sort of gently rocking from side to side. "I . . . I'll call my internist." Her fingers quivered as she dialed. "Can you see me tomorrow morning? I need a physical right away." Then, sitting more upright on the couch, she said, "There, it's done. Okay?"

Irene saw how badly Laura wanted to have her believe she was in control of herself.

For a long moment, they looked into each other's eyes, wanting to change the channel, wanting to exit the crummy reality show they found themselves in.

After a while, Irene asked, "How about if we get some dinner?"

"Okay. Yeah."

"All right! Let's order in. I'm ravenous. That lunch did-not-satisfy-me-at-all."

"Neither would he—probably has problems getting an erection and thinks you can fix him."

"Laura, stop." Irene laughed for the first time in many hours.

The Light of Redemption

ON THE WAY TO the lab, Irene decided she would talk to David about the thing with Freile. Laura's take on the whole thing had shocked her. Her BFF had lashed out from an insecure place, frightened out of her wits, not in any shape to be helpful. What Irene needed was a sane head to bounce off and some practical advice. It would have to wait until the end of the day. David had not been in the lab since Thursday night. For nearly thirty-six hours, the computers had spit out a hefty spiral of printed material.

Jason Stivik, a brilliant programmer who free-lanced out from IBM, was David's go-to IT man. He had written the elegant little algorithm responsible for the mess on the floor. She sighed. Sorting out the data spill and weaning out any significance would take up most of the morning.

David was brilliant too, and patient—eager to accept any tiny bit of communication, a syllable, a phoneme, any signal something was getting through.

Persistent drowsiness distracted her focus. Then at about two in the afternoon, the breakthrough they had been hoping for: A transmission!

David had been randomly rotating six subjects in soundproof rooms on separate floors. On the fourth floor, three people sat with insulated headphones in front of computer screens. They were to input anything they perceived to be communication, a word, a phrase—a thought. Two floors below, three others were instructed to concentrate on the messages flashing on their screens. The items were parsed to form unique phrases for each session. At 2:07, on the fourth floor, two volunteers, fingers flying over their keyboards, recorded parts of a message: Dare not look into the blinding light of redemption.

It was impossible for the subjects on the fourth floor to have guessed any of the words. But it happened; words had come through, first in bits, seemingly disparate syllables, and then, the phrase: light of redemption. David always developed distinctly different strings of sentences for each session, and the computer did the rest, so there could not have been any prior learning. Finally! At least one human transmitter, maybe three—and two human receivers.

The door to the lab flung open, and David barged in like a maniac. "We need to take a closer look at some of the histories." Irene had sealed the hard copy results of her screenings to protect the participants' privacy. On her computer, she keyed in the code which retrieved the numbers of the files. David was standing over her shoulder, practically babbling. "It's happened, but we need to be as certain as possible about the subjects before continuing. I aim to prove the validity of the activity here today. Irene, it's within our reach now."

"We'd have to duplicate the study at least once. David, how about reliability issues? It might be months before we can expand our sample. Six subjects are not sufficient." Irene was excited also but knew it was essential to address the limitations of their research. She needed to be as skeptical about their results as Freile was about her approach and modes of treatment.

The feeling they should slow down irked the back of her mind.

The truth was she wanted to shield David. He could easily be dismissed as a dilettante, at best categorized with J.B. Rhine, the modern pioneer of parapsychology, who rallied many skeptics, only to bear a barrage of criticism about his questionable scientific methodology. David would want to submit a seminal article to the *Journal of Parapsychology*, and her name would appear along with his. Her feelings for him had grown a whole lot, and the possibility her professional credibility could be at stake the moment their research became public was not important now. Yet . . . "David, are you at all concerned about ethical considerations?"

He looked a little hurt. "Didn't all the subjects sign waivers? You ruled out pathologies, and they're all adults, aren't they?"

"Ah, yes, we did rule out pathology." She hoped they were not overreaching, grasping at straws. She was at the files for a long while, carefully searching for discrepancies, hoping not to find any. "Here's something that may be significant. Subject 361A said he was an empath."

"Inconsequential. He's one of our receivers. Empaths are sensitive to feelings, not to messages on a computer screen. What are you thinking?"

Empaths had a gift, to perceive and receive emotion. Could isolation in a soundproof room expand an empath's field of perception, thereby enabling instances of telepathy? She did not want to counter, but the presence of another variable, the possibility of it, did exist. Irene frowned.

"What if the other receiver is an empath also?"

He raised an eyebrow and shrugged.

"Look, we don't have an instrument to measure it, or do we?"

"Well, the capacity to be an empath has been studied quite a bit, surveys, that kind of thing." She bounced up from her workstation and delved into the hard copy files, silently congratulating herself for the acumen of her notations. She looked up. "Safe, no one else identifies as such. Anyway, I suppose it could complicate things to try to make such determinations at this point, with surveys yet." She wanted to let go of the concern.

"Irene, if those two continue to receive, even after I scramble communications further, then we are definitely on to something. Whew!" He breathed out, then smiled. "You wouldn't want to celebrate our new success? Dinner at my place?"

"No, David; I don't think so." But even as she uttered the words, she regretted it. And it wasn't just the regret of passing up on terrific sex and the intimacy inherent in the sharing of mind and skin. She'd wanted to talk to David about her encounter with Freile. But why deflate today's success balloon? It could wait. Laura would call her stupid right about now.

⎯⎯◆⎯⎯

A glass of Merlot soothed her heart and helped her reflect on the day's events. Well, at least the research was yielding results that merited further inquiry.

Also—The contracts.

Right. Irene opened the folder, perused the real estate jargon, and called her brother. "Jaime, hi. Good news, two offers, and both are ready to go to contract."

He wanted to know if either was cash, as financing could go sour and often took more than a month to process.

"Cash? Sure. That's not going to happen. I would go with the one putting down the largest down payment. "What do you think?" Jaime told her to go for it.

Perfect. She called Laura. The phone rang repeatedly. *Oh, oh.* Nothing, not even voice mail. She dialed three times. Finally, Laura's groggy voice.

"Hello. Who is this? Irene?"

"It's me. How did it go this morning?"

"Don't worry, I showed up. My internist looked up every orifice and took blood and urine. The lab will send the results to your friend, the shrink. I doubt he'll get them in time for my appointment."

One of the little rain clouds storming around Irene's head quietly dispersed. "Great, I'm coming over."

"What?? Irene, I'm tired."

"Yes, I know, but I want to bring you the signed contracts so you can fax them to your guy. Jaime is anxious to move ahead with it and so am I." What a crock! She could have faxed them herself. The realtor's info was right on the face sheet.

"Oh, okay. Hurry up."

Irene grabbed an overnight bag and stuffed sufficient garments to get her through the rest of the weekend and dressed for work on Monday. Laura was following through. The least she could do was provide emotional support until her friend's first appointment with the therapist. The least she could do was admit she also needed some support.

Monday Morning

On Monday morning, all she hoped for was not to bump into Walter Freile. Glad to have a few more days to think about what she would say regarding his manner and the mysterious complaints, time to think through whether she should go over his head and speak to Human Resources directly. She wholeheartedly wished she had a personal contact in HR with whom she could discreetly confirm receipt of the complaint. Without someone who could be on the hush and hush about her inquiry, there was a risk of opening an ugly can of worms.

What if he'd made the whole thing up? What if he called her a liar? What if he accused her of provocative behavior? After all, she'd agreed to an intimate tête à tête. If she filed a harassment complaint, heads might roll, including her own. The PTSD unit was much too important. A scandal would surely bring it down. Risking the demise of the unit was just not worth it. Knowing she too could be fallible; she had dispassionately dissected every single scenario that may have resulted in a complaint. But no. Not that her ego couldn't sustain a blow, but she genuinely did not think there was any basis for allegations of negligence and misconduct.

By the time Marίanis showed up for her appointment in the afternoon, Irene had managed to shove the problem to a temporary folder in the back of her mind.

Maríanis was doing great. Her ex-husband had stopped the harassment. "I think he's the scared one now. The police were ready to handcuff him because of the violation. And you know, I think the kids want to be with me. They're getting more and more affectionate, closer. How is Felicia?"

Irene wished the police would handcuff Walter Freile. "Why do you ask about Felicia?"

"We talk on the phone a lot. Sometimes she sounds sad, but then it seems to go away when we get to talking about the future. We might get an apartment together and help each other out. We've been talking about going back to school."

"Really? Sounds like a plan. Felicia needs a little more time before she's discharged to outpatient follow-up." Irene was pleased to hear Maríanis say she had plans that did not exclusively revolve around her children. A woman's life should not be just about being a mother. "It's good you're thinking ahead, wanting to do something for *you*."

She doubted the court would grant her patient full custody any time soon. If it all developed into another court battle, Irene would not hesitate to testify on her behalf once more. In such cases, judges usually ordered home studies, and the process could go on for months. But the court could not ignore that, this time, Maríanis Román was petitioning from a position of strength. She had the support of the social worker's reports, and her tenacious attorney was still working the case pro bono. Even so, Maríanis would need all the hope for the future that she could muster.

Irene was in her second week of EMDR with Felicia and started Marta with it as well. Carolina was writing a lot and offering her journal to Irene during sessions, but still not talking. Melissa would be the person to have heard her say anything; they spent a lot of time together in the glasshouse.

Amanda. Well, Amanda was just too funny, Irene's instructor on girl gangs, blades, and sharp nail files. She laughed about her violent drawings and asked Irene if she thought they'd be suitable for a comic book series. EMDR was working. Amanda stopped seeing blood dripping on the walls of her dreams.

On Wednesday, Irene planned to let Walter Freile know how well things were going.

Just A Moment

As soon as Irene walked into the early morning Wednesday conference with the night crew, she felt the tension, retentive as an unreleased bowstring. Had something happened overnight? Immediately, Ana Amado came to mind and she groaned inwardly. She managed a smile, said good morning, and began to distribute the new material she hoped would motivate at least two others, besides Jackson and Reid, to volunteer for the next presentation. "Is everything all right?" She had to ask. The room was unusually quiet.

Only Jackson and Reid began to look through the material. Two pushed the stapled booklets away. No one was saying a thing. Irene placed a hand on a hip and asked, "Okay, what is it?"

Sylvia, the oldest member of her crew, a black woman of about forty-five, straightened the collar of her uniform, and stated, "Dr. Míral, with all due respect, we feel you've been using Jackson too much. You're always calling on him, and we don't think it's right."

Irene's eyebrows shot up. *Wow!* "Oh, are you speaking for the group? With all due respect to you, Sylvia, I would like to hear from everyone on this. I . . . It's important."

Ernesto got to the point, "Well, for example, take the Amado case. You put a lot of pressure on Jackson to help you with it, and you're putting pressure on us to do these presentations."

Irene breathed in, pausing before defensiveness set in. Ernesto's comment reverberated like electricity in the air. "All right, we need to work this out right now." She avoided looking at Jackson. Was this coming from him? He had always impressed her as someone with sufficient integrity to speak up for himself.

Surprised by the sentiment of those who had spoken up, and although she wanted to once again express her regard for their work, she proceeded to probe the discontent.

Jackson tried to come to her defense. Irene stopped him and stood her ground as one more disgruntled person spoke up, Liz Smith. "I agree with Sylvia."

"Anyone else have thoughts about this?" The room was quiet now. So, three out of six—possibly displaced professional insecurity on their part. Jackson was a lot to compete with. No one else said a thing. She needed to hear from Gregory Jackson. "Okay, Jackson, what do you have to say? Don't hold back. I can take it. Be honest." Irene tried to keep the edginess she was feeling from coloring her voice.

"No, I don't feel used or pressured. Dr. Míral, you gave me the option of bailing out of the Amado case, and I'm glad I chose to stay with it. Man, I was surprised when Ana spoke to me at the workshop, sane as all get out, *and* smiling. But hey, y'all, thanks for the concern. Want to say all this is a valuable learning experience for me, and I do have an excellent working relationship with Dr. Míral. Pat and I volunteered to do the workshop because we wanted to." He stopped to look around at his coworkers. "We want to do another, and please join in. The more, the merrier. No sweat."

Sylvia rolled her eyes, leaned toward Liz Smith's ear, whispering, "He's still brown-nosing-his-way-up."

Irene waited for more comments. No one said anything else.

"Team, let's get your log reports."

She took some moments to review their annotations, nodding approval as she read. "Thorough as always." Their observations of the past week proved to be further indication that the women were improving. There were no complaints about Ana. "I think we're making excellent progress, and not only with Amado. Some of the women are scheduled for discharge. First, Melissa. Any thoughts?" All agreed she was ready.

Irene ended by thanking them for the feedback and for feeling free to bring up their concerns. "I apologize if I made any team member feel uncomfortable or pressured. I am grateful for your hard work and your willingness to exchange opinions. If ever you need to speak to me privately, I'm always available." Ernesto stayed behind with Pat and Jackson. They huddled over the new material. "Guys, if you want to work on another presentation, please understand it is entirely up to you."

She left them to themselves. Irene felt hurt and disappointed. She was proud of her staff, but maybe she'd taken their cooperation for granted, assumed too much. She wanted to give Jackson a big thank you. It would have to wait. Last thing to do was play favorites in front of the group. She braced to face Freile.

Review proceeded uneventfully until she requested additional information about the complaints. Back at that meeting with the crew, she'd wondered if the complaints had come from one of them. No. They were straight-up people who would not resort to complaining behind her back. *Gregory Jackson would have mentioned something. Oh boy! If I can't trust someone like Jackson, then what?* She remembered what Amanda had said, *not everyone is your friend.*

Freile was deliberately avoiding eye contact, seemingly intent on investigating the file. *Well, he'll have to look at me now.* Irene leaned forward, inched to the edge of the chair, and stated. "I've been giving a lot of thought to what you said regarding those complaints. I need to know what I'm up against and I'm considering going to Human Resources."

He raised his gaze and very carefully removed his eyeglasses. "Irene, let's forget the whole thing. Human Resources is not overly concerned about it, and neither am I."

"Just a moment, Dr. Freile, if you do not believe it's of any concern, why did you bring it up? I want to have confidence in your judgment. But you need to understand how upsetting and potentially damaging it all can be to me, to my career."

He reiterated, "Let's forget it, shall we? It happens all the time, the reason we have malpractice insurance. Complaints about staff come in daily. Nurses, doctors, receptionists, and even custodial help can be targets of unsubstantiated booing and calumny. Let's not delve into minutiae."

Was he implying she also forget about his unwanted advances? Surely, he understood she could file a complaint, accuse him of sexual harassment. But part of her wished the whole thing to go away. She wanted the PTSD unit to move forward, be successful, and be judged on its merits, not petty gossip. She hoped that mentioning Human Resources would make it clear that she was not going to play. She looked down at her lap, not wanting to let the issue go, but nevertheless, not insisting.

Walter Freile resumed the case review, his remonstrative tone a notch softer, until he pressed regarding discharging patients. "Several cases, including Felicia's, should be on track for outpatient. Let's discuss discharge dates. Now."

Irene tapped her index fingers together. Was this the way it was going to go? *Well, I am not going to buckle.* "I think we should hold off for a few weeks, but we can discuss a timeline."

He practically spit out, "Fine!"

Irene ignored his tone. "About Felicia, I am still concerned about suicidal ideation. Although she says the nightmare of falling into a dark pit is gone, she is now reporting it as a flashback."

"Follow her up in the outpatient clinic. She is to be discharged, continued on antidepressants."

Irene counted silently to three. She would continue with the case until she was sure Felicia was out of the danger zone. Discharge plans would have to wait.

⋯❖⋯

Wednesday night, Laura called; she'd kept her appointment with the therapist. "I'll see him for just a month, beecaause . . . I'm going to P.R. and staying there for a while. Be happy. By then, the bank will have approved the buyer, and we can close the deal for you."

Just one session with the therapist and Laura seemed as self-assured as ever. A stay on the island would do her good. It might be just what she needed, miles of distance from the stupid jerk.

PART THREE

When the doors of perception are cleansed, men will see things as they really are, infinite.

—William Blake

Washington Square

THANKFULLY—THURSDAY EVENING. MOST OF a tough week was behind her. The cases were going well, but everything else wasn't. Well, not everything. There was David and the lab. Tonight, Irene was looking forward to being in the same space with him for a few hours. She boarded the IND to Washington Square. Upon exiting the station, she pulled out a collapsible umbrella from her tote bag. It was raining quite hard now, and the small umbrella shook feebly. Wet hose clung to the skin of her ankles. In another few minutes, she would be soaked. She hurried into the building.

David was nowhere in sight, likely had gone out to the deli for a bite. She wasn't hungry; she was cold. She plugged in the electric teapot and opted for a fusion of Peppermint and Echinacea. David kept the small kitchen area stocked with healthy snacks and tea, no coffee; he preferred his freshly brewed from around the corner. The security guard called in: "All the subjects have reported and should be at their respective stations."

"Where is David?" She walked out to the elevator and bumped right into him. He grabbed her by the waist and kissed her full on the mouth while balancing his cappuccino.

"David!"

She half-pulled away.

"Sorry. I didn't bring you any coffee, but I know you prefer tea when you're here." He smiled big and bright and kissed her once more.

"All the subjects are in. You need to start them." He hurried.

That first kiss was a surprise, the second a shock of pleasure. Irene's entire being wanted to meld into him. But she didn't, just didn't. Did she really mean to keep David at a distance like all the rest? She knew that this time it was different. They were quite close already. Although, he still did not know about her mother and the domestic violence, only about the young woman in the light.

Lately, she'd been deliberating contacting Alfredo Bryson again. This time it was not about a case. This time it was about her. She thought she might benefit from some therapy and hoped he could recommend someone she could trust. Her confidence had taken a beating. New insecurities hovered. Walter Freile's advances, and the intangibles of the complaints had shaken her, the mood of her relationship with the night crew staff had shifted unexpectedly—then there was David. Moonlit tides of emotions rose and ebbed. Some days, she felt as free as a bird poised to take flight into the brilliant blue of sky. But she had never been in love, so how would she really recognize it? Doubt was not comfortable. And the question of her need, the impetus to fill the empty space left by her mom.

Sometimes, in the early morning hours, she awoke from a disturbing dream, a dream much like Robert's experience on the road: She was driving in heavy rain, a branch laden with large leaves fell in front of her car, keeping her from getting through. Dreams provide insight into a person's psychological state. She was stuck. The road ahead was not clear.

She knew better but could not halt the ego mechanisms called defense, rationalizing her motivations at every turn. Yes, she could continue to delude herself by keeping her relationship with David in a comfortable compartment labeled safe and casual sex with a good friend. He was a responsive and sensual man who made beautiful love to her body. Maybe it was all she needed. Lie. So why persist in holding back? In all her bougie wisdom, Laura had always said she'd been avoiding genuine intimacy. Irene supposed it was true. Way back when, she'd made an unconscious vow to keep her heart safe from men. Hell, David's attentiveness could merely be a function of his interest in assuring she remain vested in the study—all silly fodder for a date night with Laura. No. Girl talk was not the answer.

She'd have to seek answers elsewhere. She drafted an email:

Hi Fred,

Lots of stuff going on right now,

and it all has catapulted me into Doubtlandia,

a place where I don't want to be. So, I've decided

I could benefit from a few sessions with a therapist.

Who would you recommend?

Thanks much,

Irene

She was about to click send when two screens began to light up with erratic wave patterns. She saved the message in the draft folder. "Wow," she said aloud, "there's a lot of activity going on, must be something in the night's raindrops." She was about to dial down to David and ask what the heck was up when wild spurts of data practically jumped off the screens. Amazing. Irene stood in front of the consoles like a soldier ready to do battle. She responded to the explosion of data as quickly as she could, capturing the sequence of the most active screen, thinking it would be great if Jason could write a string that would automate the process when, out of nowhere, a deep tremor echoed within the walls. Everything became eerie, translucent, and silent.

She felt as if suspended in a slow-motion movie clip, the next frame frozen, her fingers poised above the keyboard, waiting. For seconds, an air of calm reverence like that of a cathedral empty of souls settled in the heart of the room. She was about to head to the elevator when a tremendous burst of white light descended from the ceiling, inundating all corners of the space, glowing brilliant, completely blinding her before it began to gently dim and finally disperse like delicate dust. A whisper of fine white ash alighted near the entrance; the door gleamed metallic.

Irene blinked vigorously, moving her head from side to side. Her eyes stung in the glow of the afterlight. She could barely see through the bright aurora in her eyes. A most bizarre energy had coursed through the synapses of her soul, vibrating through the innermost paths of her being. Her legs felt wobbly; she sat down, waiting to regain her vision.

She stared at the bank of computers wanting to record the activity on the screens. Impossible. In her state, she could not keep up with the speed of the patterns. She swiveled her chair toward the screens and clicked To Print. She would have to annotate from the rollout of printed material.

Then as hotly as it began, it stopped. The screens dimmed. David was on the second floor. She had to call him. "David, is everything okay down there?"

"Hold on." She heard him speaking to the subjects, concern in his voice. He was sending them home. "Irene, some kind of glitch affected the equipment for a moment. Everything seems back to normal, though."

Normal? It all seemed more than just a moment. The moment had practically lifted her right off the floor. What in the world created such an incredible energy field? She needed to examine the printout. Her mouth flew open when she saw the immense instances of activity from one particular subject. Although her vision had not adjusted completely, she went straight to file 361B, the file of the twenty-five-year-old woman whose IQ was 240—Alina Andrades.

Compelled to conduct an extra interview with the subject, one more than she completed with the other volunteers, Irene had eventually cleared her for participation. Alina Andrades was tall, and although slender, possessed a powerful aura. Irene sensed a strange power in the young woman's mesmerizing gaze. Her eyes did not blink. They were large, with deep pupils of dark marine blue. While Alina was completing the first questionnaire, her irises transfigured, assuming a disturbing gray luminosity that unnerved Irene as they became the color of cold, weathered stone.

Once before, she'd witnessed something similar, albeit less dramatic. She'd dated a divorced movie director who was determined to impress her with dinners, desserts, braggadocio, and not so discrete invites to his apartment. His eyes were quite blue but at times became deep turquoise, then green—not all that unusual. However, while they blundered through yet another dinner date, his eyes suddenly became brown.

Irene thought he might be having a fit. She asked about the color of his parents' and grandparents' eyes. He said he'd lain with a Brazilian woman the night before, and he'd eaten her brain, brown eyes, and all. Irene did not appreciate his attempt at humor. She did learn his eye color genealogy. His father was the blue-eyed parent, his mother had hazel eyes, and her mother's eyes were a deep, dark brown. Irene dropped him even after he laughingly admitted the thing about the Brazilian was a bad joke.

The thing with Andrades could be genetic; the fruit-fly-phenomenon at work could account for variations in the color of her eyes. Still . . . Maybe she was mad. Eyes are attached to the brain. But the most remarkable result of Andrades' psych evaluation had been her high IQ. Irene supposed she could have missed something, hoped she hadn't erred.

She called David again. "David, are you still there? What is going on?"

"Don't know. I had to send the subjects home—the disturbance." His voice sounded shaky.

"God, I thought the whole system had blown. There was the strangest silence right before the whole place shook with a powerful explosion of light. I was right in the vortex of the brilliance and felt as if I were floating right off the floor."

"Sounds like an episode from Star Trek. A luminous cloud smothered you in white light? I watched almost every episode with my dad, fantasized about stepping into the transport capsule and traveling within seconds to another dimension—or the corner pizza parlor."

"I never watched the show, and I don't think you are taking me seriously. Look, I did not imagine it. I believe I've experienced a pre-telepathic contact. Those spikes in data transmission, hot on the screen right before the disturbance, had to be connected to the inundation of white light which overpowered me. And in that instance, the image of a woman flashed before me. It was her. I believe the intense activity came from Alina Andrades."

"Why?"

"Wait until you see the printout. So far, the feedback substantiates what I think happened. We need to take a closer look. But David, she came to mind immediately, and the sensation that all of it, the light, the energy, passed straight through me."

"Wow! That is disturbing, and especially since nothing nearly as powerful as you're describing occurred on the other floors. The fourth floor reported the lights went out, then came back on in moments. Here, on the second, the computers went dark, and the lights flickered. Andrades did not move a muscle. If all that energy came from her, I discerned nothing, except that she sat quite still, calm and composed, earphones securely in place, intently staring into the dark monitor. Apparently, whatever happened, did not affect her."

"It didn't have to. It affected me!"

"Then it's possible you also can receive telepathic messages. Andrades may have attempted a communication." The line went quiet. "Irene, Irene, can you hear me? Say something."

Didn't she just say the same thing? She'd intuited becoming a receiving vessel of some kind, and it had to do with Alina. Wasn't David listening?

He rushed up to the fifth floor and found Irene sitting stiff, staring at the door, her pupils so dilated her eyes loomed like dark gray discs. She literally looked like she'd seen a ghost. He looked at her a little wildly, "Are you okay, Irene?"

She nodded her head yes. "That light is still in my eye. I just need a few more minutes."

David squeezed her hand and kissed her cheek. Then, in a moment, he was at the computers, practically eating the screens as he searched for the file he wanted, the data they had collected the week before. "Hey, there's nothing here!"

"What's wrong?"

"Nah, just wanted to take a look at last week's stuff. Found it! But tonight's record isn't here, it would have been awesome to make a comparison. I think you're right. The erratic activity that disabled the consoles may have come from the two who reported receiving a transmission the other day."

"I'm sorry. I couldn't capture the data. That light was overwhelming. I think it all got deleted after it printed out. Weird. Although . . . Well, it could have been a momentary power failure. We can try a file recovery. Let's not get bent out of shape about it." She didn't think it was a power failure at all. She could feel it in the skin of her bones; something else was definitely going on. She handed him another length of computer paper.

"I see it. It's here." He pulled compulsively at his left ear. He was still holding the printout, looking perturbed.

"Ah . . . what if Andrades' psychic capacity became so overloaded it generated a field of tremendous energy."

"Possibly. But why? He pulled on his ear some more. He was thinking."

"There was activity from one other subject, but nothing nearly as pronounced as what I believe came from her." Irene pointed to two sections of printout while carefully avoiding David's reaction. She had gone to the woman's file, not mentioned it to David because even after examining the file, all she still had was a hunch, a hunch there was more to Alina Andrades than she'd been able to discover through assessment.

"Um . . . radio waves, if so, the spikes in activity could be evidence of telepathic reception by our two subjects from somewhere *outside* the lab. Information took a ride on an electrical or radio wave of some kind, triggering pronounced brain activity, and all the astounding fallout."

"There you go with Tesla again."

"He reported seeing blinding flashes of light, much like what you described."

"Tesla?"

"Yes, Nikola Tesla. He worked out of labs not too far from here for many years. Some say he reported having flashbacks of sorts, visions." He regarded her with sweet sadness. The woman before him, his Irene, was also exceptional.

"That's some creepy coincidence. But what are you saying? Are you saying Tesla left behind some kind of recurring energy field?"

"Um, not exactly. The uncanny flash of light could be some kind of stray reiteration. Nikola had been experimenting with all kinds of things. Maybe our lab has tapped into something similar. Are you okay now?"

"Yes." She really wasn't but didn't want him to worry. "I don't think it came from out there. The event originated right here, within these walls, from one of the two subjects we've already identified. And it should only bolster our confidence in the strength of our sample." She wanted to somehow prove it was indeed an internal event, validate a scientific instance of telepathy that had nothing to do with radio waves. Once again feeling protective of David's ambition, she continued, "Those two subjects are hot, the white light, evidence of a powerful mental energy force generated by one or both. They may be both receivers *and* transmitters, especially Andrades. We need to move forward with this."

In the aftermath of the event, Irene and David struggled to wrap their heads around the unknowns, desperately trying to identify any substantial fact they could glean from what had transpired. How could they prove it had been an internal phenomenon?

The look of consternation on David's face was evidence of how off-kilter he was feeling about the whole thing. "Irene, go home, before it gets too late. I know you're as fanatical about the research as I am, but we should stop now and come back to it when we're not shook up and confused. I'll stay for a while to double-check the equipment and make sure everything is in working order. And you, you need to rest up. Go home."

"Don't worry, I'm already recovering from the electric onslaught of preternatural communication. Ha-ha."

"Take a cab, Irene. It's on me. It's past nine already." He handed her a fifty-dollar bill.

"What? Is that tonight's gratuity? I'm worth a lot more." She tried to wink, but her eyes were still agape from the light. "Keep it, I don't need a cab. I only take taxis from the airport or if there's an emergency. So don't spoil me."

"I'm serious, Irene. Don't-do-the-subway-tonight. Jason called about an active shooter near the South Ferry station and that's only one stop away." The protective tone in his voice and the intriguing frown forming between his dark eyebrows induced little warm waves all over her. Aw, she wanted to say, you love me. She grinned, took the fifty bucks, and headed to the subway.

After the rain, the night had chilled. No one was around. She hurried west on Washington Place and across the desolate square. The fountain was silent, and the stately arch glowed with an anemic bronze cast. The metal of the park benches at the periphery of the quadrangle gleamed wet. Disparate bundles, and a homeless individual who had retired for the evening beneath layers of shiny garbage bags, occupied two adjacent benches.

Her insides singled hunger. She started to descend the steps into the West 4th Street Station, wishing hard the next train would pull in as soon as she traversed the turnstile. Ali's Deli would still be open, and she would spend some of the fifty dollars on falafel and a quinoa health salad. The offer of money had amused her, and so had his concern.

She stepped down carefully. The strips of metal edging the concrete rungs were slippery. She was nearly at the bottom of the staircase when she sensed a presence hovering, felt someone at her back, thought she saw a shadow reflected on the wet surface of the amber tiles that covered the wall on her right. For one insane moment, she thought of Peter Grantis, remembered how he'd behaved suspiciously, scurrying through the black wrought iron gate like a fugitive. Then, a few days later, she thought he'd followed her as she jogged toward the park. She whipped her head around and looked up to the top of the stairs. There was no one.

Want to Learn Jujitsu?

Irene was allowing herself a sense of achievement—bitter-sweet satisfaction given everything else going on in her life.

Carolina and Ana were finally moving out of the danger zone. Yet her radar screen was now always up and running during reviews with Freile. The possibility he might move to disband the unit stubbornly buzzed around in her mind's bonnet. She made sure the case notes were succinct and clean of any tinge of overly optimistic prognosis. She was meticulous as she updated Carolina's and Ana's files.

The day Rosalía Mateo called to ask if her niece could be discharged to the hospital's outpatient clinic, she did so only after profusely thanking Irene for bringing Carolina out of her silence.

"She's like a new person, Dr. Irene."

Sometimes individuals who wished to be on less formal terms, but still wanted to express respect, would call her Dr. Irene.

"She wants to pursue her art and a wonderful opportunity for access to studio space has become available. An artist friend of ours remembered the dreamy landscapes my niece painted a few years back and has offered to let her work out of her loft in SoHo."

Irene's lips parted in surprise. "Please be clear. Are you saying Carolina spoke to you, made a request?"

"Well, eh . . . it was not a real conversation, but she did speak a handful of words, which I tried to paraphrase, and to which she responded with one-word answers."

Paraphrase? Her loving aunt may have overinterpreted Carolina's communication. Perhaps her ambition for the girl's talent motivated her to read too much into her utterances. Rosalía had mentioned that before she went silent, Carolina was taking art classes, and her instructor had suggested an application to the Art Institute of Chicago. Perhaps the aunt's request was premature. Still, excellent news signifying meaningful progress. "Let's schedule a family conference. How about next Friday afternoon?"

The next time Carolina walked into her office, Irene remarked on the bloom on her cheeks and the smile on her face. "Good morning, Carolina. You look very pretty . . . and happy."

And then, a soft, almost inaudible thank you. Irene put an arm around the girl's shoulder. "Sit. Carolina, sit."

Ana Amado's developing proficiency in jujitsu had impressed the women, earned her considerable respect, and especially from Carolina. While Ana worked out, she always applauded vigorously, even letting out a yell when Ana Amado toppled the instructor with a skillful roundabout. Ana reported. "Dr. Míral, Carolina is better. She's like one of us now." The two had become fast friends.

"And how about you, Ana? Are you better?" Ana laughed a nice laugh and with a wink in her eye asked, "Want to learn jujitsu?"

Yes, her most challenging cases had moved forward, out of Walter Freile's range of perceived pathology. But she could not shake the feeling she was the one now lined up in the crosshairs of his scope. *Sanity is a continuum, and I am developing paranoia.*

⚬

Alfredo Bryson responded to the email she had twice saved to draft before finally hitting the send button.

Irene,

I called two friends that can see you next week.

I've known them since Yale. Please call one.

Many regards and much love,

Fred

Back home that evening, Irene sat staring at her phone before finally dialing Dr. Edith Solange. She left a message requesting an appointment.

After the call, a hot shower, and a glass of Bordeaux, the kinks in her shoulders began to loosen. But within, she remained as tense as a wind-up alarm clock. She wished to calm her thoughts and went for another glass of wine. Those complaints were Freile's fabrications. They had to be.

Her mind raced back to the disconcerting Wednesday conference with her crew. How could she be sure it wasn't someone in the group? Sylvia or Ernesto, or . . . Could not even entertain it could also be Jackson. All of them? She thought hard about her patients, how Amanda had said not everyone was a friend and stated that some of the women thought therapy was bullshit. But no. She was confident the complaints had not come from the women, and she knew of no relative who objected to their treatment. On the contrary, those who were involved seemed grateful. She could not, would not, allow a more terrible suspicion to take hold. *What if it had been someone closer, Laura? Joe Martell? Absurd! My God, I do need to talk to a therapist.*

The demeaning aspects of the whole situation rankled her to the core.

Bullshit. It was Freile. He pooh-poohed the report of complaints because there were no complaints. None. What were the words he used? Negligence and Misconduct. Was he in a cowardly way saying what he thought of her?

Facts: Freile harassed her. Laura was breaking her heart, and her mom was gone. She needed someone objective to hear her out and listen to her preoccupations and her confusing emotions regarding David.

After she brushed her teeth, she examined her gums, her lips. *What is that? Jeez, just chapped skin, just stress.* She grabbed a little tin of Blistek, unscrewed the cap, dabbed balm on her lips, popped two mega doses of vitamin C, brushed her hair, and slept for nine hours.

Things Hidden

IT WAS THE KIND of Saturday morning that invigorated, that welcomed joggers, cyclists, dog walkers, and athletic young moms run-pushing their blissful babies in tri-wheeled strollers through the pedestrian trails of Central Park. It was the kind of fall morning that no one wanted to spend cooped up indoors, the sort of day whose city air smelled fresh and clean, inviting one to open windows wide and breathe in. And that's just what Irene did. She stood in front of an open window and stretched her arms wide to the morning, enjoying the cool breeze on her face.

She opened the door to pick up the newspaper. Her neighbor Beth's new puppy pulled on his leash, coaxing his owner to walk him over to Irene's door. He was some kind of poodle mix with curly brown hair. "Good morning to you, guy." Irene petted and cooed. "He's adorable, Beth. I love his coat." The puppy's coat was soft and curly, like David's hair. She laughed, thinking he might not appreciate the comparison.

Beth had a funny look on her face. Charly had disappeared, and as adorable as her new doggie was, Beth was not getting over Charly so quickly. "Mornin' Irene, came up to talk to you, wanted to thank you for helping us look for Charly."

"Really sorry about him, Beth. Someone must have stolen him. He was a good dog."

"I think it was Grantis. I do. He complained about noise, yelled we should put socks on our dog because he could not stand to hear his claws clattering on the parquet floors." Beth was angry. "He's fucking weird. Charly isn't claws; he's a teddy bear. I think Grantis killed poor Charly. That's what I think. I want Dad to evict him, but he said no, said I had no proof Grantis had harmed the dog, said I was being hysterical, and that Charly probably ran away." Beth's eyes pooled, then she knelt over her new pooch, nuzzling his neck. "I love you, Harry. I love you so much."

Irene guessed Beth named her doggies after guys because she wanted a baby boy. Beth picked Harry up. "Oh, also wanted to tell you we're having a get-together in the courtyard on Saturday night. Alan said it would cheer me up. Join us if you're free. But I must warn you, it's six couples. No singles. You have to bring a guy." The apologetic tone in her voice was unmistakable. Irene winced; the comments were not like Beth. It was Alan speaking his mind.

"Thanks for the invite, but I'm afraid I won't be able to make it. No guy." Beth looked at her with a look close to pity. Irene could ask David, but she wouldn't. She did not like Alan, thought he was overcontrolling, changing her Beth. David would not like him either.

"Beth, maybe you should talk to your dad about Grantis again. I think he followed me to the park a few days ago. Divorced men can snap. Too many losses can make for misogyny and displaced anger. And who the hell knows why his wife didn't want him? Probably needs help, maybe your dad can convince him. The guy does seem kind of strange, won't even say hello."

"He killed Charly. I know it!"

"Beth, I miss Charly too."

"I know. Oh, downstairs, there's a large manila envelope for you. Guess it didn't fit in the mailbox, so the postman left it on the ledge."

Irene went down to pick up the correspondence. Her heart leaped. Was it from Human Resources? From the person who complained? Maybe whoever it was, was now contacting her directly. She climbed back to the third floor holding the thing up gingerly between her index finger and thumb, keeping it at arm's length as though it were something dangerous.

Well, it wasn't sales material—no logos or trademarks. The envelope appeared plainly and clearly anonymous. She poured a glass of wine and set it down on the table next to the manila envelope. *This is ridiculous! Hell, let me open it already. Beth thinks Grantis killed Charly, and I'm looking at this envelope as if it contains the doomsday report!*

The thing weighed some; the postmark was from somewhere way downtown. She supposed it could have been mailed from anywhere—no return address, only a small, printed label: Dr. Irene Míral. She went to the desk in her home office, retrieved a letter opener, and inserted it carefully under the flap.

Three photographs, and on heavy white stationery with a lovely red rose motif, a handwritten letter from Andrea.

Dear Irene,

I want to say, dear sister, but you and I know terms of endearment between us would be quite hypocritical. The link that makes us sisters was always weak. I am sorry. I know you loved Alma dearly. I am sure she loved you very much as well. And for your sake, I am sorry for her passing. And I apologize beforehand for what I'm about to say.

She was weak. Alma was a weak woman, a weak mother.

I've tried hard to think of her as mother, but there are no memories in my mind of her as such. How far back does your memory of her take you? Were you three or four or five? Fernanda said Alma abandoned me when I was three. But I cannot remember when I was one or two or three. Can you?

I know what you think of my father and his family. They indeed said unkind things about Alma. Now, I am an adult and know life, so I understand how they could exaggerate. But why?

How could a mother leave her little girl behind? It's the question I've asked myself all my life. When I asked Fernanda, she would say, "Because she was a bad woman."

I don't know about that. But I do know Alma was weak. She was a weak woman who could not fight for me, could not fight my father for me. He drank a lot, my father—must be why she left him. But she didn't have to leave me.

Do not feel sorry. In many ways, I have been blessed. I am grateful for good health and my beautiful sons.

Fernanda was a hard one, and maybe I take after her, take after her too much. But she was the mother fate provided, wasn't she? Like a substitute teacher, you know. Kind of funny because Fernanda did look like a homely schoolmarm. Alma was pretty. I know this because I found these retratos hidden in one of Fernanda's old books. I stole them when I was six. I think they belonged to my father. I hid them in one of my cuadernos, and no one missed them.

Sometimes, when I felt lonesome, I'd turn to those photographs of our pretty young mother. And our little brother who died. No pictures of the others. Seems like we've both inherited spaces empty of memories. We had other siblings; I don't even know their names, but I know they died as small children. I wish I could tell you more, but the things hidden from us remain hidden in someone else's past.

I've kept the photographs all these years, but now I want you to have them. Keep them. They are your retratos.

Best regards,

Andrea

Irene read Andrea's letter over and over again and she cried until the salty tears dried up and her cheeks were as taut as a tambourine. Andrea was talking to her from across a chasm, a vacuum, a place barren of an entire field of childhood memories. Memories of growing up together and of their deceased siblings did not exist for either of them. And if there were no memories, how could they be sisters?

She stared at the photographs of a young Alma, maybe fourteen or so. Yes, she was pretty, and she was smiling. Irene guessed the photos were taken before she married, before the abuse began, before she could blossom into a healthy woman. The third retrato was horrifying to Irene. *Why Andrea, why did you send this?* A young child lay in a small satin-lined casket that looked like a bassinet on stilts. So small, the features indistinct; Irene could not tell whether it was a baby boy or a girl. And standing behind the tiny corpse was a tall skinny man with a face as hard as a hatchet.

Irene placed the retrato of her little dead sibling back in the envelope. She should send it back. Was Andrea trying to absolve herself of the ugly truth, that her father was at the root of their grief? Was she admitting it, or deliberately being hurtful?

The pictures of her beautiful mom, she would cherish those. Irene knew exactly which frames to place them in. She stuffed the manila envelope with the awful photograph beneath a pile of old magazines. Then she picked up the phone to call Andrea. She got voice mail. "Andrea, I want to say that your letter touched me deeply. I think we should have a talk, and soon. Thank you for the photographs. Be well. Give me a call."

She'd recognized the sentiment, the underlying regret in the letter's words. If Andrea had not included the retrato of their deceased little brother, Irene would have in moments boarded a cab to her home and embraced her, and cried with her. Irene would wait for her call.

She rarely had an unrestful sleep or disturbing dreams. But for the second time in a month, she dreamt a dark dream: She and Andrea by a lake, thick black tears streaming down their cheeks.

250

Now Kiss Me Right

In a few hours, she would be at the lab. The white light in her eye had not gone away; it had appeared twice since Thursday night. Paranoia, eye doctors, and therapists.

I must be getting old. She'd called an ophthalmologist for an eye exam. It was likely some type of residual phenomenon occupying her retina. The scientist in her compelled her to rule out whatever physical explanation there might be. But she knew the answer was back at Jamison Hall.

She had an appointment with Dr. Solange on Tuesday. She hoped to gain some clarity regarding the challenges that had come her way, including her conflicting feelings for David.

And as any woman on the verge, she was curious, wanting to know about his relationships. The previous week's conversation had turned out to be most enlightening:

"Hey David, how come you're still single?" He was pushing forty, although he did not seem at all concerned about it.

He laughed. "How come I'm still single? That's a good question, and I don't have an answer. And you? How come you're still unattached?"

"Me? Looks like I'm almost there, the age of ineligibility, and sometimes I think I haven't even negotiated the age of innocence." She tried to brush off regret with a chuckle. "Guess I'm left holding the old maid card."

The brown in his eyes melted like hot chocolate, like he wanted to grab her, lift her off the floor, and gobble her up with kisses. Then he looked away. "I ah . . . I fell in love, hard, when I was a real young seventeen. She was married, lived up near Irvington, drove a silver Porsche Carrera, and often came to the city to check in with her agent. She worked as a professional photographer, her specialty, nude pictorials of affluent young people. My sister Courtney was a client. When she dumped me, I snatched the nearest object I could reach on her kitchen counter, a Corning bowl, and tried to smash my head. Once the stitches healed, my parents had me see a therapist, then, as a graduation present, a trip to Europe."

He bent his handsome head and pointed to the mass of curls above his forehead. Irene pushed the locks aside and found a faint scar beneath the thick brown waves. "Oh, no!" What other scars might he have? Some people bore invisible ones from the wounds of abuse. Irene at once thought pedophile. "Did she take nude pictures of you? Did she ask you to pose doing things?"

The alarm in her voice, the way she was trying to read his face—he gazed at her like he wanted more of her fingers through his hair. "No, nothing like that at all. She tried to dissuade me from what turned out to be inevitable, perhaps primeval. Maybe I just wanted to drive her Porsche. Anyway, we went at it for a couple of months. Looking back now, I understand she had to let me go. My therapist encouraged me to feel macho about it, practically cheered like a dad proud of his son's sexual antics. By the end of the last session, we were both laughing about the whole thing. Still, she was my first love. Or shall I say, infatuation?"

"Ignorance." For a green moment, Irene wished she'd been his first.

"But guess what? I must have developed a penchant for older women—Mrs. Robinsons. You guys are real predators." He laughed.

"Oooh!" She went over to him and gave him a little smack on the shoulder. "Are you referring to me? David, don't even call me old."

Laughing, he pulled his shoulder away, then with a mirthful expression said, "Okay, okay, Tiger. You're not a cougar." He was obviously enjoying the repartee. "The next one was in her fifties, a wealthy German who let me stay in her home in Cologne the year I spent in Europe. She seduced me with marijuana and sex so super it exhausted me, exhausted me as much as you, that last time in my apartment." He laughed some more, playfully holding both hands up like a shield.

"David, you old goat! Don't be disgusting."

"I ran out after two weeks. Must have become conscious I was in trouble. She was consuming me."

"Well, thank God. You could have become an American Gigolo in Germany. Seriously though, those experiences may have ruined you for relationships."

"Umm, I don't think I have a problem. Just had not hit it off . . . had not yet met the woman I want to spend the rest of my life with." He averted his glance with half-closed lids, pausing for a long moment. His awkward silence very much like a younger man's.

Not yet met the woman . . . Had David uttered a subtle proposal? Even as she mulled over the phrase, it occurred to her there were curious parallels between David's teenage experiences and those of her patients, women who'd been victimized since childhood. But no. David was not a victim. His affluent parents were aware and knew to protect their son. Yet maybe, just like her, he'd been compartmentalizing relationships.

David's adolescent confessions intensified feelings she'd been keeping at bay, feelings deep inside her pelvis. Smiling big, she walked over, but only kissed him on the cheek. David looked into her big gray eyes and pulled her tight against him. She felt his hardness.

"Now kiss me right."

She put her arms around his neck and found his tongue as he lifted her off the floor and onto the nearest desk.

Dr. Solange

THE TRAIN NEARED THE Columbus Circle station, and she'd
wanted to keep going, had to make a conscious physical effort to
exit the subway car. She was early and walked around, stopping at
the shop that sold dance shoes, leotards, leg warmers, and posters of
famous prima ballerinas. She thought of purchasing a pair of pointe
shoes. Thought of taking them home, imagined herself gently re-
moving them from the box, sitting on the floor, putting them on
her feet, tying the beautiful ribbons around her ankles, and rising
like a swan. How silly. How ridiculous. She knew it took years of
disciplined training to get en pointe with grace and one needed to
start early.

Her family could not afford ballet or music lessons, so classical
dance remained a fantasy. Her parents did manage Catholic school
tuition, though, starting with primary school. Alma had insisted.
She took in her piecework, and Antonio worked two jobs, one in
an auto repair shop and the other delivering newspapers in the early
morning hours. Her mom was thrifty to ridiculous levels. She passed
up on the little indulgences Antonio wished to bestow and squir-
reled away money to pay for Irene's tuition.

Irene walked a block south, made a right on Broadway, and found
the address. She entered the lobby and searched the directory: Edith
Solange, Suite 901. She gave her name at the security desk then
headed to the elevator.

Edith Solange was about forty. She was dressed in a dark rose, softly tailored pantsuit, and a crisp white blouse with a mandarin collar. Pearl drop earrings peeked out from wavy strands of dark brown hair. She was tall and elegant. Irene briefly wondered how well she knew Fred Bryson. The woman greeted Irene with an outstretched hand and a nice smile.

"Let's talk. What brings you to me?"

Irene sat. The walls of Dr. Solange's office were bare, but for three certificates on one wall. A large abstract sculpture adorned a corner, the soft white of the walls, a gentle contrast. The shades on the wide windows, translucent like smooth rice paper.

"Fred Bryson is a friend and he recommended you. I suppose I'm having something of a midlife crisis and need to work out certain things . . . difficulties."

"Relationships?"

"No. What am I saying? It's always relationships, isn't it?"

"Are you married?"

"No. Never thought too much about it until recently. But since my mother died, all kinds of things are coming at me, confusing me. I'm at a juncture in my life's journey, and the signposts are pointing in too many directions. Confusion is an unpalatable emotion."

"When? When did she pass?"

"Last month. But sometimes it seems as if it were just yesterday."

"A month is not long at all, Irene. You're still grieving."

"Yes, I suppose so. At times it's as if I'm wading on a misty shore, the waves are silent, and desolation overwhelms me. Then the feeling fades. The thing is, I need clarity and I don't like feeling vulnerable."

"What's wrong with being vulnerable? You're missing your mother quite a bit."

"Yes. I do feel like a total orphan now. Both my parents are gone and my work at the clinic has become more important than ever."

"I take it that you are not in a relationship?"

"No. Yes, there is someone. For the first time in my life, I'm having strong feelings for a man, and maybe it's because I need to fill up the vacancy left by my mother."

"Or?"

Or? *There was a choice to be made, wasn't there?* Laura's aphoristic advice came to mind. "Maybe I'm afraid to have a relationship."

"Are you?" Edith Solange opened her hands, waiting for an answer.

"Don't know. That's why I'm here."

"Tell me about him. What is his name?"

"David. David and I are working on a project, a PSI project. We've been friends for a while. We're much alike, down to our personal motivations regarding the research study. And no pressure. He understands about my mother, and it means the world to me. I never went into detail about the abuse, though. I suppose he's guessed. He understands how my work with the women at the clinic is at the center of me. He's smart and sensitive, good-looking, funny, and very sexy."

Edith Solange was nodding some kind of aha approval. Then she became serious. "Have you ever been abused, Irene?"

"No. Never. My mom suffered horrific domestic violence. Her first husband, lots of grief. Dead children, siblings I will never know. Even after she married my father, who was a saint, a real saint, her past seemed to haunt her and she often warned men were evil."

"Do you think so? That men are evil."

"Far too many inflict emotional and physical pain on women. I was not there to help my mother when it was happening to her. But I am here now, at the clinic, with my patients, and I'll work my fingers off to help those women be whole again." Irene's voice broke.

"I understand."

Irene shifted in the chair. She did not want to cry and held back about the disturbing dream that drove her to seek therapy that first time. A dream with no images or people, just sounds, a woman weeping, and a deafening scream rising from a black void. "Yes, my mother's stories have influenced how I see things, if only because I heard them so many times. I was in therapy once before—two years of it during which I repeatedly vowed no man was going to put his hands on me."

"So, Irene, you don't trust men. Is that right?"

"I know there are many good men like my father . . . and David." She wanted to add Fred Bryson's name to the shortlist of men she trusted but held back. She didn't know if his affiliation with Edith Solange went beyond the professional. And anyway, she had, in a sense, outgrown Fred. "I do think I trust David . . ."

"You trust David not to hurt you. But there is no guarantee, is there?"

"Edith, it's true. I can have an accident when I step off the curb to hail a cab. No guarantee that David and I can live happily ever after."

"But you're thinking about it. All right! Fair enough."

"Yes, I am thinking about it." Irene smiled and then was quiet for a long moment. This was not the time to measure words or be reticent. It had taken her long enough to seek badly needed guidance. "Do you happen to know Walter Freile?"

"Why do you ask?"

"He's a supervising psychiatrist at Lakeside, my boss, in a sense."

"How do you get along?"

Irene swallowed hesitation, raised both eyebrows, and divulged she thought he was going after her job. "He has never been fully on board regarding the PTSD unit I coordinate. It's a new thing, you know, one of the first programs in the country devoted exclusively to the treatment of women traumatized by violence. It may turn out to be a prototype. I fear he may move to dissolve it and I don't know what to do about it except to have my guard up twenty-four-seven. All along, he's been pushing to discharge patients I know are not ready."

"Sounds awfully frustrating."

"He claimed Human Resources received an anonymous letter complaining about my job performance but won't provide details. It's making me nuts, racking my brain about who might be alleging such. Now he's saying I should forget about it, that it was likely some kind of crank complaint."

"It sounds to me as if he's being manipulative. What are you going to do about it?"

"Been thinking about going to Human Resources to get clarification, but I'm worried about complications and consequences. Don't know yet."

Irene looked up at the ceiling, thinking she was now the same as Maríanis. She wished the put-together-confident-woman she was speaking to would tell her exactly how she needed to proceed. "Honestly, don't know what to do, except I cannot allow him to disrupt the women's progress. I have to stop him."

"It's important to fight for what we believe is right. But what's even more important is to care for ourselves so we can remain strong. Hospital politics can be tricky to navigate. I'm glad we're talking. Shall we schedule for the same time next week?" Edith jotted down the appointment on a slip from a notepad on her desk. "Irene, it's still a struggle for professional women, difficult to decide how we're going to exercise the rights we do have."

Irene had made no mention of the embarrassing scene at the restaurant. She regretted mentioning Freile's name. It would be awkward if he and Edith knew each other.

She did not regret her visit with Edith Solange. As she walked back to 59th Street and into the modern subway entrance, a smile formed on her lips. One question would cease to preoccupy her. She no longer would ask herself why she warmed with giddy anticipation each time she thought of David. The answer dawned like a gentle epiphany: She was in love.

The Incident

SOMETHING HAD BEEN KNOCKING around David's mind for a few days. He'd reviewed the time sequence with Stivik several times, but the ducks just were not lining up right.

"Irene, when I got home last Thursday, the incident at the Staten Island Ferry was all over the news."

"What incident?" She'd been so amused when he handed her the fifty dollars that she'd not paid much mind. "Oh . . . you did say something was going on by South Ferry."

"That's right. A man opened fire as the vessel was docking, helter-skelter aiming at no specific target. No one was injured. He fled. The police believe it was likely an emotionally disturbed person. It happened close to the time of our explosive little event Thursday night, really close."

The edge in his voice signaled something was up. Irene raised an eyebrow. "It's just a coincidence. What are you thinking?"

"Don't want to bruise your scientific ego, but I think our study is in trouble. Let's take another look at that night's printouts."

Irene retrieved the folded lengths of data. Each grabbed one side of the perforated sheets and, with thumbs and forefingers, scrolled down and then scrolled up again. David was first to notice it.

"Look here. There are two instances of heightened activity, half an hour in between. The first coincides precisely with the time the shooting happened at South Ferry. The news report of the shooting came in about 7:05."

She saw the activity beginning at 6:59, then nothing until 7:30 when the whole thing went haywire for two minutes, two minutes still residing in her optical nerve. "Well, yes, definitely a spike in activity at about seven, but the tremendous energy I felt here didn't happen until later. I don't see a connection." She remembered her hunch about Alina Andrades. But how could the woman be connected to the shooting? And why was David focusing on an event outside the lab?

He was looking grim. "Don't know, but I aim to find out. And you're right, that first surge caused no physical disturbance, at least not anything apparent to either of us."

Brows knitted, Irene asked, "Not apparent? What do you mean?"

"Vibrations from the barrage of gunshots may have impacted our two hot subjects and breached their receptive spheres, thereby causing the second round of pronounced activity."

"You're thinking those two experienced an acute awareness of the event, the shooting?"

"Ditto. South Ferry is not that far away."

"Maybe the times are wrong, not on our side, but on the part of the news networks. Let's take another look." He was about a head taller than she, and when she glanced up from the printouts, Irene saw he was upset. Clearly, he was still delving on that first instance when it was those two insane minutes, two minutes which shook her to the marrow and nearly blinded her, which they needed to examine.

"If a breach of their receptive spheres, then did they experience telepathic communication from outside this building? And from whom? Think, Irene, is it possible they already knew?"

"Huh? That's wild." *What made him want to go there?* "David, vibrations and the psychic sense theory are fine with me." She batted her long lashes. "Most of the unusual spikes of activity came from Andrades."

He gave her a look. "There could be . . . there may be a plausible explanation. You know we can excite our autonomic nervous system by just remembering something scary, sexy, and so on. The woman could have been thinking about what she already knew would go down, and her brain went fast forward, creating the tremendous activity we recorded. It's like when your PTSD patients experience flashbacks. An emotionally loaded trigger sets off a horrible memory and all the somatic fallout, including racing heartbeat, etc."

"I'm positive she is capable of powerful communication. But why did she direct tremendous energy up through three floors of space? I'm convinced the tremendous energy was focused on me. She wanted us, me, to know of the explosive event. Although, the news was too late; the shooting had already happened. It wasn't somatic fallout, it was intentional. David, now we need to consider precognition. She foresaw the thing."

"In that case, our research design is moot, our study is screwed, and we can open up a gypsy parlor. Precognition is not what we want to measure, is it? And also, the time frame bugs me. It's creepy. And I told you, Andrades did not waver from her screen once, no visible indication she was transmitting a thing." Nearly grimacing, he said, "She may no longer be a viable subject."

David perused the questionable night's printout once more. "Exceptional and significant activity. Incredible!" He turned to Irene, arms spread, palms up, hands and face asking, what now?

"You're really bugged about this, aren't you? Look, let's not forget the premises that motivated our work here, the potential posed by other disciplines. Quantum physicists, theories of the transcendence of time and space, conclusions that transmission of information can occur through various dimensions. What if? What if the activity spikes *are* evidence of psychic reception from somewhere outside the lab? If they're as gifted as we believe, why couldn't our two subjects be able to receive from elsewhere? What if radio waves *are* the telepathic venue. If so, it should not be all that surprising, should it? Your Tesla and all."

"Just wish we could establish that it wasn't something else."

"I hear you, but let's not split hairs. Precognition would still be a paranormal event, wouldn't it? Let's not circumscribe our thinking to fit the parameters of our research. You've said there are all kinds of waves in which communication can take a ride, electric, radio, who knows what else. Whatever happened would still be an occurrence of telepathic phenomena. I want to go with the premise that it was an internal event, and that the energy was generated by our subject's incomplete and intense telepathic activity. We need to move forward."

The impulse to protect David's ambition was strong. The emotion surprised her. She decided not to bring up the eerie occurrence of the white light again, or how she'd perceived a presence, nor confess the event had driven her to open Alina's entire file going way back to the first interview. She understood how at this moment, David would be worrying their investment, a zillion hours of work and effort, was on the line. For sure, he wished to dismiss last Thursday night's event as a freaky coincidence. But she saw he could not. His milk chocolate eyes were murky, and the corners of his mouth were not smiling.

She had to shake him. "If not an internal event, precognition, or telepathy, then what, David? What?"

"... Something else still," he said vaguely, again tugging at his ear. "It's possible that somewhere in real time, they learned the shooting was to take place."

"We are scientists, we should not jump to conclusions. That is a creepy conjecture. But go on, let's hear the rest of it."

"Who is Alina Andrades, really?"

Irene felt a rash of embarrassment descend from her cheeks to her neck and hover like an incipient fever on her chest. Had she not been sufficiently thorough in her evaluation of the subject? "What are you asking me? You're not thinking Alina Andrades is linked to the Staten Island shooter and knew what he was going to do. Are you thinking that? Wow!"

"Since you asked the question, you must be thinking the same thing."

"Because you've been pointing me to it for the last half hour! David, we may have overlooked a variable, so it's not the subject but our assessments. If you feel so strongly, then shouldn't we contact the authorities?"

"I don't know, I have to think—the confidentiality issue, and if it turns out to be nothing, we could be open to a lawsuit. It's not the kind of attention I want."

"Then let's bring her up here and ask her."

"Irene, you know they already went home. And suppose it *was* an instance of paranormal activity? We'd be scaring away the person who may be our most valuable subject. As I suggested before, it was likely a loss of mind control on her part which set off the powerful waves of energy. And thusly, the erratic wave activity that shows up on the printout." David held doubt under his breath as he spoke.

"Aha! So, what is it that we have? Let's see now, the woman could be an exceptionally powerful psychic, possibly precognition at work . . . or she could be a government operative, a spy, maybe part of a subversive cell, a criminal."

"That's not fair, Irene. Don't be mean."

The thing was getting to them. He did not want to pursue the possibility of a flaw in their study, and she did not want to continue thinking she might have received a transmission or felt a presence. Neither relished the idea that any subject was linked to the shooting.

"I'm sorry. It's just that we need to agree on this thing."

David's circular thinking was wearing her out; could be his reasoning was distorted by the memory of his sister and the Stargate connection. "Seriously, shall we call the police, inform them she may know the shooter?"

Although doubt lingered, he was not willing to go there. "We might want to monitor Andrades more closely, set up a mock transmission with radio waves, and see if she bites."

"Jeez, David, we are not the CIA. What kind of complicity could it possibly be? I believe, ultimately, it all will prove our premise of telepathic activity." Irene did not want to further complicate David's thinking, so she said nothing about how she was beginning to believe the entire event had been a warning of some kind. But no angel's kiss was apparent on either of their lips. She leaned into him and held his face in her hands. "Or we are both loco in the head."

Finally, his face broke out in a grin. "Let's get out of here and go for a drink." She grinned also, and they grabbed at each other in anticipation.

They hurried to lock up for the night, wanting distance from the perplexing events. David called security to ask if all his people had exited the building. "Affirmative, Dr. Rosen. Miss Andrades was the last one to sign out tonight."

The Light Is Near, In the Face of Darkness. Job: 18.9

Jupiter had risen in the late autumn evening sky, already the brightest body in the heavens. The air was cold, crisp like the skin of a new apple. David put his arm around Irene's waist, pulling her close to the warmth of his body. They paused in front of Jamison Hall, gazing into the deepening blue sky, their souls joining in a moment of perfect bliss.

"Look at that, David," she pointed to the luminous planet. "I can almost touch it."

"Yes, I bet we can see Callisto and Europa if we squinted or imagined."

Irene's gray eyes shimmered with the same brilliance as the planet's. He was her person. She didn't have to imagine it. It just was. "Yes," she said. She raised a hand toward the dark blue of the sky. "It seems so terribly close, doesn't it? Let's touch it."

She was about to reach for David's hand when a sudden splendor of white light filled her vision. She tried to blink it away. Then it enveloped her. Her skin glowed with a pearly sheen. He lowered his head to kiss her lips, and she whispered, "David ... there's a girl in the light . . . a beautiful girl in white light . . ." Then, a rip went through her head, and she fell.

**November 14, Weekend Broadcast
11:00 P.M.**

Today, an active shooter opened fire near the Washington Square Quadrangle by New York University and fatally wounded Psychologist and Researcher Dr. Irene Míral. The bullet ripped through her forehead and prefrontal cortex before exiting the back of her skull. She died instantaneously. David Rosen, her fiancée, suffered a shoulder wound as he leaned over and held her in his arms. The killer is deceased as well, apparently a suicide. Motive is unknown. This is a developing story; we will keep you updated as details become available . . .

11:35 PM

Reporting back about an incident in Washington Square earlier this evening. The individual who shot and killed Dr. Irene Míral still has not been identified. The police will make a statement shortly . . .

David was not conscious of the tears wetting his cheeks as he spoke to the police and EMS. He could not think straight, only wanted to know she was not gone. The medics had already covered her up. "No! Revive her. Her heart could still be beating. She's not gone." He uncovered her face, and the truth clobbered.

"Sir, move away. We have to get her into the ambulance, and you need to have that shoulder attended to."

"What?" He looked down at the blood soaking his right shoulder and felt nothing.

"It looks like a surface wound. Get in."

The sirens screeched in his ear even after the ambulance came to a halt at St. Vincent's Hospital. He hung on to the gurney, talking to Irene the whole time as they rushed her in "Hang on, please hang on."

A security guard practically pushed him away. "Sir, you cannot go in there." The man ushered David back into the emergency room.

At about five in the morning, an image of the shooter flashed on the screen of his Sony. David rose from the couch and pressed the red record button on the VCR. With the remote in hand, he peered into the television. He could not move from the spot, could not move his feet; they were cold, petrified as if they'd become one with the wood of the oak floor. He worked the remote, moving from channel to channel. The same man appeared, face blank of expression, staring out at David from the television screen. It was the annoyed guy who had come in a month ago, asking for Irene.

The rage rose in his throat like a hot wind and exploded in a violent scream. And he screamed until he could not hear the sounds coming out of his mouth any longer.

He sat back on the couch and sobbed. This was his fault. He fingered the small plastic bottle of painkillers, enough pills for a week. He should swallow them. Life was not worth living. Nothing mattered now. Maybe that man had felt the same way, felt there was nothing to do but end it all. Suicidal. But also—a killer. David walked into the bathroom, dumped the pills, and flushed three times. He wanted to feel the pain in his shoulder, wanted it to counter the pain in his heart.

Then at ten, a news flash: Several witnesses have identified the man alleged to have fatally shot Dr. Irene Míral as the same man who shot up the South Ferry Terminal, a vet by the name of Simon Smith.

David Rosen told the police and the reporters that he and Irene were engaged. It wasn't true. But it wasn't a lie.

The becoming of their love had been sweet and so right, love as natural as breathing and walking and smiling and laughing. The love he felt for Irene was not only natural but necessary, and how was he going to continue breathing and walking and smiling . . . and living. The shock of the tragedy had laid naked the truth in his heart, tearing away at the essence of hope.

He could not continue with the research, would not.

For him, it began as a professional aspiration. And along with Irene, it had become a quest to find answers to questions that haunted them, a way to share a passion and an ambition. All of it was destroyed at the steps of Jamison Hall. If the research had been the cause of Irene's death, he would not rest until he discovered why.

Simon Smith, another army veteran with a tortured soul and a mysterious past . . .

That is all the media channels were saying.

Together

MARÍANIS LEARNED OF THE tragedy first. "No, that TV station's info has to be wrong! No way. No!"

But yes, each station reported the same horrible news. It was Irene. Someone shot her, a deranged man who may have mistaken her for someone else. She let out a pitiful wail, and Felicia grabbed her before she collapsed. They clung to each other for hours.

Ana, not yet discharged to outpatient, signed herself out when she got news of Irene's assassination. Then, her rage—and the calls.

—Ana calling, and calling, urging the women to do something. And the silence on the other end, the quiet sobs.

"We have to do something. We need to."

And so, they agreed to meet.

But as they huddled at the Starbucks that had just opened on West 87th Street, all they could do was weep. Ana was still raging. "I'm glad the fucker who did this to her is dead because if he weren't, I'd kill him. We'd go after him and kill him." The other women did not react. Ana sat down, defeated by the ugly truth, a crazy man had killed Irene, and here they were, staring at their tall coffees with horror etched on their faces. Carolina, shivering like a small bird denuded of feathers, sat close to Ana. "Hang on, we're all feeling like it's a cold day in hell. Here. Take my jacket." Ana placed the garment over the girl's slender shoulders. Tears trickled down Carolina's cheeks. She tried to wipe them away as she whispered thank you. That did it. That little thank you meant everything. Images of their time at Lakeside surged—a Carolina who would not speak, a bellicose and forever fiery Ana, their raucous laughter around the ping-pong table, and their Irene, steadfast and patient, shoring up their confidence, helping them to recast their lives so they could go on, free of violent memories.

How could this happen to her?

Being with the women calmed Ana some. But the terrible need to do something continued to gnaw at her insides. "Where's Amanda?? Why isn't she here?"

Maríanis said, "I'll find her. Maybe she didn't get your message. Don't be angry. She'll surface. Maybe she can't deal with it yet."

"Yeah, well, we all need to be at the service for Irene, pay our respects, let her know how grateful we are, thank her for what she accomplished with us, and wish her a blessed journey."

Melissa kept asking the question, the question that had no answer. "Why, why has this happened? Last week, I told her I was getting engaged, and she was so happy for me, hugged me and everything." She groaned. "Oh, God. I planned to invite her to the engagement dinner. Oh, God! It's wrong, so wrong."

Each time she closed her eyes, Maríanis saw Irene, saw her transforming into a beautiful swan-like creature, majestic wings parting the air as it flew toward the sun. Then the sky filled with moonlight and peace, and she did not see anything else.

She started to tell them how Irene was going to her place, a place beyond the sun and the moon and the stars. But first, she had to convince herself. The vision had only provided temporary relief. She sensed Irene was still present. "She's been here, been here before."

Olivia pleaded, "Stop, just stop."

"Yeah, what are you talking about, don't be going nuts on us," said Marta. "Irene don't want any of us to be nuts."

"It's okay. Just that I noticed one of their containers on her desk last Monday when I came in for therapy."

273

The Parting

Gregory Jackson, brown face wet with tears, braced himself against the back wall of the room where folks were gathering to pay respects to Irene Míral.

He'd always been a little in love with Irene. Pat Reid knew that. She held on to his arm. "Let's go to her. I want her to know that we're here. Her soul is still with us. The dead don't leave this earth for seven days." They walked to Irene and knelt. Jackson whispered, "God speed, Dr. Míral, God speed. May you rest in peace and harmony, always."

David shook hands and patted backs: Jaime, Robert, the staff at the hospital, and the eight women Irene had been so proud to lead. He should have met them at their engagement, at a celebration of their love, not at a mourning.

Laura consoled Jaime and Robert. Despite her aversion to funerals, she'd steeled herself to be present. She needed to witness what she could not accept: her life's sister was gone. When she learned of the tragedy that had befallen Irene, she'd felt as if one of her limbs had been amputated, and she flayed at the air and screamed. Screamed at the God who could not possibly exist. She would stay for a while and help Jaime sort things out; she knew more about Irene's affairs than he. She'd flown in for the funeral but would never visit New York again. She would return to Isabela.

Two men were standing close to the casket. Joe Martell and a fellow with arms hanging at his side like some disabled robot. Laura knew it was David. He was tall and handsome in an unobtrusive, quiet kind of way. He was a Ph.D. also—just like Irene. Fate had brought them together only to cheat them, dispatching a thief in the night to steal their future. Why? Did God have no control over the Fates? Could he not safeguard the lives of good people? She swallowed several times to moisten the back of her throat until she could speak. "Hello, David. I'm Laura. Irene was my best friend, my sister of the heart. I cannot replace her."

Irene had never mentioned Laura. David scrutinized her face as if trying to find something he'd lost. "I cannot replace her either." And his voice, soft like a whisper of butterfly wings, made Laura cry.

She had found him. Irene found the man who would cherish her. Laura didn't know what to say to David except what she knew of her friend's heart.

"Irene had a savior in her. She saved my life when I was losing control of my existence. And she saved those women." She turned her face toward the eight women. "That's why they're here. Did you know about her mother? Irene once told me she wished she'd been able to save her from meanness, but all she could do was soothe the emotional scars by listening to her stories. Did you know about those stories?"

"Yes."

"Ironic, isn't it? As if somehow . . ." She'd hit a nerve of some kind because David winced. "Irene and I touched base at least once a week, been doing so since I don't remember when. Last week, just last week, we were on the phone for more than an hour. I told her I had finally met the man who would love me honestly, love me despite all my faults and neuroses. She was happy for me and confessed she too was in love, very much so. It was you. Irene was in love with you, David. I am sorry."

A stout woman in a black dress was at the casket. Two young men stood by her side. She bent over Irene and kissed her cheek. She mouthed a few words and gently placed a hand over the arrangement of brilliant red roses at Irene's feet. They spoke to no one and left at once.

And Beth. She stood numb before her friend. "What did you do? Irene, what did you do!?"

She stroked her friend's face. So pretty Irene was. No, she was beautiful. "Just want to tell you that Charly came back. Found his way back home from where he'd been . . ." Beth started to bawl. "I'm sorry, Irene, so sorry."

Jaime went to Beth and put his arm around her. She looked into his ashen face; the familiar flirty glitter in his eye was gone. "I ah, I brought the keys to her place," she pointed to the brassy one, "this one is for the entry downstairs, and here's the mailbox . . . Oh, God. I can't." Beth leaned on Jaime's shoulder and bawled some more. Jaime didn't say he already had her keys. Irene's belongings had been released to him, her nearest relative.

"Thanks, Beth. Laura's going to help me out with things."

"How about her sister? She told me she had a sister. Is she here?"

"She left a moment ago."

Eight women stood before the stainless-steel casket. Profound sadness would have overwhelmed them, except Irene would not want any to weaken. She had been a warrior for them, and so they stood there like faithful soldiers on a watch. Maríanis noticed the pearly sheen of a votive burning on a narrow stand. And next to it, a single white rose stood in a slender crystal vase; the card, simply signed—*Always, Alfredo.*

She knelt. "You look so serene in that delicate white dress, irenic and beautiful, your face like an angel's. Your work on this earth is done. But I sense ours has just begun. I want to be a social worker. Didn't get a chance to talk to you about how much I want to help women, didn't get a chance to say you've inspired me to do so. I'm a strong woman now, Dr. Míral, just like you wanted me to be."

The women moved closer and in unison voiced the words Maríanis Román had just uttered. They didn't see Amanda walk in.

They'd thought she wouldn't show up, but she did, garbed all in black, crying, looking lost in baggy sweats. She went to Irene, leaned over her, and in one swift motion pulled something out from under her enormous sweatshirt, placed it in the casket, and spoke some words the women couldn't hear. When she finally came to them, she joined hands with Olivia and Marta.

Olivia asked, "What did you put in there?"

"A sharp steel nail file, in case she has to fight her way back."

Amanda still wore feistiness like armadillo armor whenever she was in pain.

"Don't worry. Irene doesn't need a weapon in heaven," said Maríanis.

But eventually, grief would get them there, get them to the place where they would want to punch something.

Ana piped up, "A professional girls' Kickboxing team. That's what we need, and I'm going to start one." The women, all at once, raised their eyebrows. "It's a good way to channel energy." Anger. That's what Ana meant. Anger, like love, was hard to let go of. Maríanis' fury over the time she'd lost with her children still churned and sputtered. Yet the despair was gone. They would soon be hers again. She tightened her hold on Felicia's hand. Her temples throbbed, and she clenched her teeth, thinking about all the little successes they hadn't had a chance to share with Irene. At that last therapy session, the last time she'd seen her alive, she'd spoken more about Felicia than of how well her custody case was proceeding. "Irene, last week, she gave me a big scare. I found her on the roof, much too close to the ledge and I called out, 'Felicia! Oh, my God!' When she turned around, she was smiling like a kid. 'It's gone, Maríanis, the falling into the pit sensation is gone, I ain't never jumping. I am living.' I hugged her so hard I could have broken a rib." The suicidal flashbacks were gone; Irene had saved her life.

But did Irene get to know Carolina was having her first gallery opening soon or that one of her canvases was named *The Girl with Gray Eyes*? Did she know Marta and Olivia planned to apply for a training program to become EMS workers? Amanda had disappeared into an underground community of artists on the Lower East Side. She had not been showing up for outpatient, so Irene never knew Amanda and two artist friends had begun work on a comic book series. Maríanis closed her eyes and once more saw Irene becoming a magical swan. The throbbing at her temples began to subside.

Irene had been ripped from them before she could fully see the fruits of her work. She never knew how prophetic her words had been. "You are ready to resume your lives. You may never be entirely rid of PTSD symptoms, but you are learning to cope. You can pursue your dreams, work, and love . . ."

Questing Retribution

DAVID HAD NOT SLEPT for more than forty-eight hours and did not want to. The loss of Irene was like losing the feeling part of his being. He feared sleep because what if he still did not feel when he awoke? He yearned for the neediness, the wanting, the pain that had made him weep. Anything was better than the sickly numb sensation which had descended over him. He sat before the television screen, deadness dominating his mind.

And the guilt. Maybe it was better to feel numb than face the terrible guilt.

But he'd never been a man to wallow, and he wanted answers. He played back the recordings of the newscasts over and over again; the scientist in him coldly scrutinizing every detail. His thoughts becoming increasingly pellucid as he processed the significance of that last news report. He had work to do.

He stopped for some coffee and the newspaper. And there was Simon Smith's face again, inscrutable as a cyborg's. David didn't need the caffeine; crazy energy began to possess him, and it made no difference he hadn't slept.

Quiet and eerie, the lab now seemed surreal. Had he and Irene really been there? Working. Questioning. Laughing. Kissing. Or had it just been a dream? Yes, a dream they'd shared. But for what? Shreds, that's all it was now. He would give anything to get back into the dream and be with Irene. Wanting to be free of sentiment, he shook his head hard and smacked his forehead. Then he turned on the lights and sat before the computer consoles.

Fine silvery dust had settled on the equipment; the screens cast a nacreous light. His eyes surveyed the room: Even the floor was covered with a strange dust that seemed to disperse with his movements and each shallow breath. He rubbed his fingers together; the ephemeral silvery sediment felt slippery. He brought his fingers to his face; a scent like chalk and white roses lingered for a moment, then faded. He tried it again, but this time there was no fragrance. Nothing.

He remembered the event, the inexplicable and powerful energy that had shaken the whole place, the spectacular flash of light Irene had described. He recalled her last words, "David, there's a girl in white light . . ." He whipped his head around, expecting to see her. Maybe she would come for *him* now. There was no one. The space was as silent as a vacuum. Whatever it was or had been, descended to the street below to take Irene from him before dissolving into inconsequential dust. He scowled and rubbed his hands hard on the front of his pants until the white substance was gone from his fingers. He turned his palms up. Yes, gone. He stared at his empty hands, and the tears flowed once more. Down his cheeks, trickled from his chin, and settled in the little hollow below his Adam's apple.

No, the being in white light had not taken Irene. Simon Smith had shot her dead. David thought he might go mad. He and Irene had never made the connection that could have saved her life. It was all linked to the study. The flash of light she saw had been a warning. The illuminated female had descended over Irene to protect her, but the killer's bullet had been fleeter than her light. "All due to the damn research, my stupid ambition, and senseless hubris. Why did I even bring her into it? Fuck me. I deserve this, fuck me!"

Joe Martell had pulled David aside at the funeral. They regarded one another with tacit understanding; steely anger squared their shoulders. "The shooter, Simon Smith, I know who he is. Irene referred him. She called me and said he had PTSD."

David's shoulders sagged when Martell said the name. He remembered the man who came looking for Irene. And he fought to keep hate from taking hold in his heart for men like Simon Smith. Men who did not value life, or themselves.

"Joe, how did this happen? How could it happen?"

Martell put a hand on David's shoulder, "Are you with me? There's more. We could not find a record of his service."

Simon Smith's twisted mind had sought revenge because Irene had rejected him for the study. That had to be the motive.

But David could not close the chapter yet. Why did the guy even volunteer to take part in their research study in the first place? Where the hell had he come from? No record of service? Who was he?? Had he and Irene been targeted by the government? Yes, a government working back channels to suppress curiosity about telepathic communication. Was Simon even American? Was he an operative or a pathetic pawn? Had he been assigned to shadow them? Was it the reason he had volunteered? Had he received additional instructions on how to proceed once Irene rejected him for the study? But had it been just Simon Smith assigned to infiltrate? In his mind, he replayed their conversations, conjectures, and conundrums; how Irene had asked, "Shall we call the police and let them know we suspect a connection between the shooter and one of the volunteers?" And sadness sat tight in his chest.

He needed to act before the guilt tore his gut to pieces. Simon Smith was out of the picture, perhaps as planned by the powers that were. There would be no answers coming from him. But there had been someone else: Alina Andrades.

With icy focus, he accessed two files: Smith's and Andrades'. Irene's notes were detailed. David scanned the facts he already knew about Smith, then paused on the background paragraph: 1991—Subject separated from the military after serving as an agent in Mission E-94. Irene noted: (subject evasive about the mission and merely mentioned it had been based in the Middle East. Subject stuttered, twitch in the right eye during this interview segment.) She summarized: Subject provided no physical address, only a P.O. Box. He is likely suffering from PTSD and is not appropriate for the study. Referred to V.A. Clinic, contact: Joe Martell.

A vague recollection of something sinister hovered. David placed the feeling. The same sensation surfaced whenever he remembered his sister and the Stargate connection. 1991, the year Stargate had been terminated. *Madness to think there was a connection of some sort . . . my sister, the vet . . . might he be a Russian spy?* He closed Smith's file and moved on to Andrades. Nothing remarkable. Except, Irene had gone back to that file several times. Wait, something else. Irene had twice postponed approval of the subject's participation with no explanation. She did remark that Andrades' I.Q. was the highest of all the subjects, that she had a mesmerizing gaze and an unusual aura about her. Irene added (re: gaze and aura—examiner's subjective perception.)

She'd had more than a hunch about the woman and the event that shook the lab. He again remembered how they agonized over his suspicion that it could be linked to the shooting at South Ferry Terminal, and how they discussed the possibility that Alina Andrades had known what was going to occur and when, how their minds went from considering it as an instance of precognition to suspecting foul play, and how he'd asked Irene to take a cab home and not get on the subway, fearing for her safety while an active shooter might be lurking. Damn! Damn! Damn! He *had* been lurking. Likely watching Irene and her comings and goings, stalking silently, observing the exit of the building, waiting to strike her down.

He checked for Andrades' address, looking to see if she had the same P.O. Box as Smith. No. She lived on West 84th Street—no apparent link between the individuals. But that address bothered him. My God, she lived practically within walking distance from him and Irene. Why did that not bother her? David printed out copies of the two files and three copies of an announcement:

The research study conducted by Dr. David Rosen and Dr. Irene Míral is terminated. Many thanks for participating in our project. Interns, please consult your advisor regarding credited time.

He disconnected all the equipment, posted the announcement outside the doors of both floors, and stopped by the security desk. "Want to let you know that our project has closed. No one should be up there. Here's the information in case anyone has questions."

The man was typical of security personnel stationed in many low-risk buildings: middle-aged, amiable, self-effacing. "Sorry about Miss Irene, Dr. Rosen. It doesn't make sense, not at all. I ah . . ."

David raised an eyebrow. "Yes?"

The man lowered his eyes. "Just that it's . . . it's terrible, a terrible tragedy." He frowned and fussed with the sign-in book. "Dr. Rosen, the Thursday night before, a man was pacing in front of the building, back and forth, back and forth, finally crossed the street, then out of sight. I can't say what he looked like, don't really know. If you remember, Dr. Rosen, it was raining pretty hard about seven-thirty or so. Probably he wasn't . . . probably just a bum with no umbrella."

Seven-thirty?? David's throat tightened. He pivoted away from the man and marched to the 86th Street subway station. The crazy energy Irene had determined came from Alina coincided with the moments a suspicious individual had been pacing in the rain at the entrance of Jamison Hall! Andrades must have sensed the danger, knew the killer was outside, and her psychic force generated a warning so powerful it almost blinded Irene. Perhaps the tremendous energy field had also impeded the killer from crossing the threshold and entering their lab.

But it did not deter him from coming back days later to wait from a distance until he saw them exit and pause, lovers gazing at the new evening's sky.

The scenario presented itself clearly, the edges sharp and hurtful. What he had to do now became clear as well. He had to find Andrades.

For a moment, he wondered if he should go to the police. But what would he say? He had nothing substantial. The police would think he was out of his mind. In fact, what was he going to say to Alina Andrades? He didn't know, but he knew he wanted to face her, look into her eyes, weigh the thing Irene had called an aura. When David arrived at the address, the bottom of his stomach dropped. It was an abandoned building.

In the middle of the night, he cried. He cried for Irene, he cried for himself, and he cried for the work that would not get done. He and Irene had been onto something important but perhaps not meant to be proven. The idea that paranormal activity had been at work loomed in his mind in such a huge way that it frightened. Irene's mother had experienced the presence of a girl in white light she called Adriana, a girl who appeared during her moments of profound strife to comfort and protect.

A-D-R-I-A-N-A . . . A-L-I-N-A . . . A-N-D-R-A-D-E-S

Adriana, reincarnated in Alina Andrades to look over Irene and fill her eyes with the protective light of her soul? In those last moments, Irene spoke of her beauty and light. Hypotheses churned in his mind until the fatigue of it exhausted him, depleting him of ambition for any of it.

Investigating the woman led to a dead end. The building had been condemned for two years and was now the city's property. David's lawyer tracked down the original owner who ascertained he knew of no one by the name. Andrades had literally disappeared into thin air, disappeared into the nether, vanished.

He smote the thought that she'd taken Irene with her.

David continued to press Joe Martell for information about Simon Smith. "Joe, in 1991, a guy who was probably a double agent for the government vanished. His military profile is uncannily similar to what we know of Smith, an expert in artificial intelligence and communications who served in the Middle East. Could they be one and the same?"

Martell sighed. "Either the military covered Smith's tracks completely, or the information he provided to Irene was not accurate." Joe advised him to drop it. "There's a limit to the access that I do have to government files. David, I am a veteran also. So was my father, one of seven survivors of the 31st Infantry, Korean War. I don't want to get to the point where I might doubt my own patriotism. Our government is powerful. The payout for pushing on this thing can yield nothing but more grief. Nothing can bring Irene back. The only thing about Simon Smith I feel certain about is that he did have PTSD. God knows I've treated enough ill men to pick up on even subtle symptoms."

David looked at him like a child who had been expecting a present and though knowing he could not get it, still pressed. "Many previously classified files now appear in the public domain regularly. We could dig deeper."

The guilt trap was sucking both men in. "David, I want to kick myself also, should have made it clearer to her that Smith was bad news. I felt his sickness, but not his violence, could not have predicted . . ."

"He came around asking questions. I should have alerted security to keep an eye out."

"Let it go, let it go!" Martell reached into the inner pocket of his jacket. "Look at these. Do you know what they are? Season tickets for the Yankees. And it's been canceled. The team was having one of its best runs with a good chance at the pennant. Now, the season is canceled." The rims of David's eyes were wet. "David, I loved her too, probably since I was thirteen or so. Was as proud of her as Jaime, as her parents. But her season is over. And there is nothing we can do."

The only fruit of David's quest for retribution was becoming good friends with Joe Martell. Joe had known Irene for a long time. David felt comfort as Joe shared memories of their friendship.

"We grew up in the same Bronx neighborhood. Jamie and I attended Cardinal Hayes High School. Irene got herself a scholarship to Regis, the Ivy League school of New York City Catholic high schools. She wasn't one to hang out on the block, always on the books, quiet growing up, seemed like a wise old lady sometimes, terribly attached to her mother, calling her all the time to find out if she were all right, as if Alma were the child and she the parent. I never knew her to have boyfriends, although I secretly thought of myself as such. But really, nothing beyond platonic."

David almost smiled; Irene did have a knack for cultivating platonic friendships.

"Her father Antonio was a very nice guy, affable, open, loved both his kids to death, kind of adopted me. My father passed when I was fifteen, my older brother came back from the Nam, addicted, useless to us, died last year, Irene holding my hand." Joe was quiet then like he was trying to pull himself together. "And the mom . . . don't know, nice also, but there was something about her you couldn't quite touch. Know what I mean? It was in her eyes, half the time looking beyond some invisible horizon as if she had seen too much and her eyes could not hold much more."

Joe's words jolted. David remembered sometimes seeing that same look in Irene's eyes.

He asked David if she'd ever talk to him about Alma. "Don't know what happened to the woman, but whatever it was, it rubbed off on Irene, some mysterious wisdom rippling in her pupils by age ten."

Joe commiserated; David listened. Their conversations lasting into the early hours of many mornings. Through the fog of grief, David had sensed something special at the funeral. Those women, standing in solidarity before her casket, believed Irene had the power to heal. They were testimony to her strength and dedication.

⋅◦⋅

Within weeks, the idea of the Irene Míral Foundation took flight, a foundation dedicated to the study of PTSD. Six clinics opened in three states and Washington, D.C. Joe Martell resigned from the Veterans Administration and became national director. The generosity of David's parents ensured a substantial endowment. Through their networks, enormous sums were raised, money that would sustain the trust for decades.

If she were alive, Irene would say her true legacy was not the foundation, but the recuperation of eight women. Women who needed to believe they could heal and that an incorrect diagnosis could be reversed. She'd suceeded in meeting the challenge of Walter Freile's timetable and, most importantly, the goals of the PTSD unit she'd worked so hard to establish.

Irene had worked. And she had loved.

Lakeside Revisited

EIGHT NEW REFERRALS LAY on his desk. One bed had remained occupied: Ana Amado's. He laughed when she signed herself out. *Good luck to her, and good riddance, too.*

He had other duties to attend to at the hospital. What could Alfredo Bryson have been thinking? He pushed to institute the darned unit, then took off to London. Only politics had prevented him from turning down the responsibility of consulting psychiatrist for the new unit when Bryson left.

He'd always thought it would be a short-lived experiment and had no intention of proceeding with the new referrals. Since its inception, the unit had been irksome, like a splinter buried under his skin. Now, this scandal. The whole affair had an unpleasant scent about it. He was confident the PTSD unit had seen its last days.

Irene had begun to step on his toes. When he learned she'd gone over his head with the Felicia Monserrat case, indignation reared angry and sullen. Worse was the ego battering awareness he'd been negligent. Irene's concerns about the Monserrat woman had been correct, his recommendation premature. If Monserrat had attempted suicide, it would have been a stain on his conscience. There was no real reason he could not have agreed to hypnosis while she was still in-house. But of course, Míral handled it.

He tried to squash the sensation of self-loathing each time he remembered the anonymous complaints. He should have taken those complaints more seriously, investigated the source, and stopped the killer. Ridiculous! He needed to put the matter behind him. All too far-fetched to merit his guilt. But as the story developed in the newscasts, he understood the person who sent those letters to Human Resources was the same man who killed Irene, had to be. The link was the research study and the message in one of the complaints: "Dr. Irene Míral is conducting subversive research." A zealot who acted out a patriotic delusion.

How could an intelligent woman like Irene fail to recognize the folly of pursuing paranormal research? What could have possibly driven her to it? Why would she risk her professional standing? Inevitable that such activity, albeit not unlawful, would eventually result in negative consequences. She had done nothing illegal, but it had killed her. Her unit would be gone soon also.

He was floored when the hospital administrator informed him The Irene Míral Foundation would be funding all operations for the PTSD unit. Within hours, a succinct memorandum landed on his desk.

ATTN: Supervising Psychiatrist, Dr. Walter Freile

Two candidates have applied for Dr. Míral's position.

Please schedule interviews ASAP.

We expect a recommendation by the end of the week.

Well-entrenched in hospital politics, he understood his position was in jeopardy. Shortly after James Haggerty took command of the hospital, he'd appointed him as one of two Supervising Psychiatrists. He had Mrs. Freile to thank for it. She and Haggerty's wife were on the board of Citizens Against Human Trafficking and the husbands found themselves at the same functions several times a year. They were on a first-name basis and frequently spoke on the phone. But Haggerty hadn't called him on this one. Freile suppressed hubris and went into survival mode with the practical diligence he applied to all his professional endeavors.

The first candidate was just a year out of graduate school and already licensed, ambitious, possibly brilliant, but perhaps too young. He decided to interview the second applicant, Dr. Adriana de Rodríguez, a Harvard graduate. Her credentials were impeccable. She was giving up the chair at McGill University to return to New York. The interview went well. Cold enough, he thought, and a bit arrogant. He supposed it went along with the territory. She was tall, confident, and attractive. When he asked her why she was choosing clinical work over an already established academic career, she said, "I believe we should apply the knowledge we acquire."

Her eyes were enormous, the color of cold, weathered stone.

The Epilogue

November 2004

The little girl sitting next to her was getting fidgety. "Mommy, when are we going to McDonald's? I want to get another Happy Meals Toy." Starbucks was not her speed. Not at six years old it wasn't. "Daddy will be picking you up for McDonald's soon. Right now, I want to show you off to your *madrinas*. They'll be here in a moment."

She was a lucky little girl; most children had one madrina, Mandy I. had seven. Satisfied, little Mandy I. directed her attention to the small box she always carried, her little treasure of prizes from her favorite kids' place. She removed her collection of plastic Aladdin figurines and posed them on the table.

Melissa, Amanda, Ana, Marta, Olivia, Carolina, Felicia, and Maríanis met each November at the same place, the Starbucks where they had gathered after that awful day.

Marta and Olivia walked in and embraced Melissa. "Oh, my God, Mandy I.!" Marta gushed all over the child. "She's grown a whole foot! Right, Olivia?" She stood the child up, twirled her around, and made her laugh. "She's beautiful." Olivia produced a little purse.

"Look inside," she said with a wink. Melissa frowned. She'd asked the madrinas not to give the child cash. "It's a cute pocketbook. It matches the dress I gave Mandy I. for her birthday."

Of all the madrinas, Marta and Olivia doted on Mandy I. most. They were a couple and wanted their own child, preferably a little girl who would also have an "I" as a middle initial. "I" for Irene. But the adoption agencies in the city would not approve same-sex couples as adoptive parents. Some politely skirted around immediate disqualification with veiled excuses, feebly concluding their hours as EMS workers would not be conducive to stable parenting. Angry as hell, Marta and Olivia just grew more determined and became active in the WGC, the Women's Gay Coalition. One of the attorneys with the organization had been trying to help them through the bureaucratic blockade that stomped on their dreams of becoming parents.

"I know a couple who adopted a little girl through a Chinese adoption agency. They're still giving little girls away over there. It's awful, but maybe you should look into it."

Marta gave Olivia a look.

Melissa apologized. "Sorry, guys. Probably too complicated and expensive. Maybe you can become foster parents first."

"Melissa, you just don't get it. It's outright discrimination. Don't you know? Gays are also barred from becoming foster parents. We've been working for this city going on eight years now. Next year, we'll have enough saved up to start our own ambulance service, be our own boss, have better hours."

Olivia pecked Marta on the cheek. "Yeah, but not here. We plan to move to Massachusetts, where same-sex marriage is now legal. We'll get married. Those agencies are going to have to shut up and put up."

"But . . . You guys can't leave us. Stay."

"Don't worry, Massachusetts is not that far away, and we can drive down anytime. One day we'll be here with our own child." Marta fussed under the table and cooed. She'd snuck in a cat carrier. Three tiny kittens snuggled like one furry soft ball. Mandy I. wanted a peek. Marta nodded yes as she put a finger to her lips, indicating to Mandy to do so quietly. "Can't wait up the babies."

Melissa wasn't going to say one more thing; she'd already hurt their feelings. She was relieved when she glanced over to the entrance. "They're here!"

Right outside the Starbucks, Maríanis was mad-hugging a gang of fashionable females. They traipsed in, smiling, laughing, and crying. Carolina—still the most sensitive. "Mandy I., Mandy I." She hugged and kissed her godchild. After ten years, Carolina looked as girlish as ever, elfin in a Lily Pulitzer smock. Ana looked comfortable and elegant in designer sweat threads and a signature scarf with a logo of her gym: AB, Amado Bodyworks. After touring for five years with her championship girls' Kickboxing team, she'd opened a gym and was making a ton of money. She loved to buy gifts for her darling godchild, expensive label sneakers and sweatsuits, and one Christmas, even a dollhouse with little furniture.

"Babes, how is everyone?" Amanda slapped each woman a high five and then stooped before the little girl to give her a big kiss. "Hey, princess, what you got there?" Mandy I. grinned. Amanda was fascinating—grungy clothes, Doc Martens, punk-spiked hair, and a ring in her nose. She pulled out a Barbie-sized doll from her leather satchel and handed it to her godchild. It wasn't a Barbie doll at all, but a girl figure from one of her successful comic book series, and it looked a lot like Amanda.

"You're getting rich, bitch," blurted Ana, then apologized to Melissa before she could chastise her for using profanity in front of the child. Mandy I. didn't hear anything; she was busy conversing with her new doll. Melissa shook her head and laughed. Each of the madrinas was a good role model for her child. Each in her own way.

Carolina produced a large hardcover book and held it up. "My book. Poetry and reproductions of my artwork, many poems about Miranda—from my journal. I'm going on tour next month to promote it." There was a flurry of applause and congratulations. Ana asked, "Is the painting of me in there?"

Carolina opened the book to the chapter titled "My Friend Ana." She pointed to the full-page photographs of two paintings. "Look", she said proudly. Ana noticed the one she had not posed for. She was sitting by the lake, a big dark tear slipping down her cheek. And there was a poem: "Our Black Tears". The women were quiet. They missed Irene all over again.

Lots had happened in the last ten years. Lakeside was now a distant chapter in their lives. Yet as the women navigated through the inevitable tribulations of living, loving, and striving, they often found themselves tapping into the well of strength that resided in their memories of Irene.

For Maríanis, Irene's example served as perpetual inspiration. She worked in various clinics where she witnessed how violence against women continued to ruin lives. She chose to put her social work degree to work for change and developed a sturdy network of like-minded professionals who were determined to help abused females. With community support, she acquired a grant and established a shelter for battered women.

Her boy was ready to apply for college. He planned to become a psychologist. Her Tina's gift was kinesthetic. She moved with the grace of a gazelle. Dance studio was expensive, but Maríanis managed. Their father helped, even beyond the required support payments, but he knew to keep his distance. He remarried and seemed to have mellowed. She hoped so, for his new wife's sake. Maríanis had no time for men. She maintained a sometime relationship with a local politician who had assisted her with the grant and counted on her to garner votes among women when election time came around. She liked to think of their relationship as beneficial symbiosis. He was good to know, made sure police protection was instantly accessible in case of problems at the shelter, was good with her kids, and good to her when she needed him.

The women never spoke about men or relationships. Marta and Olivia were gay, and their love was still solid. The others seemed content to bow to Melissa, the happy wife, the happy mother. Melissa had found happiness in that sphere, but for the others in the group, men was not a topic they wished to explore or discuss. During their yearly get-together it was as if they existed in a world without men. Men were faded figures in the background of their lives. Their experiences of trauma, the connection that bound them, superseded all else.

Felicia finally got Mandy I's attention and was helping her give the little Aladdin characters a voice. She was excellent with children, had become a registered pediatric nurse, worked at Flower Fifth, and was devastated by the abandonment of infants. "I need to find myself a husband so I can go ahead and adopt some children also." She did not consider single motherhood an option. She often stated, "It's the reason why so many children have issues." But Felicia could not find a husband. She found a flaw in every relationship, mostly a flaw in him.

Maríanis reminded her, "Felicia, I'm a single mother; my kids are doing fine."

"True. You're a great mother, and you've worked hard raising your kids, but it is harder with just one parent. You happen to be an exceptional woman, so it has worked for you."

Only the little girl noticed the handsome man who stood by the entrance trying to spot his wife and child. "Daddy!" Mandy I. ran to her father. Melissa looked up and waved him over. "Girls, you remember Steve. He's taking Mandy I. to McDonald's on a quest for more Happy Meal Toys." Smiles and hellos and then goodbye kisses and little hugs for Mandy I.

Before heading out, Steve leaned over Melissa to give her abdomen a proprietary little pat. "How are you feeling, babe?" Melissa seemed embarrassed, kissed her child and her husband goodbye, then turned to the women. They were staring.

"I, ah, have news. I'm pregnant, a boy, in five months."

Ana reacted first. "A boy! Oh, no. We only want girls in this family." She laughed and went over to Melissa. "Congratulations, though, good job!" Marta looked down at the floor with a pained expression. Olivia squeezed her hand. She was always mothering, was nursing three sickly stray kittens to health, and wanted a puppy. The adoption thing was mostly her initiative. And it was all right. All right. Marta's love was big enough for three kittens, several pups, a child, and Olivia.

Ana continued to cheer, pointed to Melissa's belly, and shouted, "That one will be a Tae Kwan Do expert. Leave it to me!" Everyone laughed. Marta recouped, put her arm around Melissa, and kissed her cheek. "Now, you'll have a little couple. We'll have to think of a middle "I" name for your little boy, so he won't feel left out."

Amanda perceived Steve had smirked, and the possessive touching of Melissa's belly struck her as offensive. Nevertheless, she congratulated Melissa with an enthusiastic high five then gave her a big hug. The women still regarded her as the renegade of the group; her appearance alone was proof. Her brand. Yet, she had conformed, worked to become a savvy entrepreneur, and nurtured her contacts, male and female. Still, there was never going to be another Estéban. And the conforming had taken a while.

A new P.O. had turned out to be a creepy bastard who was itching to rub something or other in her face. The letters from the folks who produced her comic book series did not satisfy him, and he claimed photocopies of the royalty checks were not enough. "Insufficient documentation and failure to secure employment." She complained to his supervisor but got stuck with the extra year anyway.

She could not completely shake it off. Even if she were making good money and had lots of fans, she would always be an ex-con. The only time she felt legitimate was here, with the girls, felt Irene's presence, knew she was still looking out for her, for them.

They needed the meeting, and they would continue to do it because they never wanted to forget their Irene or forget her words. "The memories may remain, but they don't have to torment you. The trauma is part of your history, but it can be just that, an event in a history book."

The women said their goodbyes and reminded each other to check in, to call, and to take care. Carolina said she would need lots of luck on her book tour. Maríanis reassured, "Don't worry, Irene is rooting for you. Me too! We all are. Right, girls?" Then, teasing shout-outs from the group. "You forgot our signed copies!" The sorry startle on Carolina's face was precious, and they burst out laughing. "I'm sorry, so sorry. I'll mail you copies. My first stop is in Princeton. Come support me."

"Yuck," said Amanda, "stuck-up yuppie territory. Don't worry, I'll be there."

And so, they moved on. Busy, Involved, Living. For the first few years, they all waited in front of the Starbucks for cabs to Grand Central and boarded the train that would take them to the Westchester town where Irene was buried. But with each passing year, one or the other could not make it after the reunion.

Maríanis, though, did not miss a single year. Sometimes, Felicia came along, but not today; her shift at the hospital began in an hour. It was okay. Maríanis looked forward to the solitary trek. It was comforting, the long ride in the middle of the afternoon on the

Metro-North, the short cab ride to the cemetery, the gravel path that wound around the graves, saints, and monuments. David Rosen had wanted Irene in a mausoleum. Odd, but maybe he planned to join her there when his time came. Jaime told him he'd done enough to honor her memory, and Irene was laid to rest by her mother.

The stone was beautifully engraved: Daughter, Sister, Friend, Healer of Souls. Deeply loved. She picked up the white votive she'd placed by the headstone the year before. A ritual. She brought one to the graveside every year, placed it by the stone, without lighting it.

Once again, the pearly white wax was half-melted. Maríanis was not surprised. She cried that first year when she saw it had been lit. For Irene might still be, her soul nourished by the atmosphere surrounding her grave, particles in the air claimed by her sacrifice, and her unique light.

The afternoon's air was soft, unusual for November. Maríanis replaced the votive with a shiny new one. She stood there for a long while, holding a long stem white rose. Finally, she knelt and placed the stem by the stone.

Acknowledgements

The seminal ideas for this novel had been gestating in my mind since the late 1990s. Three years ago, The Daughter Bond finally began to take form. However, the issues I wanted to raise with my writing were so important that sometimes they obstructed the creative process. After two editorial assessments, I kept plugging along. Although, if it hadn't been for the input of some very patient and supportive people, this book would not have come to be.

I want to thank Susan Clerici for sharing her clinical expertise and taking time from her busy practice to review my work for accuracy. In addition, I am exceedingly grateful to D. Murphy and S.L. (she knows who she is) for evaluating my manuscript and steering me in the right direction. Special thanks to Ann L. Tuttle for the edits, which were eye-opening and more than valuable.

And heartfelt appreciation to all the profesionals who have generated an extensive body of research on PTSD and rape.
The following seminal studies were pertinent: Burgess and Holmstrome(1974), Kilpatrick, Veronne&Best (1985), Kilpatrick et al., (1989). Most of all I want to thank the women whose experiences inspired me to write the story in the first place. Although this novel is a work of fiction, the trauma and harassment women have suffered over generations is reality and the fight for change must continue.

Note: Titles of conferences and articles in the narrative are fictitious and do not refer to cited sources.

Afterword

The reality is staggering, the statistics shameful: sexual harassment and molestation, domestic violence, rape, and femicides, in the workplace, at home, on campuses, on the streets, in the armed services, and government institutions. Then there are the invisible cases, dead and missing women, notably, minority and Native American women.

Domestic violence, rape, and abuse continue to be significant public health concerns. In addition, gun violence is intricately linked with femicide.

The cost of the long-term and generational impact of violence on the women who physically survive is a shameful legacy.

PTSD is a serious condition for both men and women. Women are more likely than men to develop PTSD. PTSD in adolescence is more prevalent in females.

Annually, approximately 12 million women in the U.S. experience clinical depression. The highest frequency is among women ages 25-44.

Question: How many of the 12 million are suffering from undiagnosed PTSD?

Sources: Wikipedia, VPV.org/studies

Hotlines:
National Suicide Prevention:
1 800 273 TALK
The Veterans Crisis Hotline Line:
1 800 273 8255
National Domestic Violence:
1 800 799 SAFE
Suicide and Crisis Hotline:
Dial 988

About the Author

C.P. Florez has a B.A. in Spanish Literature and an
M.S. in Counseling.

She is the author of Puerto Rican Love Stories and
Nenadich Street, Poems and Passages.

www.cpflorez.com

Dear Readers,

I hope that even if you are not a Spanish speaker, you were able to discern the meaning of the Spanish words in the narrative from the context. But if you wanted to grab a dictionary at any point, then here is this glossary for you.

Madre Ausente	Absent Mother
Bendición	Blessing
Guardar luto	Mourn in black
Brujería	Witchcraft
Sagrado Corazón de Jesús	Sacred Heart of Jesus
Lo siento	I am sorry (for your loss)
Velorio	A wake
¿Qué dices?	What are you saying?
Niña	Child (girl)
Se tiene que largar	He(she) must leave
Canalla	Scoundrel (dog)
Madrina	Godmother
Agua	Water
Azucenas	Lilies
Mosquitero	Mosquito netting
Ayudame	Help me
Retratos	Photographs
Hispanoparlantes	Spanish-speaking people
Cuaderno	Student's Notebook
Flaca	Skinny female
Maduros	Ripe fried plaintains
Prontisímo	Quickly, ASAP
Cojones	Brazenness, balls
Coño!	Expletive associated with fornication; spoken in anger and frustration, _or_ voiced as heightened approval or affirmation.

DISCUSSION POINTS

The novel takes place in the early 90's, before the advent of social media and the #metoo movement. In subsequent decades, many women came forth to finally tell their stories of sexual harassment and molestation in the workplace.

Irene held back from reporting her supervisor and filing a complaint for sexual harassment. Do you think most women of her time would have proceeded similarly? What would you have done in her place?

The Daughter Bond touches on pertinent social issues such as sexual harassment, molestation, domestic violence, and mental health misdiagnoses. What do you think of the author's approach and her treatment of those issues as she tells Irene's story?

Secondary trauma is an underlying theme in the novel. Alma passed on details of her trauma by telling Irene her story, including her encounters with a presence she called Adriana. The telling influenced Irene's life choices and largely determined the trajectory of her life and the nature of her relationships. She chooses a career in psychology, dedicating her professional life to the treatment of females who have PTSD. Her mother's perceptual experiences become an obsession, causing her to doubt scientific precepts, propelling her to seek answers.

The women Irene treated at the hospital suffered direct trauma, yet they not only survived but they were restored to productive lives. Can secondary trauma be as consequential as direct trauma?

How much family history should parents share with their children?

Several secondary characters help move the narrative along.

Who is your favorite, and why?

What do you think of Irene's relationship with the men in the story? Dr. Freile is a morally gray character. Much of the conflict in the novel results from Irene pushing back against his chauvinism and questionable ethics. What morally gray character in your life has caused conflict and changed the trajectory of your life?

Notes